WITHDRAWN FROM FREE USE ...
AND WELFARE ...
THE BENEFIT ...
ONLY.
Y0-AUD-359
FOR RELIGIOUS USE ONLY
SOLD

THE PHOENIX LECTURES

THE PHOENIX LECTURES

by L. RON HUBBARD

THE CELEBRATED LECTURE SERIES GIVEN BY L. RON HUBBARD TO THE PROFESSIONAL COURSE, PHOENIX, ARIZONA, IN JULY 1954, COMPILED INTO BOOK FORM BY THE EDITORIAL STAFF OF THE PUBLICATIONS ORGANIZATION WORLD WIDE

FOR RELIGIOUS USE ONLY

THE AMERICAN ST. HILL ORGANIZATION

Published by
The American St. Hill Organization
(A branch of the Church of Scientology of California, a non-profit corporation in the U.S.A. Registered in England.)
2723 West Temple Street
Los Angeles, California 90026

Copyright © 1968, 1969
by
L. RON HUBBARD
ALL RIGHTS RESERVED

Revised Edition
Reprinted April, 1971

THE E-METER IS NOT INTENDED OR EFFECTIVE FOR THE DIAGNOSIS, TREATMENT OR PREVENTION OF ANY DISEASE

Printed in the United States of America
by Anderson, Ritchie & Simon, Los Angeles

TO THE READER:

Scientology is a religious philosophy with spiritual guidance procedures enabling an individual to attain Total Spiritual Freedom. The mission of Scientology is a simple one–it is to help the individual become aware of himself as an immortal being and to help him achieve and attain the basic truths with regard to himself, his relationship to others, his relationship to the physical universe and to the Supreme Being.

The spiritual counseling procedure used by the Church of Scientology is referred to as auditing or processing. Auditing is a spiritual exercise through which the Thetan (soul) aided by a Minister of the Church seeks total spiritual awareness. Auditing addresses the Thetan and aids him to relieve those encumbrances of a spiritual nature which inhibit the Thetan's native awareness and abilities.

Scientology addresses only the spirit, it is not medicine and does not replace competent medical treatment. If you are physically ill you will be sent to a competent medical practitioner prior to receiving spiritual counseling from a Minister of the Church of Scientology.

The Road to total freedom has indeed come to pass... and is yours for the asking.

BOARD OF DIRECTORS
CHURCH OF SCIENTOLOGY

SCIENTOLOGY is an applied philosophy possessing a technology for spiritual recovery and the increase of individual ability. The word Scientology comes from Latin and Greek roots which can be translated 'knowing how to know' or 'the study of wisdom'.

Scientology was discovered, developed and organized by L. Ron Hubbard.

IMPORTANT NOTE

In studying Scientology be very, very certain you never go past a word you do not fully understand.

The only reason a person gives up a study or becomes confused or unable to learn is that he or she has gone past a word or phrase that was not understood.

If the material becomes confusing or you can't seem to grasp it, there will be a word just earlier that you have not understood. Don't go any further, but go back to BEFORE you got into trouble, find the misunderstood word and get it defined, using the Glossary on page 311, a good dictionary or other Scientology texts.

CONTENTS

CHAPTER ONE

SCIENTOLOGY, ITS GENERAL BACKGROUND

(*Part 1*)

The word SCIENTOLOGY is one which you might say is anglicized. It comes from the Latin SCIO and the Greek LOGOS, with SCIO the most emphatic statement of KNOW we had in the western world. And OLOGY (from LOGOS) of course means "study of".

SCIO is "knowing in the fullest sense of the word" and the western world recognizes in it and in the word science something close to a truth.

This is not "science-tology"—and it is not "scio-tology", simply because that is not close enough to English.

So we use a word which is fairly easy to say, which is simply Scientology.

For quite some time we have not used the word Dianetics, but certainly not because Dianetics does not belong to Scientology. It does, one hundred per cent. It is the subject of the mind and says so. It says DIA-NETICS from DIA NOUS (with an engineering twist on it—"ETICS") and DIA NOUS means no more and no less than *through mind.*

Of course the western world thinks of mind as something that mental cases have, something of that kind, and we weren't particularly interested in continuing to concentrate upon this thing called mind, although mind is a perfectly useful word.

In Scientology we are not going "through mind", we

are talking about *knowledge*. Dianetics was a study of the mind, there's no doubt about that, and there is no doubt about it that it is a very legitimate ancestor of Scientology, but Scientology is a thing of considerable *amplitude,* where Dianetics in comparison was a very narrow thing indeed. And Dianetics belongs, in a sense, in the world of psychology, and Scientology does not belong in the world of psychology and is not "an advanced psychology" and cannot be defined in the framework of psychology. Psychology is an anglicized word, not today true to its original meaning.

Psychology is composited from *psyche* and *ology,* and *psyche* is mind or soul, but leading psychological texts begin very, very carefully by saying that today the word does not refer to the mind or to the soul. To quote one, it "has to be studied by its own history", since it no longer refers to the soul, or even to the mind. So we don't know what psychology refers to today. It simply got lost. And so we have to step out and take a word which actually means what we mean, which is a study of knowingness, a study of wisdom. We have to take the word Scientology because that is what we are doing.

Now philosophically, there is a word called epistemology, and epistemology is quite separate from ontology, another word in the same category. In philosophy matter is considered to be separate. The physical universe is considered one direction, thought another direction and so it goes. The available words do not encompass enough.

Thus we are already looking at a cloudy vocabulary when we look at the field of western philosophy. In fact, nowhere in the west can we find any qualification for a study which assumes to reach the highest possible level of knowledge which can be attained by Man or Life. We find nowhere in the western world a word or a tradition which will embrace Scientology. This makes some difficulty for an auditor (*Auditor*: trained Scientologist. Auditor means "one who listens" and is a person who applies Scientology auditing technology to individuals for their betterment) when he is trying to communicate to people in the society around him, since they want to know what Scientology is, and then he speaks to them, in the west, without this tradition.

They assume that the word psychology embraces all sorts of eccentrics found in mental behavior. They assume this so they could not possibly understand how anything related to thought could be said to exceed or not be the same as psychology, and they are left in the dilemma of non-recognition. You have just not communicated in the west when you have said "we study wisdom". You see, if you just said that, they would say, Oh yes, that's all very well, I did that in third grade.

Now, in view of the fact that you go out of communication, in a society which has no standard of communication on the subject about which you are talking, it is necessary to resort to various shifts in trying to describe what you are doing. You have to find the background which actually leads to an understanding of your subject.

There would be many ways in which this could be accomplished, but let's take up something that is quite important to us and is not limited to any ignorance that we discover in western civilization. Let us take up what amounts to probably ten thousand years of study on the part of Man of the identity of God or gods, the possibility of truth, the inner track mystery of all mysteries. In other words, the mystery of life itself. We find that for ten thousand years, which figure, by the way, does not agree today with certain historians (but then they don't know much of the data I am referring to) man has been on this track. We find that the material which is extant, even in western civilization and in Asia, has gathered to itself an enormous verbiage, you might say. There are somewhere between—and I think it would be adventurous to state an exact number—125,000 and 150,000 books which comprise the Vedic and Buddhist libraries. Now that's a lot of books. Here is a tremendous amount of data.

One could say, if all this data is in existence, then why doesn't the western world know more about it? And we have to go back and take a brief look at what happened about ten thousand years ago, and of course, that's rather cloudy too, but let's put it into the field of anthropology rather than into the field of history. And we discover that perhaps much earlier than ten thousand years ago, there was a division of peoples here on earth, and the division point was evidently the Ural Mountains. This is material that was given to me by a Professor of Ethnology at Princeton University.

There was evidently a split of races somewhere in the vicinity of the Ural Mountains. Part of the population which is now in the northern hemisphere went east, and part of it went west. The borning spot of the human race has been variously disputed but if we don't worry about the borning spot and just say—that is more or less what occurred at that time, that there was a sharp division, and that part of the northern hemisphere's people went east and part of them went west—we discover that a singular difference of personality occurred which is in the northern hemisphere *the* most observable difference.

The people who went into the steppes, into the Gobi, into China, India, and into the various islands, were faced by an enormous chain of deserts. They were faced by privations of great magnitude, and they developed a philosophy of *enduring*. That was the keynote because that was what their environment demanded of them. They had to endure and so we find these races colored in a certain way so as to thwart the onslaught of sun and snow. We find them without natural protection in their environment and therefore we find them able to survive long after those who went in the opposite direction.

And so it is, their colorations, their customs, and so on, are different from ours just to the degree that they can survive in tremendously arduous surroundings, and the surroundings of those lands *is* arduous. They are, those races that are there, able to endure. And if you said *anything* about them, this is certainly a clear statement of fact.

They also are tremendously practical. Their practicality is such as to stagger a westerner. The explanations that they will suddenly and innocently voice to a query are always of such sweeping simplicity that they leave a westerner standing there staring with a slack jaw.

Now the races which went in the opposite direction from the Urals, evidently went into a country which had a heavy forestation. It had a great deal of game and the philosophy of the western world became that of striking a hard blow. If you could strike a blow of great magnitude hard enough and fast enough you could kill game and so you could live. Because of the vegetation and because of many other factors, they did not particularly need coloration. Their own customs did not need to be as thoroughly practical and they were able to dispose of their lives much more easily, you might say, since food was plentiful, as it was not in Asia. And we discover western philosophy building up on the behavior pattern of striking a hard blow. Get in quick, hit hard, your game drops and you eat. And beyond that, not very much thought or practicality.

However the truth of this may be, here certainly is

something which is said to have preceded a period of 10,000 years ago. It might or might not have truth. But it is a very fast explanation of this—and we discover immediately, as we look at these two worlds, that one of these worlds, having to endure, being faced with enormous privation, would of course develop a certain patience and an ability to philosophize. An ability to think. It would take a long time for anyone to think all the way through something. And a man who is merely accustomed to striking a hard blow is not likely to think all the way through something. When we are up against philosophy, we are fortunately or unfortunately up against an Asian tradition.

This is a tradition which is not necessarily that of colored peoples or strangers. This by the way, would come as a great shock to some people in the western world, to discover that in India the ruling caste is quite as white as any Norseman.

Well, they have, because they have a tradition of enduring, preserved records. We do not know what went on in North America. We can only guess. We do not know what went on in South America. There are a few ruins kicking around but beyond this, we don't know very much. We get down into the Mediterranean basin and we discover that there was a certain traffic with Asia and therefore there is quite a bit known about the Mediterranean basin. This philosophy of endurance came forward into the Middle East—very poorly, but it was to be found there. The records of Europe we can hold in tremendous question. They do not, for instance, know where or when they had ice ages. They actually cannot trace from one millennia to the next, who was where and owned what. Every now and then they have to write a history, so everybody gets in a good state of agreement and somebody writes a history—but so unreliable that Voltaire dubbed history A Mississippi of Lies. Now where the western world is concerned, we have records which go back—written records—supposedly 3,500 years. This may or may not be true but certainly the schools in the western world teach us that we can go back that far with written records. And in Egypt they go back to Isis, I think, which for the west is quite early. And they have found records in that particular area and they hold these up as being very old. But be very careful, be very, very careful that you do not leave the western world, if you are looking for early records. In order to have a blackout of history and a blackout of knowledge, you have to stay west of the Ural Mountains.

East of the Urals you discover no such blackout. You discover a recorded tradition of wisdom which reaches back about 10,000 years. And that is the oldest trace that we have.

Now true enough we don't necessarily have to recognize that there are written works any older than any anthropologist in the western world knows about. It does happen, however, that there is a set of *hymns* which as I recall were introduced into the societies of earth in about 8212 B.C. (The favorite western figure puts it *after* Egyptian!) These are hymns, and it would seem that if we spoke of hymns then they would contain largely modes or rites of worship, since they are religious, but that would only be our western interpretation of what is religious. These were religious hymns and they are our earliest debt in Scientology. Our earliest debt, because the very early hymns contain much that we know today and which checks against what we have rediscovered, or what we have followed back to, and this material included such a common thing as the cycle of the physical universe, known to you in Scientology as the Cycle of Action (*Cycle of Action*: the creation, growth, conservation, decay and death or destruction of energy and matter in a space. Cycles of Action produce *time*.) And this is contained in "The Hymn to the Dawn Child", variously captioned and translated by western translators, but all this information is there.

Furthermore, we find, in that same set of hymns, the theory of evolution which was brought forward in the west only a hundred years ago, or slightly less, by Charles Darwin. In fact, as we look at these hymns, we discover almost any information you want to discover later. Whether you call it science or what you wish, here is a tremendous body of knowledge. They are supposed to have come forward in spoken tradition, memorized, from generation to generation, and finally to have been set down. Now this is a western interpretation of what happened to them. I would not care to say how exactly correct this is but I can tell you that today these hymns are still in existence. They are very hard to acquire in the western world. You have to find the specialized translations of them and they are studied as curiosa more than anything else, but we do not know *what* sciences would suddenly open their doors should someone sit down and begin to study the *Veda*. We don't know what would happen. But information seems to have leaked from that direction into the Middle East and into Europe rather constantly over the thousands of years.

Man is fond of believing that yesterday's man was unable to walk, to travel, to move. We find, however, that as late as 1200 B.C. certainly, he had horses, and horses can go almost anywhere. He was able to make his way here and there across the surface of Earth and naturally when you get this, you get a transplantation of information. For instance, today anyone who knows

China discovers nothing very strange in Italian cookery. And he would not discover it very strange that Italian cookery suddenly came into being shortly after the return of Marco Polo and many other travellers who had been in the same area. Just because one person wrote about it, is no reason a lot of people weren't there. It is always a matter of astonishment to some member of the Explorer's Club to go in and pick up all the information he needs about an area which is now wild and "completely unexplored", from a white man or a Chinese—particularly the Chinese—who has been living there for the last forty years. And the explorer brings back the information and publishes it in journals and makes it available to people. The information collected by that white man or Chinese on the ground, would probably only be told to his family when he got home and not particularly broadcast at all. So we have to recognize that certain information is broadcast broadly and some is merely carried around. Marco Polo and even Batuta happened to be writers, and like writers, they wrote, but that is no reason to assume they were the only people in motion during the last 3,500 years.

Thus it is no wonder that we discovered the various wisdoms of Egypt appearing as the earliest wisdoms of Greece. It is no wonder why we look into the Christian bibles and find ourselves reading the Egyptian *Book of the Dead*. It is no wonder that we look into the middle of the Romantic period of Europe and find that the *Arabian Nights* had just been translated and discover that European literature did a complete revolution at that point. We're not stressing that nothing has ever been thought up in Europe—but Europe has made tremendous strides forward, immediately that its doors were opened to Eastern information.

Because the Eastern tradition says that you can sit

and think, and sometimes somebody in the western world is reminded of this, and when he is reminded of it, he is struck by the fact that he can sit down and think too.

And if we have been taught anything, it is the patience of the East which permitted itself to stop acting long enough to find out how and why.

And it's that tradition alone for which we are most indebted to Asia.

But *are* we indebted to Asia? Is it to Asia at all, or is it merely to man on this planet, who, breaking into two halves, you might say, went east and went west—the common ancestors of Man. All of us have the same potentials, but it happens that the information which has been collected over the years is available in Asia. It has not been preserved in the Western world. Therefore, we look to such things as the Veda. We look to such things as the Buddhist text, to the *Tao-Teh-King* and other materials of this character from Asia, to carry forward to us information of the past. Who knows but what these materials did not come out of Europe in the first place and go over to Asia. We could follow very dubious tracks in all directions, but we do know as we sit here in the western world, that man has a tradition of wisdom which goes back about 10,000 years, which is very positively traceable. And we find Scientology's earliest certainly known ancestor in the Veda. The Veda is a very interesting work. It is a study of the whereins and whereases and who made it and why.

It is a religion. It should not be confused as anything else *but* a religion. And the very word Veda simply means: *Lookingness* or *Knowingness.* That is all it means. That is all it has ever meant. And so, we can look back across a certain span of time, across a great many minds and into a great many places where man has been able to sit still long enough to think, through this oldest record, and find where it joins up with the present and to what we, in Scientology, are rightly indebted. For to say that out of whole cloth and with no background, a Westerner such as myself should suddenly develop all you need to know to do the things they were trying to do, is an incredible and an unbelievable and an untrue statement. Had the information of the Veda not been available to me, if I had not had a very sharp cognizance of earlier information on this whole track, and if at the same time, I had never been trained in an American university, which gave me a background of science, there could not have been enough understanding of the western world to apply anything Eastern *to* and we would have simply had the Eastern world again. But the western world has to hit with a punch. It has to produce an effect. It has to get there. Nobody urged Asia to *get* there. You could sit on a mountaintop for a thousand years and it was perfectly all right with everybody in the whole neighborhood. In the west, they pick you up for vagrancy. So, we combine the collective wisdom of all those ages with a sufficient impatience and urgency, a sufficiency of scientific methodology. I think, by the way, that Gautama Sakyamuni probably had a better command of scientific methodology than any of your Chairs of Science in western universities. We had to depend, though, upon scientific methodology and mathematics to catalyze and bring to a head the ambition of 10,000 years of thinking men.

And if I have added anything to this at all, it has simply been the urgency necessary to *arrive,* which was fairly well lacking in the Eastern world.

CHAPTER TWO

SCIENTOLOGY, ITS GENERAL BACKGROUND

(*Part 2*)

Of the great body of work comprising the Veda, the Dhyantic and Buddhistic written tradition of ten thousand years, very, very little, actually, has arrived in the western world. Only a small amount of the material has been translated.

It would take someone a long time to get through the 125,000 to 150,000 volumes, and it has not been done, so that the totality of what is in those books is just not known.

The Veda itself means simply Knowingness or sacred lore and do not think that that is otherwise than a synonym. Knowingness has always been considered sacred lore, has never been otherwise than sacred lore, and has only been present a relatively short time in the western world, which is just growing up now and beginning to come out of the level where sacred lore is equated with superstition.

The Veda, should you care to look it over, is best read in a literal translation from the Sanskrit. And there are four major divisions of the Veda, all of them quite worth while. A great deal of our material in Scientology is discovered right back there. This makes the earliest part of Scientology, its sacred lore.

The next written work, which is supposed to be the *oldest* written work, according to various frames of mind, is a book called The Book of Job. It is Indian and quite ancient. It probably predates what is called early Egyptian. And we discover that this Book of Job contained in it simply the laborings and sufferings and necessity for patience of one man faced with a somewhat capricious god. Now other such works, *like* the book of Job, are scattered along the time track, and are known to us here in the western world as sacred works. They are thought to have come to us from the Middle East but that would be a very short look.

Actually, we're looking, in the Middle East, at a *relay* point of wisdom, from India and from Africa into Europe. And as you see, it follows a trade route in both directions and so you have the roadways of the world crossing through the Middle East. So we would expect such things as the Book of Job to turn up in the Middle East as holy scripture. You would expect such things as the Book of the Dead of the Egyptians to turn up in the Middle East as part of the New Testament, and so on. There could be a great deal of argument about this. Someone who is passionately devoted to practice rather than wisdom (there are two different things here that embrace religion) would argue with you. But Scientology has no interest in arguing along that line because we can make this very, very clear differentiation right here and now. The word religion itself can embrace sacred lore, wisdom, knowingness of gods and souls and spirits, and could be called, with a very broad use of the word, a philosophy. So we could say there is religious philosophy, and there is religious practice. Now religious practice could take the identical source and by interpretation put it into effect and so create various churches, all dependent upon the identical source, such as St. John. If we think of the number of Christian churches there are and we look at one book of the New Testament and realize that just one book was productive of Baptists,

Methodists, Episcopalians, Catholics, we find that a tremendous number of practices, can debase upon one wisdom.

So let's get a very clear differentiation here between religious *philosophy* and religious *practice*. When someone who comes to you and says so-and-so-and-so is actually *the* way you're supposed to worship God, you can very cleanly and very clearly and very suddenly bring this to a halt by merely mentioning to him that he is talking about religious *practice* and you are talking about religious *philosophy*.

Now, just coming down the track in a little more orderly fashion, we get to the Tao-Teh-King, which is known to us in the western world as Taoism. And we may have heard of this religious practice in China. Taoism, as currently practiced today may or may not ever have heard of the Tao-Teh-King. It may or may not ever have connected. But we are certainly talking about religious philosophy when we mention the Tao-Teh-King.

It was written by Lao-Tzu in approximately 529 B.C., something around that period. He wrote it just before he disappeared forever. And his birth and death dates are traditionalized as 604 B.C., born, to 531 B.C., died. This is the next important milestone in the roadway of knowledge itself.

Now what was the Tao: it meant *the way to solving the mystery which underlies all mysteries*. It wasn't simply *"the way"*, as the western world generally thinks of it. I would suppose this would only be the case if they were unfamiliar with the book itself. It *is* a book and it was written by a man named Lao-Tzu when he was ordered to do so by a gatekeeper.

Lao-Tzu was a very obscure fellow. Very little is known about him. His main passion was obscurity and he started to leave town one day and the gatekeeper turned him around and told him he could not leave town until he went home and he wrote this book. It is a very short book. It must not be more than six thousand characters. He merely wrote down his philosophy and gave it to the gatekeeper and went out the gate and disappeared. That is the last we ever heard of Lao-Tzu.

Well, when we have this book, we begin to see that here was somebody trying to go somewhere without going on *something*. We have the western world defining this work as "teaching conformity with a cosmic order" and "teaching simplicity in social and political organization". The Tao-Teh-King did do this and this would be a very finite goal for it, but this was actually not the Tao. The Tao simply said you can solve the mystery that lies behind all mysteries, and this more or less, would be the way you might go about it, but of course, what you're trying to solve, itself, does not possess the mechanics which you believe to be inherent to the other kinds of problems which you solve. It says that a man could seek his Taohood in various ways but he would have to practice and live in a certain way, in order to achieve Taohood.

This is an amazingly civilized piece of work. It would be the kind of thing you would expect from a very, very educated, extremely compassionate, pleasant people of a higher intellectual order than we're accustomed to. It is a very fine book. It's sort of simple. It's sort of naive and it tells you that one should be simple and economical and it tells you what would be a wise way to handle things. That, by the way, is about the only flaw there is in it, from a Scientological point of view—that you must be economical.

And if we took the Tao just as written, and knowing what we know in Scientology, simply set out to practice the Tao, I don't know but what we wouldn't get a Theta Clear. (*Theta Clear*: An individual who, as a being, is certain of his identity apart from that of the body, and who habitually operates the body from outside, or *exteriorized*.) Actually the Tao is merely a set of directions on how you would go down this way which itself has no path and no distance. In other words it teaches you that you had better get out of space and get away from objects if you're going to achieve any consciousness of beingness, or to know things as they are, and it tells you that if you could do this then you'd know the whole answer and you'd be all set. And this is exactly what we are doing in Scientology.

Tao means Knowingness. That is again a literal translation. In other words, it's an ancestor to Scientology, the study of "knowing how to know". The Tao is the way to knowing how to know but it isn't said that way—it's inverted. It's said, This is the way to achieve the mystery which lies back of all mysteries. Now, however crude this might seem to someone who has specialized in the Tao, that's really all we need to know about it, except this one thing: there is a principal known as Wu-Wei which is odd because it goes right in with the Tao, which also means the way, and you are probably vaguely familiar with a practice known as Judo, or Ju-jitsu. Wu-Wei is a principle which crudely applies to action more or less in that fashion. We find that this principle is *non-assertion* or *non-compulsion*, and that is right there in the Tao: self-determinism. You let them use their self-determinism. (A little later on with Judo, you find that if you let a man be self-determined enough, you can lick him every time, but this is outside the scope, actually, of the Tao.) That's an interesting thing to find sitting there as one of the practices which emanated from the Tao-Teh-King.

Well, it must have been that there were a lot of very, very clever people on Earth at that time because we find in the lifetime of Lao-Tzu one called Confucius, of whom you have heard so much, but unfortunately Confucius evidently never wrote a single word. Confucius is reported by those who were around him—his disciples. And he took most of his material from, or gave credit to, some ancient Chinese works, and one of them, if I remember rightly, is the Book of the Winds. And these are very, very ancient and I have seen some fragmentary translations of them. Of course Confucius himself was the great apostle of conservatism, and as such, has ever since been the very model philosopher to have in a government. He is worshipped in this century by many many levels in China and you could buy his statue with great ease throughout North China.

Now the amount of superstition which has grown up around Confucius is considerable but we had in both Lao-Tzu and Confucius two people who never otherwise than pretended to be human beings who were simply pointing out a way of life. Now Confucius is of no great interest to us because he was codifying *conduct* most of the time, and the great philosopher of that day, if less known, was Lao-Tzu.

We come then into the main period of the Dhyana. The Dhyana has, as a background, almost as legendary a distance as the Veda, appearing in India in its mythological period, legendary in its basics. Dharma was the name of a legendary Hindu sage whose many progenies were the personification of virtue and regilious rites, and we have the word Dharma almost interchangeable with the word Dhyana. But whatever you use there, you're using a word which means Knowingness. Dhyana again means Knowingness and Lookingness. The Veda, the Tao, the Dharma, all mean Knowingness. This is what they are, and these are all religious works, and this is the religion of about two thirds of the population of earth. It is a tremendous body of people that we're talking about here. We erroneously know about it as and call it Buddhism in the western world and it has very little to do with Buddha. The Dhyana is what the Buddhists talk about and is their background.

We first find this Buddha called actually *Bohdi,* and a Bohdi is one *who has attained intellectual and ethical perfection by human means.* This probably would be a Dianetic Release (*Dianetic Release*: One who in Dianetic auditing has attained good case gains, stability and can enjoy life more. Such a person is "Keyed out" or in other words released from the stimulus-response mechanisms of the reactive mind) or something of this level. Another level has been mentioned to me—*Arhat,* with which I am not particularly familiar, said to be more comparable to our idea of Theta Clear.

There were many Bohdis, or Buddhas. And the greatest of these was a fellow by the name of Gautama Sakyamuni and he lived between 563 and 483 B.C. I won't go so far as to say he'd ever read the Tao-Teh-King because there is absolutely no evidence to that effect at all, except that they certainly were riding on the same pathway. So much so that when Taoism turned into Buddhism later on they never abandoned the Tao. Taoist principles became Chinese Buddhist principles, in very large measure. And what we have just talked about in terms of knowing the way to Knowingness, is very, very closely associated here with Buddha or Lord Buddha, or Gautama Buddha, or the Blessed One, or the Enlightened one. He is looked upon, and according to my belief in the line, erroneously, as the founder of the Dhyana. I think that this was in existence for quite a long time before he came along, but that he pumped life into it, he gave it codification, he straightened it up and made it run on the right track and it has kept running in that direction ever since, he did such a thoroughly good job. He was such an excellent scientific philosopher, and he himself was so persuasive and so penetrative in his work, that nobody has ever managed to pry apart Dhyana and Gautama Buddha. This identification is such a very close one that even in areas that have no understanding whatsoever of the principles laid down by Gautama Buddha, we find him sitting there as an *idol,* which would have been a very, very amusing thing to Buddha, because he, like Lao-Tzu, never said that he was otherwise than a human being. He didn't ever announce any revelations from supernatural sources, there were no guardian angels sitting on his shoulders preaching to him, as in the case of Mohammed and some other prophets. Nobody was ever giving him the word. But he went around giving what he had to people, he never intended to be anything but a human being, and he was a teacher. A tremendously interesting man. Now we find, however, some of the things that were *written* by Gautama, find them very significantly interesting to us, completely aside from Dhyana (which could be literally translated as "Indian for Scientology", if you wished to do that).

We find in *Dharma-Parda*:

"All that we are is the result of what we have thought. It is founded upon our thoughts. It is made up of our thoughts."

Interesting, isn't it? And:

"By oneself evil is done. By oneself one suffers. By oneself evil is left undone. By oneself one is purified. Purity and impurity belong to oneself. No one can purify another."

In other words, you can't just grant beingness to, and over-awe the preclear (*Preclear*: A person who through Scientology processing is finding out more about himself and life). It means you've got to have him there working on his own self-determinism or not at all—if you want to give that *any* kind of an interpretation. In other words, you've got to restore *his* ability to grant beingness, or he does not make gains, and we know that by test.

"You yourself must make an effort. The Buddhas are only preachers. The thoughtful who enter the way are freed from the bondage of sin."

"He who does not rouse himself when it is time to rise, who, though young and strong, is full of sloth, whose will and thoughts are weak—that lazy and idle man will never find the way to enlightenment."

The common denominator of psychosis and neurosis is the inability to work.

And the next verse:

"Strenuousness is the path of immortality, sloth the path of death. Those who are strenuous do not die; those who are slothful are as if dead already."

This is some of that material, and by the way, a little bit later on in his work, in a discourse with one Ananda, we discover him announcing the fact that you have to abstain from the six pairs of things, in other words, twelve separate things, and we in Scientology would recognize them as the various fundamental parts of things such as space, making and breaking communication and so forth. They're all just named there one right after the other. But he said you had to abstain from them, and the main difficulty is of course the interpretation of exactly what he said. What did he say? What was actually written?

Because the truth of the matter is, that successfully

abstaining from these things would mean that you had to get into a position where you could tolerate them before you could abstain from them. And that is the main breaking point of all such teachings—that one did not recognize that one didn't simply negate against everything and then become pure, and the way it's been interpreted is: if you run away from all living, then you can live forever. That's the way it has been interpreted. But understand that was never the way it was said.

The religion of Buddhism, carried by its teachers, brought civilization into the existing barbarisms, as of that time, of India, China, Japan, the Near East, or about two thirds of the earth's population. This was the first civilization they had had. For instance, Japan's written language, her ability to make lacquer, silk, almost any technology which she has today, was taught to her by Buddhist monks, who emigrated over to Japan from China—the first broadcast of wisdom, which resulted in very, very high cultures. Their cultures, which ensued from Buddhism, were very easily distinguishable from those superstitions which had existed heretofore. No light thing occurred there. It was just some people who had the idea that there was wisdom, and having that wisdom, you went out and told it to people and you told them that there was a way that you could find a salvation and that way was becoming your own *mind essence*. And if you lived a fairly pure life, lacking in sensuousness and evil practices, in other words, overt acts (*Overt act*: a harmful or contra-survival action), quite possibly you could break the endless chain of birth and death, which they knew very well in those days. And in other words you could accomplish an exteriorization (*Exteriorization*: The state of the thetan, the individual himself, being outside his body. When this is done, the person achieves a certainty that he is himself and not his body.)

Now all this knowledge up to this point, was given to a world which was evidently clearly cognizant of the manifestation of exteriorization, and that one was living consecutive lives. Twenty-five hundred years later, you would expect a race to be ploughed in far enough below that level as to no longer be conscious of consecutive lives but only single ones, and so Man is. But to reach salvation in one lifetime—that was the hope of Buddhism. That hope, by various practices, was now and then, here and there, attained. But no set of precise practices ever came forward, which immediately, predictably, produced a result. You understand that many of the practices would *occasionally* produce a result. But it was a religion which to that degree, had to go forward on hope—a hope which has extended over a span of a great, great many years.

The material which was released in that time is cluttered with irrelevancies. A great deal of it is buried. You have to be very selective, and you have to know Scientology, actually, to plot it out, get it into the clear, but much less than you might expect. It was wisdom, it was really wisdom and is today the background of the religious practices, but don't think for a moment that a Buddhist in the western hills of China knows the various words of Gautama Sakyumuni. He doesn't. He has certain practices which he practices. The basic wisdom is thinned. With that as a background they have certain religious rites and they follow these. So even in China, very close to India, where this came forward—and it was sent *directly* into China from India—we have that immediate division from the wisdom into the practice, and we have almost all of China in one fashion or another, bowing down to some form of Buddhism and

a very little of the intellectual world knowing actually the real background of Buddhism. But we have there a civilization where before Buddhism we didn't have one, which is quite important to us.

Now there, so far, is your track of wisdom, which merely brings us up to the beginning of two thousand years ago.

CHAPTER THREE

SCIENTOLOGY, ITS GENERAL BACKGROUND

(*Part 3*)

When we look at Buddhism, we don't wonder that a great change took place in the operating climate of Man, which it certainly did. Rome went under just 800 years later. Now that's fast, because their *whole philosophy* shattered. The philosophy of every state operating on force alone and every barbaric society that Buddhism touched—shattered. The first one to go by the boards was, however, India itself. India at that time was a savage and barbaric area, as was China. Japan is still characterized very impolitely by the Chinese, and the civilization of Japan by Buddhism took place almost in modern times. It was completed by America. So there they meet very closely.

But now, moving forward on the time track over all of these ages, we discover that it took an awfully long time for the Veda to walk forward and emerge as a new knowledge called the Dhyana. And it took quite a little while for the work of Buddha to move out of Asia. But we see the work of Asia itself—not the work of Buddha necessarily—moving out into the Near East.

Now there were trade routes that had existed since time immemorial. Man has no real trace of his own roadways, but the trade routes were quite wide open from very, very early times. We find the Phoenician, for instance, trading very neatly and very nicely up around Great Britain and sailing out through the Pillars of

Hercules. And I was just last year standing on the edge of a Phoenician ruin which was advertised as a Roman ruin but wasn't a Roman ruin. It had its inscription in cuneiform, which was a Phoenician script. And this was 1,000 B.C. A Phoenician ship then demonstrated at least ten thousand years of sea-faring technology. It was a very complex ship. And Phoenicia spread its empire out through Europe and just from where and what and why, we have no real trace, but Phoenicia is very well within our own teachings, our own history. Well, it was a thousand years after the Phoenicians that we first began, in the western world, to actually aver to a higher level of civilization. For some time, the Hebrew in the Middle East had been worshipping in a certain direction, along certain lines, and they had as one of their sacred books, the Book of Job, and many other of their sacred works were immediately derivable from similar sources. And into this society, apparently, other teachings suddenly entered. Their holy work, known to us as the Old Testament, leans very heavily on the background of philosophy we have been looking at, but it has a rather barbaric flavor, with all due respect to the holy book. It was a long way from home.

And we discover the civilized aspect of that religion which we know of in the western world as Christianity, taking place of course at the year 1. Now we find that that's of no importance to us except that everybody who writes a date out is talking about the man we're talking about, when he puts down A.D. Now when he puts down B.C. we are dating our very calendar from this incident I am discussing here.

The principles known as Buddhism included those of course of love thy neighbor, abstain from the use of force. These principles appeared in Asia Minor at the beginning of our own date, and I am not, by the way, discounting even vaguely the work of Christ, or Christ himself.

Traditionally Christ is supposed to have studied in India. One doesn't hear of him until he is thirty years of age, and he was a carpenter and so on—one hears of a lot of things, but we also hear this persistent legend that he had studied in India. Well, this would, of course, be a very acceptable datum, in view of the fact that the basic philosophy about which he was talking was a philosophy which had been extant in India, at this time, for about 500 years. Little less than 500 years. It was about that time that it moved out of that area, having taken over, by that time, two thirds of the earth's populace, but we don't quite recognize our Europe, if we think of it as a thriving culture. It was not a culture even twelve or thirteen hundred years after Christ.

A mighty conqueror stopped abruptly at the borders of Europe because he was leaving all areas of civilization and he saw no slightest gain in attacking an area where everyone was cloaked in fur loin-cloths. That was Tamerlane—Timuri Lang.

Now when we look at the Middle Eastern picture we find ourselves looking at the rise of a philosophy which, however interpreted, however since utilized, is nevertheless a thoroughly interesting philosophy. You have told a preclear, I'm sure, to get his attention off those energy flows and to get some space. And when he could tolerate that, he then could change his considerations.

Do you suppose for a moment that a preclear can actually get anywhere if he continues to use force? Well whether we try to put this into a public practice, such as turn the other cheek, or use it for Theta Clearing —the emanicipation of exteriorization of a soul—we are certainly looking at the same fact. And we are looking at the words of Gautama Buddha, however we wish to interpret this.

Now the parables which are discovered today in the New Testament are earlier discovered, the same parables, elsewhere in many places. One of them was the Egyptian Book of the Dead, which predates the New Testament considerably. This is *love thy neighbor*. This is in effect *be civilized*. And it is *abandon the use of force*.

But at the same time, we are talking straight out of the mouth of Moses, so we evidently are at a crossroads of two philosophies, but these two philosophies are both the philosophies of wisdom.

Now the Hebrew definition of Messiah is One Who Brings Wisdom — a teacher. Messiah is from "messenger", but he is somebody with information and Moses was such a one. And then Christ became such a one. He was a bringer of information. He never announced his sources. He spoke of them as coming from God. But they might just as well have come from the god talked about in the Hymn of the Dawn Child, who, by the way, is rather hard to distinguish from gods talked about later on. The god the Christians worshipped is certainly not the Hebrew god. He looks *much* more like that one talked about in the Veda.

And we come on down from there and we find that we are talking about a meeting place, a sort of melting pot of religious practices stemming from various wisdoms, but the highest amongst those wisdoms is apparently the Veda and the teachings of Gautama Buddha. The parables coming from the Egyptian Book of the Dead and from various other places, were probably not original with the Book of the Dead, so it would not be true that the parables of Christ necessarily came from Egypt, while we know full well that Moses escaped from Egypt, and that the Jewish peoples stem their history from their freedom from bondage in Egypt—not all of their history, but the history which they speak of most in the New Testament.

Now here we have a great teacher in Moses. We have other Messiahs, and we then arrive with Christ, and the words of Christ were a lesson in compassion and they set a very fine example to the western world, compared to what the western world was doing at that moment.

What were they doing at that time? They were killing men for amusement. They were feeding men to wild beasts for amusement. In the middle reign of Claudius, we find 3,500 men being turned loose, four abreast, divided half and half across a bridge of boats, slaughtering each other for the amusement of the patricians. How long can a society stand up when it is worshipping force to this degree? However these teachings were interpreted, the vein of truth was still here: that an exclusive reliance upon force will bring about a decay and a decadence which is unimaginably terrible. And that was the truth which came through. And so we find the Buddhist principles of brotherly love and compassion, then, appearing in the west 2,000 years ago.

Now Christianity spread like wildfire throughout Europe. But it was necessary to achieve a certain agreement, and in order to achieve that agreement, many of the practices which you know of today were *incorporated into* this worship. Basic and early Christianity is not recognizable today in many church practices. It's just not recognizable. It is very clouded. But these churches themselves recognize as their original source the New Testament, which contains, aside from a few court records and a few legends, all that we know of this particular transition.

But here we have this information poorly interpreted,

badly carried, through areas which did not know how to read and write, which is quite different from Asia. And we find this church and that church having to pick up and adopt customs in order to gain any entrance into these new areas. We discover today the worship of the Winter Solstice, in our Christmas. That is German and that is also other barbaric societies. Almost every barbarism that ever existed has worshipped the departure and return of the sun in the northern hemisphere and we find this incorporated into Christianity, and over there we find something else incorporated into Christianity and each time a certain amount of superstition coming into the information line—until we don't know what was *on* the information line unless we go back to sources and trace it through clearly and purely.

Then we are again, however, working with *wisdom*. What wisdom? The wisdom of knowing how to know one's self to resolve the mystery of life.

And when this Christianity was interpreted and imported into Europe, there was considerable speculation and resurgence and an enormous amount of hope. The very same thing that the Buddhists hoped for (and this is what is very interesting) became the hope of the Christian world. Emancipation—from the body. The survival and immortality of the human soul.

And although there was a cult in Rome which had this idea, it itself had no great antiquity, and it had evidently stemmed over from Persia, which was closer yet. The Christian impact wiped out this other cult but that's because actually they were just alike and one couldn't distinguish one from the other and the Christians won.

Now we have this immortality, this hope of salvation, being expressed throughout Europe and they expound it and they find it expedient to keep extending it, because they keep promising people that it was *just about to occur*, the day of judgment was just about to occur. Now we can get this as a sort of barbaric interpretation of what Gautama Buddha was talking about, the emancipation of the soul from the cycle of births and deaths. And then we get the fact that there is going to be a day when somebody blows a horn and it's all going to occur. We don't know what barbarism that superstition came from, but we have that superstition today in our society. The Day of Judgment.

At first, Hell was only the fact that Rome was going to disappear in a sea of lava—and everyone wanted to see Rome die. And that recruited people left and right. They promised them that Rome was going to disappear in a sea of molten lava. And they tried to prove it in Nero's reign, by burning the place down. Well, they didn't have a great deal of success doing it. Rome went on surviving and was finally taken over entirely and has since been the orientation point of Christianity.

A thousand years or so after Christ they started to try to take back the actual birth place of Christ in Jerusalem, and there's been a considerable argument going on about it, back and forth, ever since.

But the orientation point was placed at the only stable point, because that was the part of the world to which all roads led, and that became the dissemination point of all this information. But Rome split off and went back to Constantinople and we had then the Constantinople branch of this church and it, however, received its biggest blow when Russia suddenly turned completely atheist. We don't hear too much of that church any more.

But we still hear a great deal in the western world of this church at Rome. It is still there.

The use of Christianity was to produce a certain

civilized state and many people would blacken Christianity by saying it reduced people down to a very low level indeed. This is not true. It took an entire world of slaves and it made free men out of them. This in itself was quite a gain. It took a world which worshipped exclusively force and matter and made it recognize that sooner or later one would have to turn to the fact that he had a soul.

Now, remember that Christianity in its basic wisdoms is still available to us in the New Testament, and that this, no matter how it has come through the line, is quickly and swiftly traceable back to the Veda. We have a consistent track here. The same message is coming through. The Christian god is actually much better characterized in the Vedic Hymns than in any subsequent publication, including the Old Testament. The Old Testament doesn't make nearly as good a statement of what the Christians think of as God as does the Veda.

We have the loss of the trade routes somewhere in the vicinity of 1,000 A.D. Now, there was an enormous period of non-communication there. What had happened was Ghengis Khan, the various hordes which had been trying to pour out of Russia had cut the trade routes time and time again, and the amount of unrest in the area, and the taking of Baghdad and Jerusalem by such people. Of course, it kept these routes cut. You couldn't travel safely between these two worlds. And we find that communication doesn't open up again, not really, until some time in the 17th century.

In the middle of the 17th century, we find certain eastern practices beginning to show up in France, and there are many books being published saying you could do this and you could do that and you'd achieve something more closely related to religious philosophy than Europe was accustomed to.

Now, quite incidentally, during this period, a navigator who should have taken more lessons but fortunately didn't, by the name of Christopher Columbus, discovered America. He was simply trying to get to Asia, because everybody knew everybody in Asia knew everything and had everything and so you had to get to Asia. And he ran into America, fortunately, because he miscomputed the size of the earth so grossly that he would have perished out in the endless oceans if there hadn't been a continent there to receive him.

He was a very wise man—he discovered among other things a variation of the compass—but he failed. It was up to the Portuguese to continue around the bottom of the Cape of Good Hope and open the lanes to Europe and as soon as we get them open, we first find all of this information flooding in, information suddenly starting to appear, parts of the Veda starting to appear, various practices of Buddhism, Zen-Buddhism, other things start to crop up in Europe and right along with this, we begin to get such things as *The Arabian Nights* and in the middle of the 18th century, we get what you might call a renaissance of literature, the birth of the novel and so forth, coincident with the introduction of *The Arabian Nights* into France. A fascinating flood of information came in at about that time and the culture had already, during the Renaissance, picked up considerably, but the Renaissance was right in there with Marco Polo and we find some other interesting routes were open during that time. People had managed to get through. This is no attempt to tell you that everything was invented by Asia, but Asia had a tradition of information. They had kept their records, which was not true of the western world, and so the information was there and you might say it was a depository of knowledge which might just as well have originated in the western world, gone to

Asia, been put on file and come back again. I don't care how you would trace this one way or the other, but we still find that it was the repository of all the wisdom there was in the world at that time. And it has more or less continued so.

Philosophers, from the early Greeks on forward, made the first division in wisdom: they said there is wisdom about the *soul,* and there is wisdom about the *physical universe,* and there is some speculation about *life.* And this is the tradition of the Greek philosopher and it has come forward to us as represented in people like Kant, Schopenhauer, or Nietzsche—interesting material, and oddly enough those writings are coincident with new releases of Asian information in Europe. If you had ever convinced Schopenhauer he was writing nothing but sacred lore he probably would have committed suicide, but he never wrote anything else.

Now where did we get this artificial breakdown? We got it right there in the Middle East. The Greek came forward, went through Rome, and the philosophic scholarly consecutive line has come to us through barbarisms. What we call science today came to us from a barbarism, Greece, which civilized itself. It's largely an independent shoot of information.

Now the western world specialized in this, and never made enough advance in the humanities with it to bother about. So that today it would gladly—just to fill another test tube full of guck—it would very, very happily blow all of Man off the face of the earth. It is completely divorced from the humanities.

Where we come to the humanities and where we have to do anything for the humanities or with the humanities, we go straight back, all the way back, as far as we can go, to the Veda, and then come on forward and as long as we're on that track, we're on a track which means better men.

And when we go on the other track, we're talking about dead men. We're talking about dead men in an arena. We're talking about dead men on battlefields. We're talking about dead men in cities under atomic bombs. That is the tradition of barbarism. The only thing that has let the western world survive at all was an entirely different track which went back to the sacred lore of 10,000 years ago.

Scientology, then, today, could not possibly be characterized as a science the way the western world understands science. Scientology carries forward a tradition of wisdom which concerns itself about the soul and the solution of mysteries of life. It has not deviated.

The only reason why I would suddenly come up and do something like this in a western culture is a very simple one. I studied in my earliest years, and the first thing I was exposed to in this life, was a rough, tough frontier society. Montana. There was nothing tougher than Montana, either in terms of weather or in terms of people. And from there I went over to the completely soft Far East and heaved a long sigh of relief and found out what it meant to be in part of a civilization and the shock was so great to me that I was very deeply impressed.

And so, although I was a young American, I did pay attention. I had many, many friends in the western hills of China, friends elsewhere, friends in India, and I was willing to listen. I was also willing to be very suspicious and I was willing to be very distrustful but I was never willing to completely turn aside from the fact that there was some possible solution to the riddle of where man came from.

Any work that I am doing or have done, and that any

Scientologist is doing, has a tremendously long and interesting background. We are delving with and working with the oldest civilized factors known to Man. Anything else is Johnny-come-lately. Scientology is a religion in the very oldest and fullest sense. Anybody who would dare try to make religion into solely a religious *practice* and not a religious *wisdom* would be neglecting the very background of Christianity. Wisdom has no great tradition in the western world.

But if we are very industrious, it will be up to us to make one.

CHAPTER FOUR

CONSIDERATION, MECHANICS AND THE THEORY BEHIND INSTRUCTION

Here we go into some items quite rapidly which we find are of considerable importance to us in Scientology. It is demonstrable material, or doctrine. This is the basic theory which underlies instruction and indoctrination.

Considerations take rank over the mechanics of space, energy and time. Considerations are senior to these things.

These mechanics are the products of agreed-upon considerations which life mutually holds. The reason we have space, energy, time, objects is that life has agreed upon certain things, and this agreement has resulted in a solidification. And so our agreed-upon material is then quite observable.

Mechanics have taken such precedence in Man that they have become more important than the considerations. "Doesn't matter what you think," is the theme. The mechanics of space, energy, objects, time, rooms, houses, earth, electricity, Ivory Soap—these things have a greater value than Man's considerations. In other words, Man has become inverted. Having agreed upon these things so long—that they are so solid—he is now *below* the level of making agreements upon them, so his considerations do not apparently pack as much power as his immediate environment. This is what over-powers a man's ability to act freely in the framework of mechanics although he invented them. His considerations are now of less impressiveness than the mechanics with which he is operating. The agreement is more solid than his new consideration. And so as he makes a new consideration he runs into the mechanics of existence—his agreements with people, space, energy, objects and time.

A primary goal of processing in Scientology is *to bring an individual into such thorough communication with the physical universe that he can regain the power and the ability of his own postulates.* We discover an individual in an inverted state—that is to say, his considerations have now less value than the wall in front of him. And in processing, for example, in Opening Procedure 8C, we put him into sufficient communication with the wall that's there in front of him—that he can then see that there *is* a wall in front of him. And at that exact point he has graduated upstairs, you might say, to a cognition of what his postulates have created. He can go on from there and can graduate up to where his considerations again have precedence over mechanics.

The mechanics are so much in his road, they are such observable barriers, that he has become unacquainted with them.

Now it would seem as if it shouldn't be necessary to do this at all. All one would really have to do would be to get an individual simply to *change his mind*—all of a sudden to have an individual who could change his mind—but that is just not the way it is. It just doesn't work out that way. The principle here is: get an individual into thorough *communication* with something, and then, when he has lost his fear of it, is no longer flinching, to demonstrate to him that he can change his mind about it.

But unless you get him over his blindness, his unreality about something he's already agreed to, he is working against himself—he's fighting his own agreements. He has agreed that there is a wall there so there's a wall there—and now he's fighting that agreement, and he's saying there is no wall there. He is fighting his own postulates, so his own postulates are therefore very weak. Because the wall *is* there—that's his own postulate. And now without undoing that postulate, he's trying to change his mind about it and say "There is no wall there, there is no wall there". And there is a wall there, all right.

So this is the state in which we find Man. He has agreed that there is a physical universe, and then having agreed upon it he's sorry about it and now he wants to change his mind about it but to change his mind about it would make him wrong. An individual who has already said that there *is* something there, if he now says, without changing the first postulate, that there is now nothing there—of course he has got to make himself wrong before he can be right, and if you're wrong, your postulates don't stick. That's what Man is up against.

Scientology is the science of knowing how to know answers. That's extended a little bit. We have defined it as the science of knowing how to know, but we'd better say *what* we're trying to know. We'll just add that it's the science of knowing how to know *answers*.

A Scientologist is expected to be able to resolve problems in a great many specialized fields, of which auditing is the first field he addresses. If you know the principles such as, for instance, the principle of A-R-C (*Principle of A-R-C*: The "A-R-C" triange is Affinity, Reality and Communication. The basic principle here is that as one raises or lowers any of the three, the others are raised or lowered, and that the key entrance point to these is *Communication*)—when you know this as the modus operandi and the mechanism of agreement (which has been agreed on itself) you can do many things. You can take an organization, an industry, a store, a troop of Boy Scouts, or whatever, and you will certainly know "how to straighten out this mess".

We know the anatomy of confusions: an unpredictability, followed by a confusion, which then goes into a mystery. There is a mystery because someone didn't *predict* something and this made them wrong. The only reason a person thinks things are mysterious is that the amount of unpredictability became too great. So he closed it all off and said: "It's a mystery!" and, "I now don't know anything about that".

If an individual knew that, and ARC—a few of the principles and applications of Scientology—he would see that in the case of this troop of Boy Scouts or this business or this disaster area, or anything else that he might be dealing with, it would be necessary to bring the individuals in it to follow a certain pattern in order to regain a communication, and having regained communication, why, he knows that other matters would remedy themselves. He would not have to be an expert in turbines to straighten out a factory which made turbines. All he'd probably have to do would be to get management in touch with the foreman and the foreman in touch with the workman and the workman in touch with the management, and the plant would make turbines. He would be a specialist in knowing how to know answers but this does not mean that he would have to accumulate an enormous amount of specialized information. What he would do would be to get the people who had the specialized information and put them into communication and the job would get done.

The world is every day more violently impressed with mechanics. The little wheel that goes spin, spin, spin is far, far more important than the little boy who is going spin, spin, spin. The care of the body and the transport of the body, the conducting of electricity—these are far more important than any activity of Life itself. The world is terribly impressed with space and energy and machines and objects which, any of them, seem to be more important than a mind—the mind which makes them. And this is curious, but it brings a person down, as he gets more and more impressed with mechanics, to lower and lower levels of *being* mechanical. So, if you could conceive it, the individual, the thetan, a life-energy-production unit, has actually dropped out of sight to such a degree that people don't even know they *are* one any more. Now that is attributable to a dependency on mechanics and the validation of mechanics. It isn't that you should just withdraw from mechanics and leave them all alone and let's all go off and quit. No, an individual has to be put back into communication with them, mostly because he's afraid of them, and after he's done this he says, "Now, lookee here, I don't have to depend on these things. That's nonsense!"

And the next thing you know he has regained some of his own power and ability.

Now, when it comes to atomic fission, there is produced in this society an enormous mystery. It couldn't help but do so. It's unpredictable. The first bomb, for example, was dropped without any warning and this was certainly an unpredictability. Nobody even knew one was being made. That's nice and unpredictable, isn't it. So that the world is living in an expectancy of an unpredicted atomic attack. Well, that looks interesting, too, doesn't it? No more unpredictability. Now let's take up subject of confusion a bit further.

What do you suppose is the picture of all of these electrons and protons and morons exploding in all directions on a random pattern—would you possibly look upon that as a confusion of particles? What would be your chance, by the way, of tracing each of these particles individually, all through the entire mass? Well, your chance of doing that, if you're in very good shape, is very good. But Johnny Q. Public knows that he can't trace one card while it's being dealt across the table (that's what card sharks thrive on) and much less billions, and billions to the billion power, electrons and morons exploding all over space. And that is a confusion to him. So here you certainly have an unpredictability and then a confusion.

What follows is mystery. And so we have everybody being very secret about all the formulas of fission. They're only available in all of the library text books that are in all of the libraries in all the world. They're very secret. They are so secret, that the notebooks of anyone who has taken a course in nuclear physics *abound* with the basic formulas, the material of atomic fission. It isn't something suddenly discovered. They just decided to *do* it. It took billions of dollars to do it and it took a long time for somebody to put up that much money. But they're being very secret about formulas that have been public property—some of them—for fifty years. And all of the material that the U.S. had on the manufacture of the atomic bomb has already been transported over to Russia by spies, who were since executed for it. So who are we keeping it secret from? Well, maybe we're not keeping it secret from *anybody*. Maybe it's just a mystery because it is unpredictable and confusing and therefore we'd better lower all our communication lines—and before you know it, government is going to be almost totally out of communication with its own people, just on this basis. You get more and more cut communication lines. There's a big mystery building up. Well, how would you solve this?

The way one might solve it would be to simply point out the fact to the government and to people that atomic disaster was not going to ruin the entire world and that if you accepted the disaster and *predicted* what was going to happen, then you could resolve the situation. Next, one would ask that the study of the manufacture of atomic fission be made a third or fourth grade subject, and get the children indoctrinated into this great mystery immediately—so it wouldn't scare the kids. Actually all they're doing is scaring the kids these days—which is not an honorable activity for big, grown men.

Now the role of Scientology is, to impede any disintegration which is going on the realm of knowingness. Just to impede it. But if a disintegration does occur, why, people who know Scientology ought to just be ready to pick up the pieces. You could have a society so organized and with such enlightenment and so functioning that it didn't disintegrate people so quickly.

You could have one where freedom itself could be achieved.

But if you, all of a sudden, were looking at the complete smearing of a state or a country or a nation, you still, knowing the principles of communication—and just what a trained Scientologist knows—could play a very large role in picking up the pieces resulting from any disintegration.

The disintegration you would be dealing with would be one not of mechanics but would be a disintegration of knowingness.

Now as far as any politics would become a concern of Scientology, I would say off-hand that it would probably hew to a democratic line—not Democratic Party—but democratic principles—because of our datum of self-determinism, but that does not make Scientology necessarily possessed of a political opinion. A body of knowledge cannot have an *opinion* on something. It simply extends what is found to be true, wherever it is found to be true—into greater truths. That's all. And if something is true, that's all right. And if something is false—well, one simply recognizes that it is false. So far as political opinion is concerned, Scientology as such, could not have, and does not have one. It knows that certain types of government could be very disintegrative to a people. It knows, for instance, that fascism, military control of areas, and so forth, would result in a knock-down of communication lines, which would be very, very unhealthy for that particular area.

But this is in the field of Scientology, not in the field of politics. And one should remember well that Scientology has no political opinions or allegiances. If one political practice works better than another one, according to Scientology, that's fine, but what's working is Scientology—not the political practice. Don't ever get detoured on this one, because if you do—you get lost.

Now the next one that comes up is—does Scientology have any religious conviction? Well, again we have the fact that a body of data does not have an opinion. I've known a lot of witchdoctors who make more sense than a lot of priests. And I know a lot of priests who make more sense than a lot of preachers. I've seen the historical records and found that the Roman Empire didn't kill many Christians. As a matter of fact in one year of *that* confusion Christians killed more Christians in the city of Alexandria than the Roman Empire executed during all its existence. One hundred thousand Christians were killed in one year by Christians in Alexandria. Well that's because of a conviction—force without wisdom. There must have been some kind of a conviction running counter to some kind of a conviction, and —as far as having an opinion on this sort of thing is concerned, you can look at it on the basis of: this demonstrates that there must have been real bad ARC around there someplace! But beyond that it might be slightly amusing to you as a datum but it actually means *nothing* in relation to the body of *data*.

So a Scientologist's or anyone's social, religious and political convictions would be those that he held to be true and that he had been oriented to. Trained to be democratic in his viewpoint, and trained to be a protestant, why then he's certainly democratic in his viewpoint, and a protestant, unless he sees fit to alter his convictions to some degree because a greater wisdom seems to have penetrated those very convictions. What would he do in that case? He'd probably simply modify for the better his convictions.

But one of the oldest things that was ever given into the training of wise men that I know of was simply this —the basic faith in which the individual has been trained and the basic political allegiance of the individual must not be tampered with by the Order training him. And it was the Order itself which laid that down. That's an old, old one. They were training very wise men and that was the first thing that they made sure not to do. They did not tamper with these things. If the individual cared to alter these things himself nobody was going to tell him to or tell him not to. Nobody was even vaguely persuading him. It might be in the course of his study that he found certain things that men did laughable, or confusing, or he found certain things that men did remediable—but nobody was standing there trying to lead him into a higher religious or political *conviction*. And that is the case with Scientology.

If you were to teach a tribal population on the banks of the Yap-Yap River Scientology, and they believed in the Great God Boogoo-Boogoo you would just be wasting your time to start in by training them on the basis that the great God Boogoo-Boogoo was nine feet tall not twelve feet tall. That's about *all* you'd probably accomplish, too. You'd probably convince them he was *not quite* so tall, or something of that sort. A Scientologist has no business fooling around with a savage tribesman's political or religious convictions or a very, very cultured, super-cultivated Oriental Potentate's religious or political convictions. His customs are definitely his. You would produce at best new convictions, but that's force, and that's not the way to free a thetan!

There are very, very many ways to live. All of them can be derived from the same source and the same sources. Just because they can be so derived doesn't mean they're not different, one from another. So Scientology does not tamper with an individual's religious or political convictions.

The total empire of a Scientologist and of Scientology and its organizations is an empire of *wisdom.*

Now on the basis of mechanics, an auditor is expected to follow the Auditor's Code of 1954. That is a very solid compilation of things an auditor can do wrong and it says don't do them. Each one of those things has considerable importance. There is the one which tells you to run an auditing command until the Comm Lag is flat ("*Comm Lag is flat*": Comm Lag is Communication Lag: the time it takes for a preclear to give an answer to the exact auditing question or to carry out the exact auditing command. "Flat Comm Lag" is the point at which the auditing question or command is no longer producing change of communication lag).

And then there is the one which tells you to run a *process* until the process is flat. ("*Process is flat*": A process is continued as long as it produces change and no longer, at which time the process is "flat").

These are the two most important parts of that Code. Very, very much the two most important parts of the Code. You should know that Code. It was put together to keep us from making mistakes. It depends for its authority only upon this—that when it is disobeyed in processing an auditor has a lot more work to do. That's its total authority. It enforces itself.

Not so the Code of a Scientologist. The Code of a Scientologist is put together on this basis: an aberrated society has in it a few who would try to keep the organization and organizations of Scientology from doing their job—*by cutting their affinity lines*. And the first part of the Code of a Scientologist, *To hear or speak no word of disparagement to the press, public or preclears concerning any of my fellow Scientologists, our professional organization or those whose names are closely connected to this science,* is simply an arbitrary slid in front of that one. When we don't allow our affinity lines to be cut, auditor to auditor, auditors to organizations, and organizations to auditors, we certainly thrive much better and we survive much better and we are certainly a lot happier. And as we go down the line, on the various parts of this Code, this again is simply knowledge which if we had started following from the very beginning, we would have had far less difficulty than we sometimes have had.

And the last paragraph of the Code of a Scientologist says don't engage in unseemly disputes on the subject of Scientology with the uninformed. That is no effort to keep the material of Scientology closed up. That's not what it's about. We keep the lines open and flowing. But when somebody comes along—perhaps he's a major in Phrenology at the university of something or other—and starts protesting, "Well, I don't believe," and "Is your conviction . . .?"—why don't you just start talking about the weather. That is, please, an invitation not to go into a fight on the subject of demonstrating to somebody who doesn't have any awareness to talk to anyhow—all about Scientology. We have always gotten ahead faster when we haven't sat down and entered into verbal fisticuffs with everybody who disagreed with us on the subject of Dianetics and Scientology. He hasn't any information on it, and now you're going to sit there and give him a complete Professional Auditor course? Well, do you have any idea of how much work and organization it requires to bring somebody up along through the level of HCA? (*HCA*: Hubbard Certified Auditor) A lot of work is expended to bring someone that far. Nowadays, with codified training, it can be done easier, but you're not going to do that in a drawing room.

And this part of the Code says in effect: please recognize this and don't make the party awful for eight other people while you and a psychology student argue.

A reporter comes in—he "wants to know all about it," although he's going to write something different entirely or more likely—his story is already written before he comes to "find out all about it". He comes from a profession which works this way. You'll do best telling *him* all about the weather.

You should never depend on anybody's industry with regard to a society at large or carrying the word in the society. Never depend on anyone's industry but your own. Other people, organizations and so forth are going to help you all they can. But don't depend on that help. Depend on yourself.

CHAPTER FIVE

CONSIDERATION AND IS-NESS

Now here is the most fundamental fundamental that there can be fundamental below the level of consideration. I haven't written very much about considerations. There really isn't very much to say about the subject of consideration. If anyone is confused on the subject it is because consideration is consideration and all things are a consideration of the consideration so that if you consider something which is considerable, why—you have considered it.

Phenomena such as space and energy, time, matter and so forth are produced on the basis of consideration.

Consideration of A is senior to A. Consideration of R is senior to R and consideration of any and all parts of C are of course senior to any and all parts of C.

When you're dealing with A, R and C (Affinity, Reality and Communication) you have entered into a very early level of anatomy as far as the business of life is concerned, but you are not into the first and immediate level of anatomy as far as mechanics are concerned.

There is a level lying between considerations and A, R and C and this is Is-ness. It's the consideration of Is-ness. Things are because you consider that they are and therefore something that is, is *considered* is. If you don't consider that it is, it of course can be considered to be something else. But if you recognize that it is a consideration you only have to recognize that it *is*. And if you recognize that something is, then you have recognized merely that it is a consideration. As soon as you have recognized that something is, IS, you have reduced it to a consideration, and that's that. One has affinity because he considers he has affinity. One has reality because he considers he has reality. One has agreement because he considers he has agreement. One has disagreement because he considers he has disagreement. One has a Dynamic (*A Dynamic*: any one of the eight subdivisions of the Dynamic Principle of Existence—SURVIVE—which are: The urge to survive as, or to the survival of, (1) Self, (2) Sex and family, (3) One's group, (4) Mankind, (5) Any life forms, (6) MEST: Matter, Energy, Space, Time—the physical universe, (7) Theta, spirit; the Thetan, a spiritual being, thought, etc., (8) Supreme Being—the "Infinity Dynamic")—one has a Dynamic because one *considers* he has a Dynamic.

Any of the eight parts of the Dynamic Principle of Existence, any part of the Cycle of Action, of Create-Survive-Destroy, of Affinity-Reality-Communication (The ARC Triangle), the Chart of Attitudes top and bottom—(*Chart of Attitudes*: a chart on which in 1951 L. Ron Hubbard plotted with the numerical values of the Emotional Tone Scale the gradient of attitudes which fall between the highest and lowest states of consideration about life. Example : top—CAUSE; bottom—FULL EFFECT.) the entire scale of emotions (The Emotional Tone Scale), the Know-to-Mystery Scale (*Know-to-Mystery Scale*: the scale of Affinity from Knowingness down through Lookingness, Emotingness, Effortingness, Thinkingness, Symbolizingness, Eatingness, Sexingness, and so through to not-Knowingness—Mystery. The Know-to-Sex scale was the earlier version of this scale)—all these are preceded by a consideration. In other words they are postulated into existence. But right with consideration we have the most native and intimate mechanic which precedes all other mechanics and that mechanic is Is-ness. We have to consider that we can consider before we can consider an Is-ness. One considers that one considers and therefore what one considers is, IS ! ! Anything that is, is considered as being. What is, is, as it is considered to be.

Now the moment you recognize, then, the Is-ness of anything, it will disappear. To have something, to have anything over a long period of time particularly, you have to beware of recognizing what it is. Because if you look at it with a recognition of what it is, simply its Is-ness, this simple recognition will of course vanish it. So you have to be careful, if you want something, not to recognize what it is. Now one of the best ways to have something for a long time is to put something in your pocket and then forget that it is there and you'll have something in your pocket. You'll have something in your pocket even though you've forgotten it's there. And that's the safest method of possession, to forget that you have it, because if you remember that you have it you won't have it.

Now this would all be hopeless if there weren't another factor way above consideration, and that is Knowingness. You know anything you want to know and you know anything that has gone on.

Now let's take the person who is using facsimiles (*Facsimile*: A mental image picture) in order tell him what has happened. He looks at the facsimile, the facsimile has certain pictures and symbols in it, so then he knows what took place. Well, he had to know what took place in order for a facsimile of that incident to be created. Now, he did know what took place, so he could create a facsimile of the incident, and he does this on an unknowingness level. And above this level he can then look at the picture and know what took place. But he had to know what took place before he made the picture.

Now if the picture was gone utterly and completely he would still know what took place, unless he had the consideration that he has to have a picture in order to prove to himself what took place.

Anybody would know anything that was going on if he didn't have to prove it. Proof, conviction, is itself a very early level of aberration. As soon as you have to start proving things and convincing people of things, why then you have to get into agreement with them and in order to do this—you have to Alter-is. You have to have something persist long enough for them to see it, so that they can then understand what it is. So in order for them to really understand what it is you can't possibly put up something that they understand what is, because if they saw completely what it was it would disappear, so you would not have been able to have proven it.

I hope you follow this very closely! Because actually what I am talking about here makes sense easily if strung together and looked at in a rational way. But if you try to Alter-is it, if you try to change it around, then you'll be able to remember it perfectly, but if you merely accept exactly what I am saying at each and every point, you know this already, so it won't exist. Now this is a very bad thing, I realize, so the best thing for me to do would be to color, if I really wanted this material to be remembered, to color the material so that it appeared to be something else than what it was. I could do that, for instance, by talking about your egg libidol, and your re-conscious. I could quote authorities who didn't exist. That's always best, you know. That's *really* a curve, you see. Nobody could ever see those, so they can't ever disappear. And I could quote these authorities which didn't exist but which you couldn't disprove and we could go on about the counter-reflex of the seratopol palsy and the og libidol, the bog libidol, the sog libidol and the mog libidol and how we would categorize these things as explanatory to the behavior of a feeshee preservation on the part of young alligators, and this nonsense of course would then be utterly comprehensible because it could be so remembered in every detail, particularly if it were altered from what I was really talking about—in trying to talk to you about turbo-electric systems, for example, with that amount of data injected into it.

We could go that far afield and you would find that you would start hanging up on these non sequitur facts. You have experienced this sort of thing.

As a person becomes unable to recognize the Is-ness of things he can't get jokes any more. Every datum that comes in must have a significance. It never occurs to him that it doesn't have a significance, and he is sure there must be a deeper significance so that something will remain. This accounts for the badly jammed facsimile bank (*Facsimile bank*: mental image pictures; the contents of the reactive mind; colloquially, "bank") of an individual, particularly when that facsimile bank of the individual is badly jammed.

He will *add* significance to everything and he will certainly achieve a preservation of data. He, in adding all that significance to things, is Alter-is-ing. So he gets: *preservation of facsimile bank.*

Now let's look at the various categories of Is-ness. We find that each one has a gradient scale and first there is As-is-ness. This is the first level that we encounter and is actually the disappearance level.

As we are content with and can accept things as they are, they won't exist. That is absolute.

Why? The simple recognition of their existence would blow them into a consideration. A wall. What wall? When we really know what a wall is, there isn't going to be a wall. That's As-is-ness, and we can see that mechanically. We have a lower, mechanical strata on that which is a *perfect duplicate*. If we make a perfect duplicate of a wall—boom—no wall. All right, that may be just for the thetan but it's certainly *no wall*. Anyway, I at least will lead you down the track to believing that you are not about to destroy the physical universe.

I wouldn't want you to shy off from the processes which come from this data just because they knocked out the physical universe.

The next stage down the line from As-is-ness is Alter-is-ness, the effort to preserve something by altering its characteristics. We make it as a simple consideration and then we alter the method by which we made it. In other words "Let's dodge on it." Having mocked it up we will now dodge and say Joe mocked it up. Well this is just as far from truth as is necessary, to get something to exist, but you have altered an As-is-ness slightly in order to keep it from being perfectly duplicated in its own time, its own space, with its own energy and mass, thus ceasing to exist.

So we enter into the field of Alter-is-ness as a method of preservation. And one seeks, when he makes an object or a space, to get it to exist simply by saying somebody else did it, or it is a different kind of space, or its method of construction was different. The consideration is altered just enough so that one will get a continuation of it.

We say "God made it", or anything that would throw somebody off this track. Well, supposing God did make it, that would be all right. It would then cease persisting if you looked at it recognizing that God made it.

People get into Alter-is-ness—simply by the experience of having had too many things disappear.

So we see a person who has lost many things then trying to change everything. He's trying to shift the As-is-ness of everything. He's trying to shift from As-is-ness to Alter-is-ness and he's got to change the significances and structure and background and everything around him so that then these things will continue to exist, and that is his first impulse.

For example, we build a brick house and then cover it up with shingles, and then insist that it is built out of lumber. You would get into enough of an argument with people trying to buy the house who could observably see that it was not totally a lumber house for them to get upset and worried about it, and that house is likely to persist in one's ownership for some time, if he just did that sort of thing. So we see Alter-is-ness then, totally mechanically, as a method of getting things to continue their existence, and that's an important fact.

Although the nomenclature here is simply chosen at random it's a pretty good nomenclature because it says *exactly* what it means.

The control case, the person obsessively controlling things, *and* himself, is an Alter-ist. He's got to change, change. Well he's lost too much. Now he's got to change everything but he's not satisfied with anything. If he were walking down the street in a limber and loose fashion he would think he had to walk in a tight fashion, etc. He's become anxious about things disappearing so he of course has to alter everything he sees in order to keep these things from disappearing.

Now let's get to the next category—Not-is-ness. Here is someone who has altered things up to the point where they are beginning to persist. In fact he's upset about their continuous persistence. He doesn't think this is a good thing, to have a black box staring him in the face all the time, or to have the walls of the room appear to be 180 feet tall although they're only nine feet tall. It's not a good thing, that Alter-is-ness, he has concluded. He has changed too many things and lost track. He isn't quite secure about what the things were in the first place, he's shifted them so often. He's like the small boy who's told so many lies that he can no longer remember what lies he has told and so he's stuck with the lies—and so becomes a human being. Now the next step along that line, Not-is-ness, is manifested as and is in itself the mechanism we know as *unreality*.

There is a category of just plain Is-ness. This of course is not a bad thing. This, in its highest level, is what we call reality. But we could spell this with bigger and bigger caps. We could keep spelling "IS" there with bigger caps and bigger caps and finally give it an exclamation point —which would represent a psycho. There is a dragon in the middle of the room, and he knows this. There are many other things which he doesn't know, but he knows this. If you ask him to mock up an anchor point to define a space he makes a pyramid out of solid iron. And when he is asked to move one of his own mock-ups, a knowingly created object or space, he *knows* he doesn't have that much strength. The world is too real.

Once in a while when somebody's just about to kill you or cut your throat or eat you up or arrest you or do something of this sort you get an enormous flash of Is-ness, a recognition of the situation. Boy, this is *it is real*—GULP! A moment after that you're likely to get or postulate an immediate reaction of Not-is-ness. "It's not real". A fellow will flare up and daze from Is-ness to Not-is-ness very swiftly in a sudden emergency.

Now Alter-is-ness, Not-is-ness and Is-ness would be then the categories which can be aberrated but remember these are not basically aberration. They become aberration only when they go entirely beyond the ability of the person to re-recognize As-is-ness. When a person has lost his ability entirely to recognize As-is-ness, he's gone. He's stuck with and has only Alter-is-ness, Not-is-ness and Is-ness—all three, or one or two of the three—some such combination—with no As-is-ness left. Therefore he gets everything persisting around him. He gets everything less and less changeable, and he goes into a dwindling spiral, because he has lost his quality of As-is-ness. That is all he has lost.

Have him touch a few walls. You just have him go around and touch walls for a little while and all of a sudden he'll say, "It's a wall!" And right then he feels much better.

He knows he's in communication. Well, he has a case of Not-is-ness—"There are no walls"—or Is-ness—"There are walls all through the room and all through my mind and I have barriers everywhere, everywhere, everywhere", or "There are no barriers anywhere, anywhere, anywhere". Just variations of Not-is-ness and Is-ness. And you've now shown him that there were walls and these were agreed upon walls and of course that's way up scale because you have demonstrated to him something closer to an As-is-ness. Now each one of these is a gradient scale and you know that you can recognize poorly enough the actual As-is-ness of something. You just draw back just a tiny bit from the As-is-ness of something, in other words indulge in just a little bit of Alter-is-ness or just a little bit of Not-is-ness or just a little bit of Is-ness—making it a little bit *more*—and it'll persist with great satisfactoryness. Of course if you walk up to it and simply hit it with As-is-ness it's not there any more.

Follow this very carefully, because it's quite important, and the technology which we're using is elementary, and you discover that many philosophies could be adjudicated out of these four categories. And believe me, any philosophy there is *has* been adjudicated from these four categories. This is the make-route of all philosophy as well as all existence and you're standing right there at the tiniest co-point between mechanics and considerations that we have so far attained.

You could then develop many philosophies out of this and the first and most dangerous of them would simply be this one: "Well, I just have to accept everything as it is and therefore what we're really supposed to produce out of this is an apathy, because if I had to accept everything as is there would be nothing left but apathy because if I can't . . . or . . . something or other . . . , but I'll go into apathy. Yeah, I know what the auditor wants, he wants me to be apathetic about the whole thing." This is too easy a philosophy. This is the philosophy of Zeno. You can't do anything about it so you might as well accept it and everybody go into apathy and cut his throat anyhow.

We have an enormous number of things which we could say, list or categorize in terms of the philosophy of this and this is only one of those which will hit your preclear. You see he has to be able to accept his own restlessness before he can be restless. He has to accept his own dislike of things before he can dislike things. He has to accept something before he can have it, because he has to get *back* some As-is-ness before he can have *any* As-is-ness. He has to get back some As-is-ness before he can become fluid in his practice of As-is-ness, Alter-is-ness, Not-is-ness and Is-ness.

The business of life requires that he be quite able in all four categories, not just As-is-ness.

You're not particularly specializing in this. But when it comes to this universe you will discover that as you return your preclear to As-is-ness things disappear. That may be regrettable, it may be interesting, it may be this and that but those things too, just like opinions of art are merely considerations.

Now the first step that we would adventure upon in this would be a step which would be immediately addressed to such a thing as exteriorization. Recovering the thetan's ability to *be,* outside the body. You would merely in auditing find what part of the body was acceptable to the preclear. What part of the body was he able to accept as is. And we would go on asking this question and asking this question and asking this question.

We could vary it by asking what part of the body would he be at liberty to alter as to its position or shape.

Or what part of the body would be acceptable to him on an absent basis. What part of the body would be acceptable to him on a much more present basis—for instance, just a hand walking around all by itself.

Indicated processes. Actually this processing is so good that you can almost take any part of it and just work with that. An indicated process on As-is-ness is simply done with that command, "What part of your body is acceptable to you?" or, "What part of the environment would be acceptable to you?" And you merely have him improve his considerations, and if he hangs up too long you could say, "Can you accept your dislike of . . ." and of course it just involutes. He could just watch it. It just sort of goes away. It's terrible! The first thing he can recognize is the fact that he disliked the environment? All right. Well can he *accept* his dislike of the environment? The second he does this he has recognized the As-is-ness of his dislike, at which moment it will blow. You can get him to recognize the existence of anything as such and it'll disappear. Just getting him to accept parts of the body on this simple auditing command,

"What part of the body could you accept? Give me another part of the body you could accept"—there are tremendous comm lags on this. You could say, "How would it have to be altered for you to accept it?" or "What would it be fine to have absent about this body?" Then we can turn around and say, "What's the acceptance level (*Acceptance level*: the degree of a person's actual willingness to accept people or things, monitored and determined by his consideration of the state or condition that those people or things must be in for him to be able to do so) of your body about a *thetan*?" He doesn't do this by mock-ups, you understand. That's the trick. Get him to concentrate on the actual body. Does it accept the thetan this way or that way or how? "What *distance* could your face tolerate to a thetan?" We already have this on exteriorization processing, but without this one fact stressed, which in this case makes the difference between a workable technique and a non-workable technique. What distance is acceptable? What distance would be comfortable from your face to the thetan? Where would your face accept a thetan? And the first thing you know you have spotted the preclear (the face seems to have spotted him) then he spots himself. But the whole thing would run out without any such complexity of command at all. You would merely ask him, "What is acceptable to you in the environment?" Look around, and simply go over it one item after another item and his considerations will improve, which is the modus operandi behind 8C Opening Procedure. Do this long enough on a preclear and he would find the entire environment, even working in it, certainly very, very acceptable to him. We could just continue to run this as "What part of the environment is acceptable to you?" and he would begin to check them off and he would eventually get down to his body and having gotten down to that and taken care of the space around the body—we'd take it by parts of the body—what parts of the body are acceptable to you, and just on and on and on—and he'd be out there standing in back of his head. Now that's the easiest method of exteriorization I know and the method which I commonly use when I am balked by a preclear. It's an easy and certain process. It's a rather short process, really. You just ask him to pick up the As-is-ness of his environment and body and if he really recognizes it believe me he will be outside. Once in a while he says, "Well, I really dislike" this and that. Run "Can you accept your dislike of it?" This'll *involute* it, which is the only additional command I have ever used. So we have As-is-ness, Alter-is-ness, Not-is-ness and Is-ness. All cases fall into these categories.

CHAPTER SIX

IS-NESS

We start out at the beginning or anywhere along the road with this as the highest truth. We are dealing with *a static which can consider.* That it can consider and then perceive what it considers, makes it a space-energy-mass-time production unit.

Now don't ever get hung up on whether or not the actuality that is made is an actuality. This is the wrong way to approach this problem. It's the way people have been approaching this problem for so long that the problem has remained wholly abstruse. That you can perceive something and that you can perceive that somebody else also perceives something qualifies only one of these conditions of existence, and that's Is-ness. And that is reality: *Is-ness.*

Now, that you simply say something is there, and then perceive that it is there, means simply that you have put something there and perceived that it is there. That's what it means. It's no less an Is-ness. That nobody is there to agree with you at the time you do this does not reduce the fact that you have created an Is-ness. It is an Is-ness. It exists. It exists, not "just for you". It just exists, you see. Now if you were to desire that that persisted, you would then have to go through a certain mechanical step, you would have to make sure that you did not *perfectly duplicate* it. That is: *create it again in the same time in the same space with the same mass and the same energy*—because it would no longer be there.

But what have you done really when you've done that?

You've just taken a thorough look.

And what you create will vanish if you simply look at it, unless you pull this trick: unless you pull the trick that it is alterable, and that you have altered it. Now if you say that you have altered it, and now that you have forgotten the exact instant it was made and the character of it, it of course then can persist. Because you can look at it all you please—with your first look, you might say—and it won't vanish.

Don't look at it however with your second look because it will be gone.

For instance—if we looked at the front of a room and saw an object we would simply have to look at it and conceive ourselves to have made its exact duplicate, or counterpart, which is to say conceived ourselves to have made it. No more, no less than that. And of course it will get *rather thin*. To some who are having a rough time with conditions of existence it will first get brighter and brighter and brighter, and then get thinner and thinner and thinner, and it'll disappear for one. This is a curious thing, but is immediately subjected to and you can subject it to a very exacting proof.

Let's look at this very carefully—at what reality is. Reality is a *postulated* reality.

Reality does not have to persist to be a reality. The condition of reality is simply Is-ness. That is the total condition of reality.

Now we get a more complex reality when we enter into the formula of communication because this takes *somebody else*. We have to say we are somebody else now viewing this and that we don't know when it was made or where it was made, to get a persistence of the object for that somebody else.

But let us say we just more or less accidentally go into communication with somebody else, and we have an argument, a chitter-chatter back and forth, about what this thing is.

If that other person perfectly duplicates exactly what we have created, it will, again, disappear.

It doesn't matter really who created it, he only has to *assume* that he created it for it to disappear for him. In other words he has to duplicate it in its same space, same energy, same mass at the same instant it was created and it will disappear for him. So you and he had better alter this thing which you made so that you can both perceive it.

And then we get what is known as an agreed upon reality, and that is an Is-ness with agreement.

Now actually the word reality itself is commonly accepted to mean that which we perceive. This then is the real definition for reality, the one which is commonly used, and that would be: an agreed upon Is-ness. That would be a reality.

A NOT-IS-NESS is a *protest*. The common practice of existence of course is to try to vanish Is-ness by using it to destroy itself—taking a mockup such as a building or something of the sort and trying to destroy it by blowing it down with dynamite. This is very practical application, this material. It isn't esoteric, it doesn't apply only to the Engram Bank (*Engram*: A mental image picture of an experience containing pain, unconsciousness, and a real or fancied threat to survival; it is a recording in the reactive mind of something which actually happened to an individual in the past and which contained pain and unconsciousness, both of which are recorded in the mental image picture called an engram. "Engram bank" is a colloquial name for the reactive mind. It is that portion of a person's mind which works on a stimulus-response basis)—this is just existence.

Is-ness can be translated quite generally as existence. We get a *Not*-is-ness being enforced upon an Is-ness by the quality of the Is-ness itself, or, by a new postulate with which the individual is saying it's not there.

This new postulate, in which you simply say "It's not there" does not pattern itself with the mechanics of the creation of the Is-ness, the exact time of creation, the exact space, the exact continuance, same mass, same space, same time. And as a consequence, saying, "All right, it's not there", it will probably dim down for you. But you have to do something else. You have to put a black screen up or push it away, or chew it up, or do anything to it here rather than giving it a perfect duplicate.

So its a Not-is-ness when we say something doesn't exist which we know full well does exist.

Now you have to know something does exist before you can try to postulate it out of existence and thus create a Not-is-ness.

The definition of Not-is-ness would be simply: trying to put out of existence by postulate or force something which one knows priorly, exists. One is trying to talk against his own agreements and postulates with his new postulates, or is trying to spray down something with the force of other Is-nesses in order to cause a cessation of the Is-ness he objects to.

And this is the use of mass to handle mass, of force to handle force, and is definitely and positively wrong if you ever want to destroy anything.

That is the way to destroy yourself, which is why nations engage in it. Force versus Force. We see a very badly misunderstood rendition of this in early Christian times with the introduction of the idea that if you were hit you should turn the other cheek. The truth of the matter is that if it were rendered in this wise it would have made much more sense: when you encounter force don't apply more and new force to conquer the force which has been exerted because if you do you will then be left with a chaos of force, and pretty soon you won't be able to trace anything through this chaos of force. So turn the other cheek is actually very workable if it's simply translated to mean force must not be used to combat force. The way to properly handle such a situation is just to duplicate it perfectly.

Now, let's go into this business of *a perfect duplicate.* A perfect duplicate, again, is creating the thing once more in the same time, in the same space with the same energy and the same mass. A perfect duplicate is not made by mocking the thing up alongside of itself. That is a copy, or more technically a facsimile, a made facsimile. Copy and facsimile, by the way, are synonymous, but a *facsimile* we conceive to be a picture which was unknowingly or automatically made of the physical universe, and a *copy* would be something that a thetan on his own volition simply made of an object in the physical universe with full knowingness. In other words, he copies it and knows he is copying it. A facsimile can be made without one's knowledge by mental machinery or the body or something of that character.

What we are talking about here is a perfect duplicate, mechanically, but it is more important to recognize it in the terms of our four categories of existence. It's AS-IS-NESS. If we can recognize the total As-is-ness of anything, it will vanish. Sometimes, if it had many component parts, we would have to recognize the total As-is-ness as including the As-is-ness of each component part of it. And in that lies the secret of destroying actual matter. And actual matter can be destroyed by a thetan if he is willing to include into the As-is-ness which he is now postulating toward any objects which exist—toward any Is-ness—the As-is-ness of each component part.

A thetan created a mockup, and this mockup was agreed upon very widely, and another process, Alter-is-ness was addressed to it and it became more and more solid and more and more solid—and then one day somebody cut it in half and dragged part of it up the hill to make somebody's doorstep.

That's already, you see, out of location. *Same place* is part of a duplication, and it's already been removed from the place where it was mocked up and moved up to the top of the hill and now it's making somebody's doorstep. Those people themselves wouldn't quite remember where the doorstep came from if asked suddenly, but after a while those houses up there—by the way, just mockups like everything else—are torn down, and somebody picks up this doorstep and chews it up for road ballast, throws it out in the road to be used as road.

And the road they make with it just runs just fine, and it runs alongside of some wharves, and one day the road is no longer being used. They now have a big long steel pier coming out there, and somebody uses a steam shovel to pick up a load of rocks and gravel, dumps them into the hold of a ship which is going to South Africa, and they unload this ballast in South Africa, and the natives use it to gravel the garden, and at length there's a volcanic explosion, it's buried under twelve feet of lava, and time marches on, and this thing is getting more and more remote from its agreed upon time, its agreed upon original position—and the moment it was postulated, as related to the time span of the people who were agreeing upon it.

You see they've agreed upon a time span, so this thing is aging and they've agreed upon this space too and it's getting moved around in this space, and here atom by atom as the eons move along, this object which was part of an original mockup is now distributed all over the planet.

It would all be fairly hard to trace unless as a thetan you suddenly took a good look at it and sort of asked it —or just located it easily.

And the law of conservation of energy blows up right here.

In view of the fact that the time itself is a postulate, it's very easy to reassume the first time of anything. Just as you ask a person in Dianetic auditing to "go back to the moment when", he could reassume the time, and if we had just added "the place where" and then said "Okay, now *duplicate it with* its own energy", why it would have blown up.

This is not a process we would use today particularly, but is one you should know about.

To create an As-is-ness one would have to create the As-is-ness of the object itself and all of its parts, and only at that moment would he escape the law of conservation of energy. Conservation of energy depends upon the chaos of all parts of all things being mixed up with all the parts of all the things. In other words we couldn't have any conservation of energy unless we were all completely uncertain as to where this atom or that atom originated. And if we were totally uncertain as to the original creation spot in the space of the atom, molecule, proton, whatever—if we were to remain totally ignorant, we of course could not destroy it, because force will not destroy it. Force will not destroy anything made of force.

In view of the fact that you would have to make as many postulates, practically as many As-is-nesses, as there are atoms in the object, why it looks awfully complex unless you could span your attention that wide and that fast, at which point you would be capable of doing an As-is-ness of it and your operational level would be such that the conservation of energy (itself a consideration) is exceeded.

Now we've taken care of As-is-ness by the mechanics of a perfect duplicate. The As-is-ness would be the condition created again in the same time, in the same space, with the same energy and the same mass, the same motion and the same time continuum.

This last, the same time continuum, is only incidentally important. It only comes up as important when you're crossing between universes, and particles do not cross between universes. A particle is only as good as it's riding on its own time continuum. Destroy the time continuum, and of course no activities can take place from that moment forward.

Let's say that Group A has made a set of postulates which gives them certain energy and mass, and over here is Group B, and they get together and mutually agree to accept each other's masses. This would never get to the point where the mass created by Group A and the mass created by Group B would interchange. Somebody has to be around always who was part and parcel of the creation of the mass looked at, at least by agreement—and then we would get a time continuum, we would get a continuous consciousness. It's this they are talking about when they talk about Cosmic Consciousness, which is a very fancy word for saying, "Well, we've all been here for a long time".

Now let's take this As-is-ness and let's discover that a

thing will disappear if a *mockup* will disappear, and that too can be subjected to proof very easily.

If a mockup can be vanished simply by creating it in the same time and the same space with the same energy and the same mass, in other words by just repeating the postulate, if it would disappear the moment you applied As-is-ness, then people would begin to avoid As-is-ness in order to have an Is-ness, and that is done by Alter-is-ness.

We have to change the character of something, we have to lie about it for it to exist, and so we get any universe being a universe of lies.

When this universe of lies compels you to tell its truths you can get very confused.

Going back in history, we find people on every hand telling us, "Well, maybe there was such a person as Christ, and maybe there wasn't, and maybe he said this and maybe he didn't and maybe the material came from here or came from there", and boy are they giving him survival! Survival itself is dependent upon *Alter-is-ness.*

In order to get an As-is-ness to persist it is absolutely necessary that its moment of creation be masked. Its moment, space, mass and energy, if duplicated, would cause that to cease to exist. The recognition of As-is-ness will bring about a none-ness—a disappearance. In other words, a return to the basic postulate. You'd have to make the postulate all over again, and then, to get it to exist any further, why you would then have to go forward and change it in such a way that people would not actually be able to recognize its source at all. You have to thoroughly obscure the source to get a persistence. Be sure you see that. You'd have to say it came from somewhere and someone other than the actual source.

People have done this with such things as Dianetics.

One rave on the subject claimed it was really invented in the late part of the eighteenth century by a fellow by the name of Hicklehogger or Persilhozer or something of the sort. This is a fact. Here we had something which could be unmocked very easily because it was set up to be unmocked, to get at the As-is-ness of things, and in view of the fact that it was set up to unmock, then it becomes very, very easy to simply say that its As-is-ness was such and such and so and so, and it would have practically disappeared if you'd continued to assert that its As-is-ness was what its As-is-ness actually was. In order to get a persistence of it of any kind, we would have had to have done something very strange and peculiar, we would have had to alter it. We would have had to enter the practice of Alter-is-ness. And if we try to alter something bad—then, too, we'll make *that* persist.

Knowing that life is basically a consideration of a Static which is not located in time-space, which has no mass, energy or wavelength, and knowing also that As-is-ness is a condition which will unmock or disappear, that you have to practice Alter-is-ness in order to get an Is-ness, and that after an Is-ness has occurred the mechanism of handling it is to postulate a Not-is-ness, or use force to bring about a Not-is-ness, and that any further Alter-is-ness practiced on it will only continue to create an Is-ness of this new condition, and that every new Is-ness is going to be met by the postulated or force-handled Not-is-ness, and that every Not-is-ness is going to be followed by an Alter-is-ness which is going to result in a persistence of what we now have, we begin to see after a while that there is no way out of this giddy little maze of mirrors except this recognition that we have a static that can consider, and that the pattern by which we arrived at what we call reality, solidity, is contained in these four conditions.

The cycle of existence is, then, for a static to consider an Is-ness as an As-is-ness. It just says: *There is.* And then to alter the As-is-ness even to his own recognition and obscure his knowingness as to that As-is-ness to procure an Is-ness. Then, having procured an Is-ness, he usually can be counted upon sooner or later to practice a Not-is-ness, and not liking the result since the Is-ness he was contesting doesn't disappear, it simply hangs up, and he gets unhappy about it. He now would practice a new Alter-is-ness, which would get a confirmation of the Not-is-ness he now has, which would then persist.

And we find that life can enter itself upon a very, very dizzy cycle and these inversions then follow: the new Is-ness is treated with an Alter-is-ness, is followed by a Not-is-ness, and is followed again by a new condition, which is persisting—a new Is-ness. And so we get this back-and-forth and see-sawing around.

Now all this depends upon a basic postulate that we agree that things proceed in a fairly orderly fashion or uniform rate of spacing or at speed or at tolerance or something of the sort.

Time has to be entered in there, and we must have had a postulate right in there ahead of all of these Is-nesses that would determine *when*, and in the absence of that one you'd get no time continuum, so there'd never be any such thing as a persistence. So time fits right in there.

Now do you see this progress of these various conditions? I think that the problem of existence now narrows down just to this: an examination of Is-nesses. But the agreements as to time itself are conditional upon what was created in the time stream, and we get a basic postulate in there resistant to all effects as being *time itself*.

Well, these are the four conditions of Is-nesses and the various definitions which accompany them and will explain any manifestation of life, human behavior, matter, energy, space or time.

CHAPTER SEVEN

THE FOUR CONDITIONS OF EXISTENCE

(*Part 1*)

All we need to know about existence is that it is. Whatever complexity it has, it still *is*. It isn't ever *was*, which is a most interesting thing about this particular nomenclature. There isn't any will-be-ness and there is no wasness. There is simply Is-ness. Speak about existence, and people spontaneously add to it will-be-ness and wasness. So existence is not the word we want. We want the word Is-ness. We want just the word we're using. We want that which is.

The *Dhyana* makes the error of "beginningless and endless time" but that's not really an error. Probably it is an error as far as the translation of the symbols is concerned. We don't know that the symbols that were used by Gautama to describe this manifestation add up into English as beginningless and endless time. We've already crossed one language jump and so we know that much less of what he was actually saying. But it was an interesting thing that you could represent this by a continuous line which joined itself. Any kind of a complexity of circle, in other words, would represent the fact that we had a beginningless and endless somethingness.

Now, that is too complicated an explanation. In view of the fact that time depends upon a postulate you could say, yes it is beginningless and endless. You could say as well that it is linear. You could say, as well, that it is continuous. You could say as well that it is Eastern

Standard, or Sidereal—it doesn't matter now how you qualify it, having once made the postulate, you can then go on making further postulates. Nobody is going to limit anybody in making postulates.

But there happens to be, strangely enough, a true flying back of time. Time is a postulate. It doesn't even have to be agreed on. You could have a time span all by yourself. You could shut your eyes and say, "and now I've sat here for a million years".

"In the next two seconds", you could say, "I'm going to sit here for a million years". There's nothing unheard of about this—that's real time. Don't be too baffled if you dream for five seconds about a five hour time span. You've just repostulated some time, that's all.

Unless you continue to postulate time, you haven't got any. And that's the first and foremost thing you can know about time.

That fellow who depends on a clock up there to move time for him, is going to get in trouble sooner or later. He's going to get, "stuck on the track", and "out of pace with his fellow man", because he's depending upon their agreement on time to give him time. The only way he can have time is to continue to postulate time.

One of the roughest things that you will discover with anybody who is having trouble with his case is to have him put something on the future time track. He'll look at that and say, "OH NO!" You say to someone, "Let's make an appointment. Let's make it at 2.05 this afternoon".

Oh no. That's upsetting. That's why when you talk to somebody on the street, you don't tell him to come around to "see you later at your office". You've undoubtedly picked up somebody who has attention on the subject of postulating time. The thing for you to do is take him right over to your office right now, if you possibly can. Don't put something on the future time track for him any more than you can help, because the person here who is really in difficulty, who has all the usual human difficulties, psychosomatic ills and so forth, has stopped postulating time.

And the moment he stops postulating time, he doesn't have any.

Now, how much time has the fellow got and how much time is he rushing and how much time is he sitting still with—all these questions are very interesting except that it all depends on just this one fact: your individual is or is not postulating time for himself.

Looking over a very busy career I can see definitely the speed factor of composition as derived from strictly one postulate. I used to write about 100,000 words a month by writing three hours a day three days a week. Now, that's a lot of words, but it never occurred to me that it was a lot of words. If you simply postulate that there's that much action and it can fit into that much time, you have postulated the time. There's nobody sitting there agreeing with you or disagreeing with you. Actually, you're just walking free. Well, one might as well postulate eight million words in one hour per month. This was just saying how much physical universe time could be allocated to the time span which I was using in which to compose. You get that as a difference.

Let's take somebody doing a job of work—you will find something very, very peculiar. You find somebody who is working like mad, he's just working, working, working, he's just got to get it all done got to get it all done—and the end of the day comes and he's got nothing done. It's all in a confusion. He was awfully busy all day but nothing happened.

And the next day he goes out and he's so busy, he's

just *got* to do this and he's got to do that, and eventually you find him just sitting still, presenting a very funny and silly picture. He's sitting still, not even moving, not even talking, not even writing, accomplishing absolutely nothing, and now he is telling you how awfully busy he is and how he hasn't got any time and he'll eventually collapse down to the point where he has no time of any kind whatsoever to employ on anything, and that's why he's sitting there. But that is perfectly reasonable to him. That's perfectly reasonable.

He'll get so that he can't *start* anything. He has no time in which to start it, much less to finish it. So he starts in originally by saying, Well, I haven't got time to finish it, then, I haven't got time to do it well, then, I haven't got time to do it, then, I haven't even got time to start it. Then finally, I can't think about doing it.

And that's what happens to a person's doingness. It's his ability to postulate the amount of time, and the only confusion that you get into about this is the fact that we have an agreed upon time span.

But you might recognize that the time for an entire nation and an entire earth could thereby go awry.

How much can you do in an hour? What's an hour? An hour is the length of time it takes for the sun to move fifteen degrees in the sky. Now the *sun* isn't doing anything. What's this co-ordination?

When a country can still postulate time or a world can still postulate time, then an hour would be a tremendous amount of doingness. They would have a festival at sunrise and a couple of games, and then along about noon, why, have a feast, and that leaves them all afternoon, that leaves them *all afternoon* completely empty and that would be a good time to go boating, and then they would have time to practice up for the dance they were giving that night. And then they would finish up about midnight and say, my, what an idle day! This is the amount of time they could postulate in terms of doingness.

Do we have time to do it, or don't we? That is the question.

Now in view of the fact that time itself is merely a postulate this is very simple to understand. If it's a postulate—does it have an anatomy as such? Well, yes—it's a complexity of postulates, the way you look at it in this particular universe at this time, but not really very complex. Time depends on change. In order to have time, you have to alter things, because Is-ness has a condition following it called Alter-is-ness—which has to take place for something to persist. This is the way the postulates have gone together which make up this universe—not the theoretical way in which they *could* go together to make up a universe.

Get these as different things. You could go about this just all out in an entirely different fashion and postulate time and still have time, but it would not necessarily be the postulates which were made, and are made, and are in this universe right here and now. It wouldn't necessarily be the same set of postulates, if we suddenly just dreamed it up.

So we have to subject the postulates of time to a little subjective proof, and get ourselves a test on it. And we find that we can make things persist by changing them. If we keep on changing something and change it and change it and change it and change it we're getting persistence. But actually, what we're doing is postulating the time for it to persist in.

And when an individual has stopped postulating time he has stopped perceiving. Perception and the postulate of time are identical phenomena. Perception and postulation are the same thing here.

You should recognize, in auditing, very clearly, that time is a postulate. When you are working with a preclear who is having difficulty perceiving, you know that there is something wrong with the time postulate. Therefore there is something wrong with change.

Alter-is-ness is that part of the time postulate which we can most evenly and closely observe. And we find that changing things brings time into being. It causes a persistence and the mechanism of Alter-is-ness gives us a perception of time.

We find that somebody who is in a state where he believes he is about to perish will then try to change everything in his vicinity, right up to the point where he knows certainly that he is perishing, at which moment he will simply succumb, bang, and he will cease to exist or persist as that particular individuality and he as himself without that individuality will proceed on and pick up another body.

We get the tremendous amount of change or accomplishment which has to take place immediately before death. Here we have people all around the place who aren't doing anything. Their affairs are in horrible condition.

If we were to carry a little black bag and a stethoscope (that's the Badge of Office—a little black bag and a stethoscope. One doesn't quite know what they *do* with the stethoscope but it's *interesting*. It won't detect even whether a person is dead or not. A stethoscope is actually a reactive dramatization of the Serpent of Caduceus) and we walk up to somebody and say, "My dear fellow I must inform you," having tapped the stethoscope against his chest so he knows he's being hit by a snake, "I must inform you that we have just learned through this diagnosis that you only have three months to live." The odd thing about this is that you would see a busy man promptly. He'll really get busy. He'll sit down in a slump for a moment or two. That's just the impact. And then he'll say, Let's see. Time. Time. Oh. Alter-is-ness, Alter-is-ness, Alter-is-ness, Alter-is-ness, Alter-is-ness, change, change, got to get my will straight, got to get this straight, got to get that straight, got to get Mary moved out of that house into the other house I'm having built. Gotta have this and that, and the months go by and the years go by and he's still alive.

Well, he'd say the doctor was wrong. No, the doctor wasn't wrong, as of the conditions of that moment, the experience of the doctor demonstrated to him that people who had this illness (who had not been told that they had only three months to live) died in three months. What he's left out of it is the factor on people who have been told they only have three months to live. You tell somebody that he has only three months to live and he will throw into gear the only mechanism available to him to cause persistence in this universe. And that is Alter-is-ness. And he would change, change, change. He right away has to change his condition. That is the first thing he thinks of. One might think that it is just natural that he would do that. No. We're talking on a higher echelon of philosophy. You tell him he's only got three months to live, this is an unacceptable fact to him you say, therefore he's got to change his condition. No—worse than that. Worse than that. If he has no *time persistence* he has to change his *condition*. The one thing he can do from which he can gain persistence is Alter-is-ness. If he would simply change the furniture around in his office because he can do that successfully, he'd live a little longer. It's *unsuccessful* changes which fixate a person and cause a Not-is-ness to occur.

Now unsuccessful and successful are themselves postulates. "I am this individual and this individual is supposed to persist" versus "I am this individual and this individual's not supposed to persist". You could make up your postulate that way just as well as the other way.

But the accepted chain of considerations which go to make up, for example, art criticism, appreciation, win-lose and so on—we just have a set of considerations. These changes are successful as long as *the individual is doing it,* and the changes are unsuccessful as long as somebody or something *else* is doing it. And that's very much part of the win-lose factor and also of the time factor. That's self-determinism. One merely has made the postulate that as long as one does it one is successful. As long as one is able to accomplish the postulate this makes up wins. I am now going to pick up my right finger. I pick up my right finger. I won. That is, I made the postulate good.

What has happened to the preclear is that he has made the postulate and then something has contraried the postulate to such a degree that he is fixed. He is fixed and cannot change.

It just works out that way in this universe—not necessarily the most optimum set-up that could be made. When you made a postulate and then didn't accomplish the goal postulated in that postulate (remember you were postulating time to postulate a goal) when you were unable to reach that particular attainment, then, of course, you hadn't changed anything.

Time is made by changing the position of something in space and so we get all of the neutrons and the morons vibrating at a vast rate of speed, but a uniform rate of speed, changing their positions in space. Well then we can look around at several of these particles such as the sun, earth and other things, see that they're changing their relationships to each other in space at a uniform rate, and having perceived this, why then of course, we are looking at a change in time.

There is no such commodity as time, it isn't anything that could be poured from one bucket to the other but then *this* does not take place until a postulate is made concerning it. And in this universe the postulate had to do with change of location in space. And when it occurred, then time occurred.

You could change the location of something in space simply by lying about it. And you'd get a persistence. You'd come off of the As-is-ness. The moment you change something's location in space you come away from As-is-ness and it doesn't unmock and so you get persistence.

Now an individual is as well off as he can change things in location in space. Looking at the Pre-Logics, which precede the Logics and Axioms of Dianetics, we find that they have to do with an energy, and they tell you that a thetan is an energy-space production unit, that a thetan can change objects in location in space, and right next to that we have the fact that a thetan can create objects to change in space of his own creation. In other words, he can do all of these things and we get, in this universe (and this is pretty common in universes) those postulates as the conditional postulates upon the universe. Then one makes another postulate, that something can persist, and this postulate is represented as time, so when we locate something in space we are actually working with the time postulate. Persistence.

If you observe that somebody has failed often, then what do you mean by failed? He has decided to move something in space and then hasn't. In this universe, that's the total anatomy of failure.

Of course, he could simply postulate that he'd fail and that's another anatomy of failure. He's always free to do that. You can yourself do that. Not to remedy anything as an auditing procedure or anything of the sort—just simply say to yourself that you failed, for any cause, reason or anything else, just, "I failed and therefore I have to feel a certain way" and then feel that way.

You could do that, or you could simply postulate, I've won, I've not won something, just postulate that you've won, and the conditions of winning are feeling good, which is part of the woof and warp of postulates, "And therefore, I feel good"—giving you a reason to feel good.

Why don't you just postulate that you feel good?

It doesn't matter whether you are a winner, doing this. There is no sensible concatenation here, we are only talking about an *agreed* upon concatenation. This universe, and the postulates which formed it, is not necessarily the best universe that could be made. It just happens to be the universe we're sitting in and it happens to be the universe in which our postulates are being made and unmade and it just happens that it went together on these four conditions of As-is-ness, Alter-is-ness, Is-ness and Not-is-ness, and these four conditions woven together make this universe act as it does and behave as it does and give you ideas of what a win is and what a lose is and it's all on a postulate basis.

But the most curious manifestation in all of this is the manifestation of time, and we have this matter of time occupying a considerable part of the field of abberation. And that is because time is the one postulate when an individual begins to depend on other-determinisms more than any other.

We see the sun moving and we take our cue from the sun as to how much time we have. We see clocks moving and we take our cue from them as to how much time we have. And that tells us how much persistence we have. So we're being told by these objects whether we can live or not. And that's just the most curious of things in this universe, that one would take his cue as to whether or not he was going to persist, from whether or not the sun moved a certain direction and distance. It's idiotic. So the sun did a figure eight. If I'm not dependent upon sunlight I am certainly not going to cease to live just because of the sun. And a thetan is not dependent upon sunlight. Quite the contrary, a thetan is dependent for his well-being on manufacturing his own jolly old energy. He's not dependent on the sun manufacturing his energy for him. That's just an intricate hook-together. And that again depends on postulates.

The postulate of time could be simply cleanly made, in some universe, saying "Well, there will now be a continuance for one and all", and that would be that. But that wasn't the way it was made in this universe. It was made on the basis that when As-is-ness is postulated, in order to get a persistence, we have to practice Alter-is-ness. We have to change the location of something to get a persistence.

People get inverted on this in this universe, so that they take an Is-ness and they change it in location and it starts *disappearing.*

Suppose you have a person move a postulate around with a mass of energy. He starts moving it around—and the energy mass starts disappearing.

But what started disappearing was the energy mass, wasn't it? It was not the postulate, particularly. He just got used to that postulate and he finally took it over as his own postulate. And a person could finally say, well if I move something around, it will disappear.

He has made a counter-postulate.

He is perfectly at liberty to make a counter postulate,

but this is not the postulate on which this universe is made. This universe is rigged so that that postulate will avail not, to an individual. That's part of the considerations that make it up. If you've got something and then you say it doesn't exist—you're stuck with it.

That's this universe.

Alter-is-ness produces a persistence, but then we get two types of persistence. We get persistence as Is-ness and we get a persistence as Not-is-ness. The fellow is persisting but he doesn't want to be there. Well, he's persisting *because* he doesn't want to be there. This, too, is a change, although he's fixed in a locale. And secondly there is the fellow who is persisting because he *wants* to be there and he's persisting because of change. They're both Alter-is-nesses. An individual's desire to change continues his persistence in the spot he's in, if he cannot move. But he had to postulate that he couldn't move before this could happen. And so we get the dwindling spiral of the MEST universe.

We sometimes see the manifestation of accumulating energy on a preclear. Every time a preclear has said, Now I am going to move, and hasn't moved, or has said, Now I am moving and I am going to continue moving, and he is stopped (walking down the street, walks into a lamp post)—any time this has occurred, he has lost, which is to say, he has got a counter-postulate. So he adds up *loss* as *stationary*.

This universe, you see, brands everything which isn't moving as innocent. And things that are moving are guilty, always. So he's lost. Well how do you lose, then? By getting fixed in a location. That's how you lose. An individual who is unable to move objects out of a certain location eventually gets to a position where, when he is trying to move these objects out of this location, he recognizes a failure and so he goes into apathy. He says, "I don't have enough energy to do this".

What nonsense! If he doesn't have energy enough to move energy, why doesn't he just postulate it some place else? But that's another thing. He could say it is as it is and it would disappear and then he could postulate its existence somewhere else, and then change that around so it couldn't be disappeared again and he'd be all set. What's he doing picking things up?

A drill—simply in moving things and putting them back in the same place again—will resolve this consistent continuous failure and so you get a process such as Opening Procedure by Duplication and its tremendous effectiveness. If it is done with a little bit heavier objects than is ordinary then an individual recognizes very thoroughly that he can pick up and put back into place the same object and win, not fail. You've changed the basic postulate by which he is working in this universe, which is saying that if he can't move, and that he has failed.

However that may be we have these various conditions and the immediate point here is that time depends, in this universe, on Alter-is-ness. At least the *desire* to change. Anybody who is desiring to change is persisting in time, and people who do not want to change do not persist in time.

The whole universe is rigged around these postulates.

CHAPTER EIGHT

THE FOUR CONDITIONS OF EXISTENCE

(*Part 2*)

There are extremely elemental processes we discover could be designed when we look at the various factors in Scientology which we would call very upper echelon factors.

How much in the way of processes could we get just out of the concept of Is-ness? Just that one datum. Well, actually we could get a very great many.

But let me call your attention abruptly to the singular fact that to give a thetan exercise in *getting ideas* is of minimal use. A thetan can always shift around his considerations one way or the other, but it all depends upon the scope he is willing to shift them around on.

An individual on one point, let's say the receipt point in the communication formula, would feel himself limited to the degree that he had to be on receipt point. So he would then feel that the consideration that he was on receipt point or was being the effect of existence would monitor his ability to make considerations.

That is to say: he would not feel then that he was free to make any other considerations above the level of the fact that he was on receipt point. And all of his other considerations would fall below this level.

The formula of communication—"Cause-Distance-Effect" is the most elementary statement of it—"and involving attention and duplication". We would discover that if an individual were monitoring himself with one basic consideration, his considerations would then fall *below*, and his ability to change his mind would then fall below, that basic consideration.

A basic consideration could be "I am on an effect point. I am being the effect of many blows"—and messages and that sort of thing—*"and this is very bad"*. His considerations are various. "I must get off this point". Or, "I am on this effect point and I do not like this". Therefore he makes the consideration that he must get off of this point. Well, what is monitoring the consideration that he must get off that point?

The fact that he's on it, of course.

Now let's take it reverse end to, and let's get an individual who finds himself on *source* point. There he sits on source point and he's being cause. He's being the source of the impulses or particles which are going across the distance and hitting effect point. And then this individual is saying: "Well now I mustn't cause anything bad. I must cause only good things" and he must do this and that for this or for that.

And what is this host of considerations being monitored by? Of course, the fact that he is on a cause point. He's on a source point of a communication. (Synonymous here: cause and source, effect and receipt.) And if he discovers himself suddenly on the receipt end of something, this fellow is really dismayed. Here he has this basic consideration that he's being cause point, and then all of a sudden he *receives* something! Now that would be a breakdown—basically and primarily—of his Is-ness. His reality.

He then can have a break of reality only to the degree that other-determinism brings into question the postulate on which he is operating. You see, you could have a break of reality only to the degree that other-determined-hammer-pound brings about an invalidation of the postulate on which he is basically running.

He says, I am cause and I am being a good fellow and I am doing this and doing that—and all of a sudden he gets jailed. My, this is upsetting. But what is his basic consideration? That he is occupying a cause point.

Let's take the example of somebody who is in a condition and who is trying to change this condition. Now we've entered into another level. We've entered into Not-is-ness and then we've entered into Alter-is-ness, you see. He has a terrible ill. He has this mental difficulty. He has some other difficulty or other and he now says it mustn't exist. And in his next statement he says, All right now, *don't exist.*

Well, what do you know, it keeps on existing. Well, all right, he says, I'll change it on a gradient scale. I'll chip away at the corners of it.

He'll at length decide that he can't do anything about it.

One of the actions that he would finally do would be to draw a black curtain over the whole thing. That's one of the basic reactions of Not-is-ness. He says, Now, look, I can't change it at all, so he's trying to effect a Not-is-ness by using Alter-is-ness. Not-is-ness would not take place by a postulate, he discovered (or thought he discovered), so the basic thing he must do immediately then is start changing it on a gradient scale, which is to say Alter-is-ness—and it just stays right there. And he is already running on a failed postulate of Not-is-ness. His activity of change is then proceeding from the basic postulate that it must not be, which is proceeding from another basic postulate, that it is, which is proceeding from the basic postulate that he's there in the first place. You see that we're just proceeding from the basic postulate that there must be a there for him to be at.

So we trace back these basic postulates and we discover a little rule here. *An individual has a condition and the condition continues to exist as long as the individual has a condition.* It sounds like an idiotic little rule but it's a very, very true little rule. It will continue as long as he has a condition. Well, why does he have a condition? He must have a postulate about the condition before he has the condition. So every time you find a condition there's a postulate.

In order to get over something you have to have postulated that you have it. In order to recover you must postulate that you have something from which to recover. In order to go through the actions of emptying a pocket-book you had to have postulated that it was full and should be emptied.

One is all too prone to look at existence and say, well, there's existence there and now we'll make some postulates. No. This is not quite the direction of drift. You'd have to make the postulate to have existence there so that you could make some postulates to recover from having the existence there. And any condition to have any existence or persistence must be based on time of some sort. There must be a time postulate.

And we find that an individual doesn't have time unless he continues to postulate it and ceases to have time to the degree that he ceases to postulate it.

When I say cease to postulate time, I wouldn't want you for a moment to get the idea that there is any witch-craft involved, that you have to go out with spider-webs and mix them up with four quarts of morning sunlight and stir them all up with a whisker. There's no witch-craft involved in making this postulate. It's simply this kind of a postulate: *Continue*: Just get the notion of continuing something and you'll have a time continuum. Get the idea of a piece of space out in front of you and have the notion, Continue, about this piece of space. That's making time. You've made time. That's all the postulate there is. There isn't even the words, "Now I am going to make some time and I am going to cause the time to persist and continue." No, its just continue. You didn't *say* continue.

This time continuum is a tremendously interesting thing particularly in view of the fact that so many people have agreed upon it, but their apparent agreement with it leads them to depend on other people, finally, to carry on the agreement while they just sit there. And what do you know, eventually they do just sit there. You'll find many a person in this state, simply sitting at home in his bedroom, just sitting there. Well, he couldn't have any motion, he says.

Motion consists of this: *consecutive positions in a space*. He'd have to conceive that he had some space, and that he'd have consecutive motions in it.

If you could just ask such a person to go out and trim the hedge, just no more and no less than that, or if you asked him to go out and put pieces of chalk on the sidewalk all the way around the block every five feet—you would see considerable recovery in his case. Why? Well, he knows that he'd have to go all the way around the block or he knows that he would have to finish trimming the hedge, or he would have to come around to his door again in the block, or come around to the other side of the yard. In other words, he can continue to postulate a time continuum against the objects that are already there.

You could just say to this fellow, Get the idea of moving this dish. Now move it. Now get the idea of moving this dish again. Get the position you're going to move it to now. Now move it. Now get the idea of moving this dish, now get the place you're going to move it to, and move it. Surprisingly enough an individual will sometimes turn on a violent body reaction on this.

What's kicking back there? It is the thetan's agreement with the body, to the point where he's saying he *is* the body, the body is himself—therefore everything that happens to the body is what happens to himself and everything that happens to himself happens to the body. In other words, he's in a super-identification. And he would come through this to where he could have some future.

What postulate is this individual already riding with? Let's take a look at the Is-ness of this. He has to conceive that he has a body before he can recover from one.

And we get the salient and horrible fact that this whole thing is monitored by Is-ness. No matter how much NOT-is-ness is taking place, you see Not-is-ness always pursuant to Is-ness. No matter how much Alter-is-ness takes place—you've got an As-is-ness, then Alter-is-ness has to take place to get an Is-ness. Is-ness is something that is persisting on a continuum. That is our basic definition of Is-ness. As-is-ness is something that is just postulated, or just being duplicated—no alteration taking place.

As-is-ness contains no life continuum, no time continuum. It will just *go*—every time you postulate a perfect duplicate for anything: same space, same object, same time—boom! If you postulated it all the way through, without any limiter postulate hanging around at all, it would just be gone and that's all there is to it. It would be gone for everybody else, too.

Now this, then, Is-ness, is your monitoring postulate. An individual couldn't possibly get into trouble with As-is-ness. Unless you considered losing everything trouble—but it would be losing things which you either now didn't want, or had just postulated into existence.

All As-is-ness is doing is merely accepting responsibility for having created it, and anybody can accept the responsibility for anything. That's all As-is-ness is, when it operates as a perfect duplicate.

There are two kinds of As-is-ness:

There is the As-is-ness where you postulate it in the space and time—you postulate it right there, and there it exists.

And then there is the As-is-ness where you repostulate it. You just postulate it again.

The object already exists, there is an Is-ness being approximated as an As-is-ness, and then it becomes an As-is that isn't. It becomes, then, an actual Not-is-ness. So if you created it, if you just created it as an As-is-ness, unless you altered it rapidly you'd get this Not-is-ness. And if you exactly approximated an Is-ness as an As-is-ness, you would again get the same result. Same result both times—Not-is-ness. As-is-ness, perfectly done, if not followed by Alter-is-ness, becomes a Not-is-ness. Quickly and immediately. You've seen that as an auditor, erasing parts of the reactive bank-facsimiles, etc.

It hasn't occurred to anybody yet, fortunately, to simply exactly approximate the body! Treat the body as an As-is-ness and go your way. Well, you say the body has a lot of facsimiles and so forth. All right, treat them as the same As-is-ness, all in one operation—boom. Of course you had to assume you had a body before you could possibly As-is it.

Now, existence goes this way—this is the only error you could make, and this is another method, slightly, of getting a continuation, because it is an Alter-is-ness. There is an Alter-is-ness right there between Is-ness and Not-is-ness. The moment you say, "There it is, now I don't want it and it doesn't exist", you've postulated that you're changing it. It's a very abrupt and particular kind of Is-ness—it's a *Not*-is-ness.

If instead of following Is-nesses with Not-is-nesses,

we followed them with As-is-nesses, nobody could ever possibly get into any trouble. The way you get into trouble is to follow an Is-ness with a blunt, thud, Not-is-ness. (1) There it is. (2) I don't want it. (3) It isn't. Oh ho! What's the difference between these two operations? It's a very interesting difference:

You've got an Is-ness. You have an ash tray, you don't want the ash tray any more, so the one operation, a correct one as far as you are concerned if you just really didn't want it any more, would be simply to do an As-is-ness. A perfect duplicate. Gone. You haven't got an ash tray any more. To follow an Is-ness with an As-is-ness, brings you into an *actual* Not-is-ness right there.

Or, on the other hand, you *didn't* do an As-is-ness. And you've done what? You have refused the responsibility for having created it, and you have said, Somebody else creates it and I don't want it. You've said *somebody else*. You've postulated the existence of somebody else with regard to this thing and you've said, "Another determinism is placing this thing before me and therefore I don't want it, so I'm going to say that it isn't, but it really belongs to somebody else. We have to postulate another determinism, which is to say, refuse the responsibility for having created the object, before we can get such a thing as a Not-is-ness.

Now, an individual can fail utterly. This is a very curious lot of phenomena that we are looking at here, and of course, we had no serious intent with this phenomena, which is a fortunate thing. Otherwise, somebody realizing exactly how this is done, would sooner or later perhaps unmock the Republican Party or Russia, leave a hole, and of course to do that, you would have to accept the viewpoint of 200 million Russians. You could unmock Russia if you did that, but you would have to take full responsibility.

What is full responsibility? Full responsibility merely says: I created it. When you ask somebody to make a perfect duplicate of it he's going through the mechanics of creating it, therefore it disappears. He knows, unless he throws some other-determinism in on the thing, in other words practices some Alter-ism on its creator, that it's not going to exist at all.

The physical universe as we look at it right around us here is an Is-ness for one reason only. We all agree that somebody else created it, whether that is God or Mugjub or Bill. We agree that somebody else brought these conditions into existence, and so long as we are totally agreed on this, boy have we got everything *solid*. And the moment we agree otherwise, and we say, Well, we made it—it starts to get thin. This will worry a preclear for a moment. It's just as if he feels he could never make another one. It'll get *thin*.

In the processing of reality, then, if you handled Is-ness all by itself, you would simply have an individual start looking at what he considers to exist. And the most solid manifestation of that would be the space in the vicinity, the walls in the vicinity, and so on. That would be the most elementary process that we could do. Just start spotting spaces and walls, and let what happens happen. That's all. Just ask the individual to keep on spotting things, very permissively. Suppose he kept on looking at them with his physical vision—we find that he would get up to a certain level and then he'd start to have body somatics (*Somatics*: perceptions, stemming from the Reactive Bank, of past physical pain or discomfort, restimulated in present time) because making the body do this continually is actually processing a reality vaguely in the direction of an As-is-ness. It's not bluntly or sharply in the direction of As-is-ness. It's just asking them to process it a little bit in that direction:

"Let's take the spaces around here just as you see them." And of course after a while, the walls are going to get brighter and brighter and duller and duller and—gone.

Well, when they get brighter, that's all right. The body will still feel all right, but when it starts dulling down the body doesn't like this. It does not think this is the best thing to do. It would not recommend this as subject matter for an article in a body-building magazine. Because the body knows it will fall if it stands in space. Therefore this very, very simple process would not necessarily have to be completed by remedying havingness, but just by getting the fellow to close his eyes, and spot anything he could see, no matter how vaguely, *as a thetan.* Just spot anything he sees. If he sees a nothingness, O.K., if he sees a somethingness, O.K. Just get him spotting. We don't care what he sees. We might indicate various directions but we would make a very bad mistake if we indicated them as body directions. On your right. On your left. Above your head. Oh no, no. We just ask him to look around, and what he sees, spot a couple of spots on it. Did you do that? Now something else, spot a couple more spots on that. Well, we know already that if we've run it permissively in the environment, he's had to point them out and walk around to them. He will obey orders. Now that we've got him to a point where he will physically obey commands we can trust him to close his eyes and spot spots or spot spaces or spot anything he wants to spot with his eyes closed. We just simply keep on spotting them, and that would be the most elementary process there is in Scientology.

CHAPTER NINE

THE FOUR CONDITIONS OF EXISTENCE

(*Part 3*)

The four conditions of existence are actually variations of existence itself. They are certain attitudes about existence, and they are the basic attitudes about existence. Now we could include a great many more attitudes, and we would find that we were deriving them all from these four. But we could take these four and find out that we were deriving them all from one—Is-ness, or reality.

There has to be an Is-ness before you can do an Alter-is-ness. There has to be an Is-ness before you can do a Not-is-ness—unless of course you want to postulate it in reverse.

But we are talking now about this particular universe and how it got here and we discover as we look along the track, that these four conditions of existence, that all existence, presupposes the postulate known as TIME.

Now time is just a plain ordinary postulate which says that out of a non-consecutive beingness, which doesn't exist forever, we would get then a parade of time. A time continuum.

There's no forever, it would just be there—no forever, no instant involved. There just isn't any consecutive existence at all. And then out of this we would have to make a postulate that there would now be consecutive existence, existences, or a consecutive series of states.

Now an individual who is simply occupying space

without any energy involved whatsoever doesn't have a good feeling about this. Without any space he could have a good feeling about it. No space, no energy, no continuum—he could have a fairly good feeling about this, but when he gets into the occupying of a space, now he has this feeling of foreverness unmocked. He makes that uncomfortable for himself, so he will now go on creating consecutive states of existence. He can have a game. Space is necessary to start this game but when you've just got space and nothing else, it's rather unbearable. You're already occupying, so there is an existence there, but it isn't an existence which has any consecutive difference of state. And that's real poor. This is a kind of feeling you run into in space-opera.

Here we have, then, a state of existence being conditional upon a time postulate which would include a space-energy manifestation, and this would be a simultaneousness.

There would be no question about whether you made the postulate for space and energy before you made the postulate of time. There is no question of any postulate before or after because you have not postulated the postulate which causes a before or after, and that postulate would be time. So actually, to have a game, there must be a simultaneous action whereby you postulate space-energy-time—space, energy, continuous existence. Which is an As-is-ness of space—altered, energy—altered, time—altered. So these items have to have the time postulate with Alter-is-ness in them in order to get a persistence. That's how it's done in this universe. You don't "just have to do this all the time". But when those three consecutive postulates are made simultaneously, why we then have a continuum of existence, demarked by differences of position of the particle in the space and we have time being marked out for us very neatly. We have to alter positions in order to get a continuousness. We have to say it is here, now it's here, now it's here, now it's here.

There's another way of making time come true. We say space, no space, space, no space, space, no space, space, no space. You're postulating, however, that you can do this before you can say space, no space, space, no space. Well now, this postulate is so easy for a thetan to make, it might be considered a native part of his makeup. So we have before this an ideal state, that is to say an idealized or theoretical state. We have this theoretical state whereby we merely have a Static which has no space, no mass, no wave length, no motion, no time, which has the ability to consider, and we are dealing with the basic stuff of life. Just by definition.

It is very peculiar that: "We, mixed up in all of this energy and so forth and way on down the track from the time this postulate was made"—do you see anything specious about the way that remark hangs together—"Way on down the track from the time this postulate was made"—"Very difficult and very strange that we could even *discuss* this higher state of existence which was made trillions of years ago"? No. You see, it must have been concurrent with this, right here, and so we don't use the word existence, we use the word "is". We don't use the word "then" or "will be", we don't go back into the past or go into the future for this continuousness at all. It just is.

Now, in past ages it was just: "Well, reality is reality and you'll have to accept it. There's nothing more you can know about it than that." Oh yes, there is a lot more you could know about reality than simply, it is.

So, "is" is not a complete and embrasive definition of reality. It's not complete and embrasive because reality has a certain mechanical structure and that structure is composed of these four states of existence. And it would actually take all these four states of existence to make the kind of existence which we are now living and that is to say, we would have to have Is-ness then Not-is-ness and Alter-is-ness and did it strike you before that we might have forgotten and might never have known about and it might not have had called to our attention directly, this other state? We've always had these three states, Alter-is-ness, Not-is-ness and Is-ness.

Alter-is-ness and Not-is-ness, of course, are variations of Is-ness and depend upon Is-ness. But there is a fourth one and that is As-is-ness. And that condition natively exists at an instant of creation, yet it also can be made to exist again any time anybody wants to make it exist again, simply by saying AS IS. If anybody had truly and actually accepted reality and had got all of his fellow beings to simply accept reality, we wouldn't have any. But whose reality? Whose reality in each case? Somebody else's. So this reality was actually another condition, *other-determined As-is-ness*. Other determined. Which is *Not-is-ness!*

The way you get Not-is-ness is to say "as is created by you". That's an awful one, that's a big curve, and that is Not-is-ness. It's an As-is-ness created by somebody else, which of course isn't an As-is-ness at all. It's a very specious As-is-ness, and naturally the world would sort of look unreal to everybody if Joe Blow and Doctor Stinkwater and the Heavily Laden Order of Pyramids all said "This is reality and this is As It Is and you'd better accept it." That's a Not-is-ness, isn't it?

So if everything starts to sort of dim down on you and you kind of find things going out, and getting sort of resistively thin—all transparent-but-they're-there, or, they're "all hung with black sheets"—you must assume at that time that you have faced up to too many As-isnesses which somebody else created.

Somebody else says, "This is the way things are." And you've had that. You get that operation in conversation: "And yesterday you said to me, just when I got up, you said to me, you never work, you are a dirty loafer, you remember that, don't you?" I think every familial unit of thetans should always have, not a Bible, but so and so's Rules of Evidence, lying right there to be resorted to at any time, and there ought to be a Court in every neighborhood to which you could repair and decide whether or not this was an As-is-ness or a Not-is-ness.

Now what is a Not-is-ness? A Not-is-ness comes about in that exact manifestation, or simply by the separate postulate: "Well, it is and I regret it. It isn't." You know, *you* could have made it and then said it wasn't. Oddly enough, if you made it and you *know* you made it, you have a special case of being in a position to say any time, "It doesn't exist now," and it won't—if you have also accepted responsibility for having created something and said, "I made it." So we see that there are two different conditions of Not-is-ness.

One is just vanishment.

The other one is an Is-ness which somebody is trying to postulate out of existence by simply saying "It isn't."

A Not-is-ness, in our terminology, would be this second specialized case of *an individual trying to vanish something without taking responsibility for having created it.* Definitive, positive and precise definition.

And the only result of doing this is to make it all unreal. To make it forgotten. To make it "back of the black screen". To make it transparent. To make it dull down. To give it over to a machine. To wear glasses. Anything that you could possibly do to get a dimming-down of an Is-ness.

And that is done by saying just this, just this precise operation and no other operation: "I didn't make it. It isn't." "I didn't do it, so it doesn't exist."

And that will always bring about this second condition, the one we give the term of Not-is-ness.

"I didn't create it. I had nothing to do with it. I have no responsibility for this at all, so it doesn't exist as far as I am concerned."

An individual doesn't have to operate on these postulates at all, but he *is* running on this makeup of postulates. He, of course, then will trigger in all the rest of his postulates and they'll cross-reference into sticking him right there with it. He's Not-ised it and he's got it.

Now he thinks the only way he can get rid of it is to dim it down, dim it down.

You can process a preclear on a gradient scale of change on something—and this is of great interest to us —*if the gradient scale is back toward his acceptance of responsibility for having created it.* It would not be far enough to go, as in Dianetics, simply to find out that your mother did it, that "it was what your mother said". That wouldn't be far enough to go. This is built into the woof and warp of the track, the very composite of postulates on which an individual is running.

You would have to go back this far: you would have to postulate: (1) that the time Mother said it was NOW, and, (2) that the time when Mother said it caused the time when I said it (a million or fifteen billion years ago) to key in. (*Key in* (*Verb*): An earlier moment of upset or painful experience is activated, restimulated, by the similarity of a later situation, action or environment to the earlier one.)

Every time somebody else can put one of your own pieces of mental machinery or one of your engrams into restimulation, it is only because he can work on something which was natively created by yourself. All things carry the germ of their own destruction.

So any engram, as we were operating with it in Dianetics, was actually a key-in. When I discovered that the whole track ran back, back, back, back, BACK, it was, "Oh! We're back to where the guy did it in the first place!" Well, that was very interesting, and one result was the essay on responsibility in *Advanced Procedure and Axioms.** The essay on full responsibility.

Well, a fellow did. He created the condition from which he is now suffering, and he didn't even create it in other wise than he is now suffering it. But it has been keyed in and he has consented even to its being keyed in.

Nothing, really is sneaking up on anybody. That's a horrible thing, isn't it? People haven't even made it worse. But we're having a good game. If that game is a game called psychosomatic illness, bereft lover, neglected baby, it's still a game. And as such, the individual is still playing all roles.

Now what happens is that as an individual goes along the line, he starts identifying himself with the source point and receipt point of the communication line. As a child, he identifies himself as the one who is talked to. Very seldom do you discover a little child giving mother a good lecture. If you had, you probably would remember with great satisfaction, the good lecture you gave your mother.

Here is a condition in which the individual has identified himself with a continuous effect point, or a continuous cause point, and having said "I am now on this point," he now makes his considerations below the level of that point. He has *considered* he is on that

* *Advanced Procedure and Axioms* by L. Ron Hubbard, 1951. See book list in back of this book.

point. Henceforth all further considerations are monitored by this consideration that he's on the point, as long as he considers he's on that point. And he would have to recognize that he was *on* the point (an As-is-ness) before he would come *off* the point.

A process immediately occurs to us on such a level. If you just simply ask an individual a question such as this over and over and over and over:

"Where could you be, where you would be willing to recognize and realize that you were?"

And you would just run a gradient scale all the way back up the line, to the point where the individual recognizes, finally, "You know, I'm sitting right here!" There wouldn't be any mysticism involved in this.

Now, these conditions of existence are composited up in an inter-dependency one upon another. An Is-ness exists only because of As-is-ness. As-is-ness took place in the first place. It got created. Then we had to alter it slightly to get an Is-ness. We had to give up some responsibility for it and we had to shift it around. A Not-is-ness then exists in order to provide a game.

A game is an Is-ness which is being handled by Not-is-nesses. A football game could be added up in terms of these conditions existence. One side has the ball and the other side must Not-is the side that has the ball, and the side that has the ball has to win—in other words, has to arrive at a receipt point.

We get the communication formula itself as being below the conditions of existence and we get affinity, reality and communication as simply being the methods by which existence is conducted. It is not the interplay of existences. So we're dealing with a higher echelon than ARC right now.

Affinity really is merely the consideration of *how well it's going*. In the agreement or reality itself we're talking about Is-ness and that is the corner where we enter this ARC triangle. We just slide into that triangle of Affinity-Reality-Communication on that Is-ness point of reality, and then it is modified by affinity and communication, which of course come in simultaneously with it. We discover then that these conditions of existence would add up to all manifestations of behavior. There would be a great many of them. There would be a finite number, however. It would be the number of possible combinations, singly, doubly, trebly or quadruply, of these four conditions of existence. We get this individual who in only 75% of his life is trying to say Not-is to, another 10% of his life he's giving an Alter-is, one hundredth of one per cent he's giving an As-is, or trying to give an As-is to—and the remainder is Reality. Acceptable reality. And that would be just one makeup of a personality.

If we say that there is a gradient scale of Is-ness, a gradient scale of Alter-is-ness, a gradient scale of As-is-ness (which there isn't) and a gradient scale of Not-is-ness, why we can see then that you could take these gradient scales and in one combination and another, have a character composited from them.

Characterization must be made up, in great degree, from these conditions of existence. Some space, some energy, and his considerations of Is-ness, Not-is-ness and Alter-is-ness. We would not say that any part of his characterization was made up of As-is-ness, because if it was it wouldn't be there.

One also has been trained to believe that loss is bad. This is just a reverse postulate, made just to keep life interesting. Loss is bad, therefore he has a tendency to avoid As-is-ness. Therefore he will avoid duplication—he'll avoid all kinds of things. He's afraid he'll unmock. He's afraid he'll vanish. Here he is struck in, eighteen feet thick, and you couldn't get him out with a pneumatic drill, all scheduled to go back to the between-lives area (*Between-lives area*: The experiences of a thetan during the period of time between the loss of a body and the assumption of another. See *A History of Man* by L. Ron Hubbard) and pick up another baby. Silly, isn't it? But it doesn't matter too much. Any life or continuance, to him, has begun to be better than no life at all.

You could say, well then why would you process somebody? Well, let's look at that. In order to accomplish a two way communication, just after the basic and most rudimentary chitterchat, I would start asking somebody why he was being processed. And you know, I'm just wicked enough to go on asking the person why he's being processed for *hours*. Until he can at least find one reason why he is being processed. It's a very interesting process. A preclear comes in saying, "Process me," and you have always supposed they knew. Well, at this point they don't have any idea at all why they want to be processed.

A process which would be quite powerful would be: "What wrongness or what wrong thing would you find other people would accept from you?" or "What could you do that was wrong that other people would accept?" and then "What wrongness could you accept from other people?"—back and forth and back and forth. Here goes the guy's manners, his social pattern, his behavior pattern, and everything else will just go by the boards running that process but he won't be able to tell you, first and foremost, why he's being processed.

He won't be able to tell you he wants to feel freer. He won't articulate any of these things. He'll just sit there and want to be processed. What toward? Until you've gotten him to put a little time on the track, he will use "forever" in processing, because he's sitting in forever.

He isn't moving on the time continuum. Well, if you can't get him processing toward some goal or other or in some direction, he just makes processing the end all of everything and he'll just go on being processed forever. But if he's going to be processed forever, he'll have to hold onto his aberrations forever, otherwise he couldn't be processed forever, could he? And that's why some cases stay so long in processing. It's actually as elementary as that.

So I have been sorely tempted to alter that early auditing step to just this: "Well now, give me some goals you have in processing."

And just keep it up until it's no longer forever, and the preclear has a future.

CHAPTER TEN

THE FOUR CONDITIONS OF EXISTENCE

(*Part 4*)

Here we take up the various reasons why.

We have in Scientology a lot to do with reasons why, but the fact is that a fellow who goes around always looking for reasons why is usually not in particularly good shape.

But there are a lot of reasons why the states of existence and conditions of existence are put together the way they are in this outrageous fashion in which As-is-ness followed by Alter-is-ness gives us Is-ness, followed by an Alter-is-ness, or desire to, which brings us into Not-is-ness, and which then brings us into Alter-is-ness, which brings us into Not-is-ness which brings us into Alter-is-ness, which brings us into Not-is-ness.

There's a good reason for all this. An excellent reason for all this.

We are talking right here about the fundamental of all aberration, which is incidentally the fundamental of all existence.

There is found a strange condition here. If a thetan were to remain with an As-is-ness, he would thereafter have nothing. Therefore, immediately after the postulation of some object, it is necessary, by mechanics, and it is just happens to be so in this universe it's not reasonable, it's just the way it is in this universe —which puts you right in the field of mechanics) that the As-is-ness must immediately be altered in order to become what we call a reality. And thus people attempt various mechanisms.

One of those mechanisms is the device of God. Now then, we're not saying that there is not a God. But if there were never any type of alter ego of this character there wouldn't be any permanent reality.

It's one thing for there to be a God and quite another thing for everybody to blame everything on him. The most barbaric manifestations that we have, generally includes a deity. The savage out in the Gullaby Isles is practising this—he says that the fault is the trees and the River Sprite and so forth. I'm talking to you now about the mechanism of use of, rather than the identity of, when I mention God.

All right, God, then, is to blame. If we make something and have some hard luck, something like that, the way it looks to us here at this stage of development, we can then say, "Well, God did it to us and He has afflicted us."

Quite in addition to that, every primitive people has the legend of a *creator*. They have to have a legend of a creator, otherwise they would never have anything. The immediate and intimate use of the legend of the creator is *to continue in existence*.

Whether you built it or not, you can cause something to vanish simply by looking at it as it is. Somebody else can put up a mock-up of one kind or another and merely by your perceiving it and making a perfect duplicate of it, you can vanish it. It is not necessary that you exclusively devote yourself to the vanishment of those things which you yourself have made. That is not necessary in order to carry through this cycle. Somebody else could have made it and you could have made a perfect duplicate of it—an As-is-ness—and it would have vanished.

Now we are talking about something which is very easy to work with and which can be put to objective proof. I can ask you to make a perfect duplicate of something, which is to say, get it in the same space, same time continuum, using the same mass, and your perfect duplicate will cause it first, probably, if you're having a hard time of it, to brighten up—and then it'll fade. Well, the next thing you know, even though you've made very poor perfect duplicate, why, you sort of get the idea, of *looking through* this item—and so it is with all of existence. Unless, in other words, there was a legend of other creation than your own, you would not at any time be able to have anything.

The first and most fundamental principle of havingness is: *it must have been created by somebody else.* And thus we get Is-ness. When you ask a person to *remedy his own havingness,* this is perfectly all right. You're asking him to make nothing of something. He actually can. But the reason it does him so much good is he's forgotten that he can.

In a Remedy of Havingness you ask the preclear to mock something up and pull it in. In other words, you ask him to mock it up and *alter* it. Why doesn't it remedy a person's havingness simply to mock something up—just get a mockup? It doesn't remedy his havingness because if he leaves it there, it will simply disappear. Many a preclear gets very upset because his mockups all disappear. He puts up a mockup and it disappears. Well, that's because he doesn't alter it in position. He puts the mockup up and leaves it right where it is and of course it dissipates and disappears. Now those preclears who put up a mockup and leave it in the same place, which does not disappear, are working on mental machinery which does their mockups for them and for which machine they have "No responsibility". He's doing them with a machine not because he's crazy but because this is the only possible way he could make them persist. The machine changes them and he himself knows that he did not put up the mockup. He knows this. If he didn't know that, the mockup again would disappear. So it is not a very undercover fact with which we are working.

Let's take this legend of the creator. We discover that it is quite uniform. It is found in every savage tribe. It is found across the face of the world. And it is found throughout this universe. The legend of the creator. Very well, we can say there was a creator and he created everything and that's fine. And if this were the case, why, that's fine, too, because it wouldn't unmock. In other words, things would not disappear if there were a creator who made everything. You could even use this as a tremendous argument to prove that there was such a thing as a creator and he made everything, just by the fact that it's here and if *you* had made it and continued to accept your responsibility for it, it wouldn't be here, so there must have been a creator. You could go at it with this type of logic. However, it works this way: if somebody else, other than yourself, made a mass of energy, all you would have to do would be to come along and fish around for its approximate moment of creation and duplicate it and it would then disappear. So whether the creator created everything or not, it's a certainty that you, in order to continue with a physical universe, have to, to some degree, lay the blame on some other identity.

Therefore this postulate, he created it or you created it, does not enter the question at all. If you duplicated it, it would go away regardless of who created it. We're talking now about a very basic fundamental, that it is necessary for you to carry around the postulate that somebody else created it in order for it to exist.

Now it's a little bit difficult to prove this. You have to work with a preclear for a short time. But the main difficulty of proof which lies on this track is simply proving who made the mockup in the first place. You see, if it disappeared because you duplicated it, why then, you probably made it. But it doesn't matter then whether we use this one way or the other. We don't have to admit that you could make anything disappear whether you made it or not. We don't have to admit that, to continue along with this proof. What we are coming down to here is this matter of responsibility.

We learned in Dianetics that people would not accept responsibility for their own acts, and actually they're *as bad off as* they will not accept responsibility for their own acts. And individuals are other-determined to the degree that they will not accept such responsibility.

As a matter of fact, you discover a complete dianometry, scientometry, anything you want to call it, a complete set of tests, which will demonstrate that there is a direct ratio between the health and ability of the person and his willingness to accept responsibility. But the funny part of it is, this only goes up to a certain point and when you achieve that point of acceptance of responsibility, then havingness as such, and the universe, or that part of one's interest in the universe, would vanish.

Now here is the Bodhi. Here is the individual who aspires to the attainment of perfect serenity—he can't have perfect serenity and *have* something, because he'd have to give away a certain amount of his responsibility in order to continue it in existence. Havingness would only persist so long as he felt somebody else had had a hand in creating it. And the moment he said "I created this" one hundred percent all the way along the line, he wouldn't have a thing. The perfect duplicate here is what we are looking at, again. Therefore, the condition of becoming a Bodhi is the condition of having nothing.

A thetan is very able to have something or nothing at will. But it happens that he is appealed to very often on the basis that all somethingnesses, including space, would vanish. He thinks this might be a good thing. The only protest a thetan has, actually, is somethingness.

If you want to say what is wrong with a thetan, you'd say, "somethingness", and you have stated it. He *has* something. There is something in existence.

He is perfectly willing to have many somethings, but after a while, the communication formula comes into effect, and he becomes frantic about it. This is something that is terribly elementary. In spite of the fact that it is as deeply pervasive as it is in life and existence, it is terribly simple. It is one of these idiotically elementary factors that everybody could have overlooked forever. They would have *had* to have overlooked it. They didn't even dare tread on the edges of it for fear that everything would blow up or disappear.

All right. A thetan makes something, and he himself natively is a Static, capable of consideration, has no mass, no form—as a spirit he has no form—he has no wave-length, he only has potentials. He has the potential of locating objects in space, and the potential of creating space, energy and objects and the action of locating those objects in that space.

And with this as his potential, the moment that he makes something, he violates his own communication formula.

A thetan in excellent condition is able to communicate easily with something. He can simply change his mind about anything and work it around. But the formula of communication becomes native to the creation of space, energy and mass, and that formula is, of course, *Cause-Distance-Effect, with a perfect duplication taking place at Effect of that which emanated from Cause.*

That is the Communication Formula. And that becomes the formula the moment you have space. Up until that time, you have all cause and all effect capable of occupying exactly the same location, since there is no location.

So a thetan is perfectly able, way up the scale, to occupy the space of anything, and so duplicate that thing. But his formula when he's doing this is not cause-distance-effect. It's just cause, effect. That would be the formula he's operating with because he wouldn't communicate across a distance to something, since he wouldn't be occupying any cause or effect points.

But he can't have a game if he does this.

He can't have mass if he does this.

If every time he selects out an enemy and then communicates to the enemy and simply *becomes* the enemy at that point, he couldn't have an enemy very long, could he?

If he said I am fully responsible for everything and I will now make a plot of land, and he mocked up some space and a plot of land, and he's fully responsible for it—what happens?

It's gone. If he had mocked it up and altered it or changed it, he could then bring about the phenomenon of persistence, which is itself time.

When you say survive, you're saying time. Just put those two together and make them synonyms and you understand all you want to know about time. It's *a consideration which leads to the persistence of something,* and you can enter all the mechanics into time that you want to, and you can paint it up in any way you want to and you can write textbooks on it and test it and buy very fancy watches and chronometers and set up observatories to measure the movement of the stars, and you still have "Time is a consideration which brings about persistence". And the mechanic of bringing about that persistence is, by alteration. And so we have Alter-is-ness taking place immediately after an As-is-ness is created, and so we get persistence. In other words, we have to change the location of a particle in space.

Let's get back to this communication formula.

A perfect duplication would be cause and effect in the same point in space, wouldn't it? So communication as we consider it through space is not a perfect communication system.

You on one point in space communicate with something at another point in space and if you continue to interpose a distance in between the things or space in between the things, you get even then the basic of persistence. All you've got to do is get that distance in there, and we have this taking place.

A thetan cannot duplicate a mass. That is to say he cannot himself actually be a mass. He can conceive that he is by saying now look at all this mass that somebody else put on me. I didn't create this mass.

He can *conceive* himself as mass. But he starts to get very unhappy about communicating with somethingnesses because here is this distance factor and he is a nothingness. Now if he can be the somethingness on the same point in space where that exists, then he feels very, very good about things. He feels all right simply because he's occupying the same space. Well that's perfect communication for him. That's a perfect duplicate. But if he totally occupied it at its instant of inception it would disappear.

So he gets caught between not wanting to communicate with something and wanting to have something. You see, that to really have something he would have to occupy the same space. To communicate with something he has to stand off at a distance and pretend to be a something. Communication, as we know it in this universe, is *cause, distance, effect.* Perfect communication, like a perfect duplication, is: the point, the point, there's something on this point. The thetan can also occupy this point, therefore he can have something, he can communicate with something, but if he says it belongs utterly to him and he's occupying its basic point, it will disappear.

Therefore, he has to have another creator. He has to have some other author of the universe. If he doesn't have, why, it will disappear.

Now, we could enquire at some length into the tremendous complexity of this and why is this. A thetan should simply be able to say by postulate, well, it's as it is, and it's going to persist as it is, and we'll just make this postulate and that will be that. But the funny thing is that it just doesn't work this way, and it looks here as though we have an arbitrary which has been entered in from one quarter or another, which we don't fully comprehend even at this moment. But this universe went together on this basis of: AS-IS equals VANISHMENT. You make one just as it is—all you have to do is *pretend* as if you were making it at this moment—and boom, it's gone.

You then see the necessity, at least in this universe, to have another determinism at work. Well, that's just one point. We see it in terms then of the Creator. That's fine. This does not enter the question of whether there is or is not a God. We are talking about whether or not people *blame* God, or why they blame God, or why they put things onto God.

Well, if they didn't they wouldn't have anything.

The other point involved here is people blaming *each other*. They stand there and one says: You said that, and That's your fault, and this is why we have this fight, and so forth. And the other person says, No, that wasn't the way it was, that's an entirely different situation, you actually were the one that started all this.

We talk to a preclear and we want to know what's wrong with this preclear. Well, it's "what Mother did" to him, not what he did to himself. We can't conceive that an individual could actually become aberrated without his own consent, and sure enough he can't. He can't become aberrated or upset, or thin or lean or fat or thick or stupid or anything else without his own consent because he is part of the agreement pattern, and unless he has agreed himself to other entities of agreement, why he won't get stuck with *any* kind of a pattern.

Now let's look at how that adds up. We find that if an individual to have something went into agreement with other determinisms and said these other determinisms caused all this, he could sit there comfortably with something persisting. But what did he have to do? Basically he said: in order to have anything I've got to go into communication with these other-determinisms and blame them or fix the responsibility of causation upon these others.

So the child blames his parents. He gets up into the age of puberty, he runs into sex, sex tells him he can't survive—that's the basic manifestation of sex—tells him he can't survive and he begins to worry about this fact. Why, here he is all equipped to make another generation, he's hardly started living this one, and that's a confusing and upsetting fact. He's already warned in advance that some day he's going to die. To see something really morbid, read some teen-age writings. You never saw such complete sadness anywhere. Well, they've been told they can die, and the appearance of sex, physiologically, told them they could die. They become anxious then about surviving, so they have to turn around and blame somebody for something, anything, and simply by blaming somebody they obtain a continuance of whatever condition they are in at the moment. In other words, they can continue to survive simply by turning around and saying, Well, the trouble with me is all what my father and mother did to me. So if you were to take somebody and bring him very, very close to death and cause the chilly breath to draught down his neck, you would find him very shortly blaming something else but himself. But he runs in a cycle on this. He discovers that the situation is untenable. Then he'll blame himself.

Why does he blame himself at that point?

He wants to unmock it. And he actually has forgotten the mechanisms of unmocking. By blaming himself, by taking it upon himself, by holding it all close to his own bosom, he thinks: Now that it's my fault it will all unmock, and he's a very surprised person when it doesn't unmock. He merely gets upset. And the other one is, he finds his condition of survival desirable, and when he finds it even vaguely desirable—it doesn't matter if he's a slave in the bottom of a salt mine working out a sentence for having voted, or whatever—the fact is that this individual obtains continuance by blaming others. So he goes through a cycle of, Blame somebody else, that means I've got to or I want to, or I haven't any other choice but to, survive, and the best answer is survive, therefore I'll just blame everybody else.

And the mechanism of blaming oneself is unmocking oneself. Unmocking oneself and the mass with which he is immediately and intimately surrounded. People go through these two cycles and they invert, and that is the basic inversion. They start in by saying, Somebody else was responsible for the creation of all this. They're quite happy about all this and they stand off and look at it and then they begin to get tired of communicating with these somethingnesses, because they cannot enter into a perfect duplication. They are nothing, that's a something, they begin to get impatient about it after a while, so they decide to unmock it. They look at it and say: I did it. Well, there's something wrong here. Come on, come on, come on. I did it. It goes right on. They don't mock it up in the same part of a space in which it was initially mocked up, they don't try to duplicate it with its original mass.

They omit some of the basic steps of saying I did it and they're trying to go up against the postulate with which they did it.

Having made this postulate and said already that it belonged to somebody else, now they try to take it back, and their next move is to try to squash up these energy masses, use more force in order to flatten force, and he is on his way, this thetan, right away, you see, he's on his way. Because the more he tries to use energy to knock out energy, the more energy he's going to have, and the more dislocated the basic particles of that energy are going to be, and he'll just get more and more and more persistence, and if he keeps on protesting all the way on down, it will just become more solid, and more solid and more solid, and more solid, because he's protesting that it's other-determinism, then he protests by saying it's my fault. Now I'm going to disappear and die and that will make you sorry. But again he's entering a protest into the line.

So we get this basic thing of other men's responsibility, or "God is responsible", as the fundamental of persistence and survival. We have to have other-determinism at work or we get no persistence whatsoever.

And so we get these postulated other-determinisms, and when you recognize this clearly in your preclear and in creation itself, it will cease to be as entirely baffling as it may have been in the past.

CHAPTER ELEVEN

THE FOUR CONDITIONS OF EXISTENCE

(*Part 5*)

With the data we have on these conditions we can talk a little bit here about how your preclear might possibly recover from the state which he conceives himself to be in.

We consider now that the pattern of existence through which he has been is a very definite track. It is a track which starts with As-is-ness, and this of course includes space. You might possibly completely miss in auditing a preclear if you didn't realize that As-is-ness has to start with space. One could get so concentrated on and frantic about objects and energy, this factor of space might be completely missed. A thetan can communicate with space with great ease. The body has gone too far on this track to do this easily. The body finds it quite sickening to communicate with space,. but a thetan can communicate with space rather easily, and the As-is-ness begins with space, and then it gets into, of course simultaneously, energy, and mass.

Now space, energy, mass, consideration of, are all simultaneous. There is no consideration here related to time.

We have to move the anchor points of the space, in order to get a continuance of the space, and move the energy itself in the space, and change them in one fashion or another in order to get a continuance of that energy, and when this has not been introduced we have not postulated time. A thetan doing this would theoretically pass from As-is-ness into Alter-is-ness just immediately. He'd have to, or he would have no continuation of any kind.

In other words it wouldn't exist unless he intended to change it. He would have to make the intention of change simultaneous with the action of creation. And if he did not he would get a disappearance immediately of that mass.

He passes then into Alter-is-ness, which is a simultaneous action with As-is-ness at first, and then of course immediately becomes an action of continuation, and we get Is-ness, which is this reality that we talk about—space, energy, objects.

Just exactly why we consider this combination to be a reality, that reality is Is-ness, is a little bit dull, because the fact of the matter is that reality itself to continue as a reality would not be an Is-ness at all but a continuous Alter-is-ness.

So we get Is-ness actually as a hypothetical state.

Now the fact that the thetan is a Static—that's not hypothetical or theoretical. The fact that he is a Static that can consider, and can produce space and energy and objects, is not hypothetical. That's true.

We have facts, facts, all the way along here, until we get to this thing called reality and we suddenly discover that Is-ness is hypothetical.

In the whole field of As-is-ness, the creation of space, energy, objects, of Alter-is-ness, Is-ness, Not-is-ness and more Alter-is-ness, there is only one hypothetical state. And that's Is-ness. It never exists. It can't ever exist. It has to be Alter-is-ness or As-is-ness, and of course As-is-ness *can* exist. As-is-ness can exist. It really would have to be able to exist, if you can repeat it. It must be in existence if you can repeat it and cause a vanishment of mockups or objects or spaces, so it obviously exists.

But this is not true of Is-ness.

Reality does not exist. Because it says there is a stop. And there just isn't any stop. It is continuous Alter-is-ness and when people stop altering the positions of things and stop altering anchor points, and stop pushing things around one way or the other whether they say they're doing it or they say it's being done on another determinism, or however, the moment they just relax on this whole thing, they get the condition which your preclear quite commonly is found in, of no longer postulating time. You see, the mechanism of saying "It will continue because I'm saying someone else is responsible" is of limited use. It's of very limited use.

Let's go into that a little more clearly—you set up this machine—or something to go on and shift and change the anchor points of the space, manufacture the energy involved and take care of the objects. You set up this machine and you say: I'm no longer responsible for this. I have no further responsibility for this now, and therefore it's other space and it will go on happening, and therefore I can continue to have this space because somebody else is making it. You see we could get into that rather shifty by-pass, and so we could then have—not over too long a time—but we could have a consistent Alter-is-ness, and this alteration would continue to take place as long as he at least kept one tiny little fingernail on the machine over here. We weren't looking to see that we had, but as long as we had that fingernail just touching that machine we were all right. We said just that much of it is ours.

The moment that an individual entirely relaxes and he says I have everything all set up, it's beautifully set up, and it will all run automatically, and I don't have to worry about it any more, after all a fellow created this universe, other people are the ones who caused time to take place, they tell me when to get up, when to go to bed and I've just got everything all set and it's totally other-determined now—it becomes just that totally other-determined, but it also, for the individual, passes by the board.

He's no longer postulating a persistence, he's no longer changing any objects in space, and so he will simply sit still. Everything gets very dim, everything gets very thin. Well, the funny part of it is that in that state he couldn't even keep an aberration going. But his Alter-is-ness has been practiced so long after the fact of Not-is-ness that even though he sits still he'll keep on changing something, and that condition is known as figuring, thinking, thinking. He tries to change something, and he feels, Well, I will just sit here and think, and that will keep the universe moving, it will keep time going. The only one trouble with this is, he is dealing basically with the root stuff of what makes universes but now that he is sunk into that category where he is doing nothing but consider again, not creating or moving anything, he is going to have a very difficult time of it. In fact everything is going to get dimmer and dimmer and less real and less real.

What will persist there is that which he is still changing, which is his worry about aberrations.

This is not esoteric or difficult. The only thing which goes on persisting is that which a person is actively working to change. You can only have those things which you handle. You can only have those things which you move around.

But an individual gets into a tremendous protest against *mass*. He has decided that the continuous survival of things is very bad. In other words he starts to fight survival itself with Not-is-ness. Now, as you know, Not-is-ness is a highly specialized activity. It is the activity actually of causing something to vanish or dull down or become less, simply because it IS too much. There's too much Is-ness, the fellow considers. He's got too much persistency, too much survival—Joe Jinks that got him across the barrel in a bank and took all his money away from him, and, well, there was just too much Is-ness, and the best thing to do about that is to cause a Not-is-ness, and let's just fight everything.

For an example, let's take a war. A war is just simply each side saying the other side must cease to exist, and they are doing it with shot, shell, lead, dynamite, spears, arrows, deadfalls, and they're using energy to make other things cease to exist. Well, it was perfectly all right as long as you were building your camp, you see, but if you suddenly started to fight a war with somebody on the other side of the mountain, whereby you were saying he must cease to exist, you were fighting persistence by causing persistence. If you want to know why a war which shouldn't take more than a couple of days, goes on and on, and on, and on, and on—they got so bad a few centuries ago that they had a hundred years of nothing but war—everybody was saying everybody else mustn't exist, and they kept moving objects around to cause existence to cease. Now you see how these postulates could become completely tangled.

And the thetan does this because he so loves the problem, and that is the most problem there is. The thetan loves a problem, and that is the basic of problems. You move masses around, which basically causes persistence, in order to cause persistence to cease. One hundred per cent paradox. Cannot exist, can't ever happen, never has happened, and yet he will do this. But he is never happy doing it. There is no serenity involved in this. It becomes nothing but a complete chaos. Probably the only joy any soldier ever gets out of a war (and don't spread this around, because the society doesn't believe you should tell this) the only joy anybody ever gets out of a war is by kidding himself that he has made absolutely nothing out of something. Whether it's enemy troops, or tanks, or ships, or anything, there's a big WHEE in there some place, a big thrill. Combat troops know about this. It's only when they cease to make nothing at will, apparently, that they become very downhearted.

Hardly anybody would be able to comprehend what is known as a military rout, whereby a body of troops, suddenly, and instantly and immediately disheartened, just completely, completely quits. It's a strange phenomenon. It has been rather incomprehensible how fast troops will go into a complete headlong retreat. Let's say they keep shooting at a castle on a hill. And they just keep shooting at this castle, and shooting at this castle, the castle keeps shooting back, and they keep firing at the castle, and the castle keeps shooting back. Well, they start to go to pieces in morale. They can't make nothing out of something. Observably—the castle continues to live. They bog down on that rather badly, they get to be rather 1.5, and actually that is the manifestation of 1.5 on the Tone Scale. People using force to make nothing of something which continues to exist in spite of it. And they'll suddenly drop. It isn't a slow curve. They enter it rather slowly, and then they will just suddenly go to pieces, because the only compensation they have for war is the fact that as thetans, you see, they can observe that they are at least going through the motions of and have the manifestation of *making nothing of form.*

And the sadness underlying it to them is the fact that they don't make nothing of it really.

Beyond this point still, all kinds of suffering takes

place, and sadness, and it goes on and on, but you start moving that many particles with that much velocity, such as a German 88, and you'll get persistence. That shell bursts, and we don't find that the fellow in whose vicinity it hit is still there, but there's persistence. Somebody's got to go through his effects, and then somebody's got to write a letter home and say he died a hero, and somebody else has got to carry the news through, and then there are people at home, and he's left a hole in the society one way or the other, and this goes on and on and on, and then years later they dig up what's left of him and ship him back over and put him into a cemetery. There's persistence occasioning here. And what's persisting? Well, there was that particle—it certainly was moving fast, and when we get a particle moving with this much velocity, we get some persistence, and in a war all they can think of is terms of more and more and more particles, moving with more and more velocity to cause less and less persistence on the part of the enemy.

If you wanted to know why the German nation keeps fighting and keeps overrunning its borders, well it can't do anything else by this time. From Legion times forward people have been going in there saying, "You mustn't persist, and these fast-moving particles which we're making you handle will make it so." Oh really? This can't be, you see.

When we find anything about which Man is extremely puzzled, we lead directly into the one little formula which is the mechanism of making things persist: we're going to use particles to make things not persist.

And any time you find anybody in difficulty or in the middle of a problem, just look at the basic anatomy of a problem which is that anatomy.

It's, "We're going to cause a non-persistence by the use of the mechanisms which cause persistence."

And you're going to get a game—there's undoubtedly going to be a game occur here. There are going to be lots of problems.

If you want to know how to take apart a problem, just look where the person is using particles which you know by changing them will cause persistence, in order to make a non-persistence.

He'll be using Alter-is-ness to create a Not-is-ness, and of course will be getting consistently and continually an Is-ness. Which is a continuous state. It's a hypothetical state, because you can never stop it, you can never arrest it, you can never take a look at it. You know that any time you really recognize an Is-ness—not in a state of change—why, it will disappear, it will vanish or it will dim down, something will happen with relationship to it, so you always have to look at the *change*.

This is the fellow living up the time track, this is the fellow living in the past. He's looking at the changes and he isn't looking at the reality.

Actually that's a very healthy state of mind.

The fellow's looking at the changes, he's looking at what will be, he's very cheerful about how many particles he can move around and cause to come into existence or persist. Or he knows the proper *modus operandi* for mocking things up that he wants to destroy, just As-is-ness. And that would destroy it perfectly adequately, and he could start in again.

To look at the basic mechanics of any problem which is causing any trouble, just find the matter of the particles, the particle motion, the Alter-is-ness in other words, which is aimed with the goal of Not-is-ness and is an impossibility. You'll find that's your preclear who's hanging fire in processing. He's doing this. He's using particles to knock down ridges (*Ridges*: Solid accumulation of old, inactive mental energy suspended in space and time), something on this order.

Actually he'd feel a lot better if he'd simply go out and trim the hedge. Let him move something around not quite as damaging but with the same goal, because if he's all messed up with his engram bank, and he's all messed up with tremendous ridges and black ridges and that sort of thing, and he sits there as a thetan creating particles and bombarding these ridges, what is he going to get? He's going to get a persistence of ridges. That's why we *never use flows in processing*. You can process objects if you want to, you can process space if you want to, but we'll just stay away as a general principle from flows.

Now your thetan has a great objection, because of the communication formula as used in this universe, a great objection to somethingnesses. He looks across a distance and he sees a somethingness and this begins to tell him after a while that he has to be a something too, and he doesn't like this. He doesn't enjoy this really, because it's an other-determined something that he has to be. It's looking at a wall, he has to be a wall, you see. And that's what this universe is dictating to him. Well, actually, because it's all a consideration in the first place, he doesn't have to fall into that little grave. He doesn't have to do that kind of a shift, at all. He could simply say I'm looking at the wall, you see. But after a while he gets into the mechanics of perception, the mechanics of communication. He's using energy in order to communicate with energy. There's nothing wrong with that, except to the degree that he loses his fluidity on it. As long as he could maintain the idea that he was simply communicating by postulate, that *he* was communicating, he's doing all right, but when he drops below that level—and you get him forced to communication, when he's made to stand still and be talked to, when he's made to stand to and hold that ridge, when he's made to sit there and absorb that textbook, any of these things, he gets under this bombardment, and he starts fighting the communication formula.

Of course we get a persistence then of this universe's communication formula.

Remember that this universe has a communication formula, and that that formula is based on the fact that two things can't occupy the same space, so immediately we fall away from cause, effect and no distance. Cause-and-effect with no distance is not the same thing as the bottom-scale manifestation, where complete identification never actually occurs. There's still a slight distance no matter how downscale you go; it's only *way* upscale that you can get a perfect identification between cause point and effect point. These two points can be coincident way upscale. Well, if they can be coincident way upscale, the individual could put a distance on them or whatever he liked, but to the degree that he began to agree with this universe, we would get the manifestation of "have to have a distance across which to look" because he can't occupy the same space as the object at which he's looking.

That is this universe's formula, and that by the way is native to a lot of universes—it's how you keep everything stretched apart. You say two things can't occupy the same space, therefore we've got to have a lot of spaces and things more or less fixed in these spaces, and we've got to keep them all apart and therefore they are separate objects and we go into the communication formula. Cause, Distance, Effect.

As the individual agrees that two things can't occupy the same space, and as he agrees with this communication formula, he then gets into a situation where he says, "Now look at all these somethings around here. And I am actually basically a nothing, and therefore if I have to duplicate these by becoming a something, I don't like that. I can't retain my own native form. I'm in a bad shape here. I can't fly around and be a spirit. I've got to be pinned down here. I've got to be an energy mass in order to look at those energy masses," and he doesn't like it. He objects to it. And so we get to the other manifestation on the track.

The only objection a thetan has to anything, if he's having a big objection, is to *something*. Just any something. Then this of course will invert and having objected to a something hard enough, you see, he'll turn around after a while and start objecting to a nothing.

Now how is it then that we get any change at all if Not-is-ness doesn't work? Well, there is the system known as valences: one ceases to be himself and becomes something else as his sole method of change. You see that? He is causing a persistence by saying things mustn't persist, and he keeps saying, mustn't persist, mustn't persist, and it goes on persisting, and he uses more particles and more particles and more particles—and pretty soon the United States Army is wearing coal-scuttle helmets. Just like that. And the Government says, "Down with Karl Marx, down with Karl Marx, down with Karl Marx—and everybody is now going to be taxed according to his ability to pay."

So we get another type of change. Two things can't occupy the same space, therefore we are an identity persisting, therefore the best way to get it changed and get an utter change is simply to be somebody else. In other words completely shift the valence, and because we want to win all the time, why naturally, shift to winning valences compared to oneself. If one thinks one is losing then *anything* can start looking like a winning valence. A beggar utterly penniless about to die would look like a winning valence to some people. And we get valence-shifting going right along with "two things can't occupy the same space". So an individual goes out of one spot and over onto another spot and when he is running a lot of Not-is-ness you can expect him to do a lot of valence shifting. He can't continue to be himself, because he's in communication with nothing.

At that time he will start to believe that he must have nothingness. And he goes from there into having to have somethingnesses and he goes from there into having to have nothingnesses by change of valence, and actually there is no other deep significance to it.

CHAPTER TWELVE

TIME

Time is the subject which was introduced very early into this universe, and it has been with it ever since.

The very obviousness of time has obfuscated time.

Time is something that one can easily not have enough of and at the same time have too much of.

And at the same time not be in.

The whole subject of time is a confusing subject because it is a consideration which took place *along with*—not after or before—because there wasn't any time at the moment the consideration called time was made. It took place along with space-energy.

So it was space-energy-time or energy-space and time.

Time was created immediately after these basic postulates with the postulate of change, or the introduction of policy, and as soon as policy comes in or new considerations come in then we begin to get consecutive time.

The first few Board Minutes of any corporation are more or less nebulous with regard to time. They might as well have all taken place in zero minutes at the beginning of the world. You see that it doesn't matter. The people who elect the Board of Directors are the Board of Directors before they elect the Board of Directors.

Now you *are* the space before you make the space. You are the energy before you make the energy. After you make the energy you are before the energy. The time which is postulated at that point is postulated at a time when there is no time, which is not any time at all, which might as well be now as then. You might as well be postulating time just this very instant which is the time you postulated at the beginning of this universe.

This instant in absence of the consideration called time is the instant of the creation of this universe, is the instant of the end of this universe. If no time has been postulated, then all time would be one time.

A preclear who ceases to postulate time ceases to have time. And that's the first thing you can learn about time. Unless you're putting things on the future time track consistently and continually, you will not have any time track, because—was there a Board of Directors or a single Director at the beginning of track of this universe who made all the postulates, then elected you to the Board afterwards? Or were you part of the Board?

Well, you could be running on this very well simply being recruited to this particular organization called Physical Universe. You could be—and have been—recruited to it afterwards, but the moment you were recruited to it you could only have been recruited to it if you had agreed to its time continuum. In other words, if you had agreed to a uniform rate of change, and had you agreed to this uniform rate of change you would then have a uniform rate of change. Otherwise you'd be in 1776, or 2060, while everybody else was in 1954. You see, you'd be somewhere, something, and sometime.

Well, in view of the fact that the particles themselves of this universe are a matter of consideration, stem from consideration, are themselves consideration—the space in which those particles exist are themselves considerations—we are not then at any time dealing with anything else but considerations.

We're dealing with considerations, and these considerations are only complicated and fixed to the degree that they are agreed upon.

If you have agreed solidly with these considerations why then, you have the considerations with which you've agreed.

It was not necessary for you to be the prime mover to be part of this universe.

The moment you have agreed to the considerations which compose this universe, you are at its inception, you are at its end, you are at its present, but you are running under the consideration that time is taking place. And as long as you are running under that consideration you say fine, we'll go along the time track. Wonderful. Time is progressing. You start looking at clocks. Clocks are keeping time for me, the bus schedule's keeping time for me, the motion of the earth is keeping time for me, the precession of planets and stars are keeping time for me, everything is keeping time for me, my wife keeps time for me by serving breakfast at a certain time, everybody keeps time for me . . . time? Time? Time . . . what . . . what time? What time is it? Do I have any time?

No, you've become motionless. You became dependent on everything else to keep time and make the considerations and then you didn't continue to agree with those considerations that are made. All you'd have to do is just go on agreeing with those considerations—you'd move right on along the time track, just as nice as you please. But if you just drop out of the basis of consideration, drop your own consideration of the fact that time is taking place—at that moment time ceases to take place.

Because time is a consideration and these other things are consideration, it doesn't mean then that after this consideration was made all considerations start moving. Should we make a consideration that there is time, then this doesn't immediately put all considerations in motion or create anything more than that which is already created with considerations, with the changing factor of time.

The definition of time itself is very important to you. Time is the co-action of particles. You can't have action of particles at all unless you have space. If you have space, then you can have change in space, and when you have a change in space then you have a different time.

There's the time from the moment the particle was at position A—that's one time, now another time when the particle has been moved to position B. There could have been no motion taking place whatsoever unless you had made a postulate of motion from position A to position B, and if you had made this consideration "from position A to position B", then you would have motion and you would have time, because you said position B is then a later time than position A.

A later time—what is this word time? You might as well have said this: "there's a consecutive shift of position". You ask somebody, "What consecutive shift of position is it?" And if he answered you truly, he would say, "It is the 15th degree position past zenith of the sun on its 200th revolution since its Winter Solstice." Quarter after twelve to you. 200th day of the year. That's time. If the sun hadn't shifted 200 times you wouldn't have had 200 days.

But it isn't that that is making it simply because it marks it. Let's look at that now. Just because it's doing it is no reason it is creating it. It is simply a particle which is moving in space. Earth is a particle which is revolving in space.

And the sun wouldn't be there, unless we were running on the basic consideration and agreement that it was there.

Here is an example of that simple change-of-position idea: I pick up a book, and just consider at this moment everything's static, no motion at this instant—no time, no motion. A new instant. You see that it does not require articulation or verbalization or anything else. It's so simple that it is overlooked. In order to conceive that this book can move from a position on the desk over to a second position, one must simply have conceived a new set of considerations which are consecutive in each position of motion over to this new position. And each one of these is *after* the consideration that the book was here. Now it's very embarrassing when an auditor is running the process Opening Procedure by Duplication and he tells the preclear, every time he picks up an object, to duplicate it—if the auditor forgets to have him consider that it's there again, because it's an invalidation of the preclear—the preclear makes a perfect duplicate of it and the object isn't there. When going back to that object a new time the auditor, if he's using "make a perfect duplicate of it" as part of his routine, had better then also say just before he sends him back toward this book: "Consider there's a book over there". Because as far as the preclear's concerned he's just unmocked it, and if you're working with a preclear who's getting into good shape, that book will be invisible. So he has to consider there's a book there, then he has to consider that he has moved across to it there, and he has to consider that all these things are taking place, and if he does he has time. Time is the co-action of particles.

Now the time that we're dealing with is a time with which we can stay in good agreement. It's a uniform rate of change. In other words, we are considering and considering and considering and considering and considering. We could be doing it very rapidly with regard to a particle for instance in the wall. We consider that it's there, and let's say the wall is being pulled this way—we consider it's there, it's there, there, there, in other words we keep considering that that particle is coming closer. It takes a brand new consideration every time to have a particle and to have a space to move it in. Every time you see a particle move, actually somewhere in some automatic fashion and so on, we don't care about the mechanism, you have to consider: space-particle-position, space-particle-position, space-particle-position, space-particle-position. You get motion. You'll get an aeroplane going overhead, and for you to see it go overhead you'll have to be saying space-aeroplane-position, space-aeroplane-position, space-aeroplane-position, space-aeroplane-position—and you'll see a jet plane go across the sky. But if you aren't at least agreed to this, you won't see any aeroplane go across the sky, you won't have any space, and it certainly will have no position.

Now what happens to an individual when his time factor starts to go to pieces? He gets stuck in time. He gets stuck at those moments when he is sufficiently rattled, confused or upset, in other words is given a new consideration that all is confused, and he doesn't at that moment have time to make new considerations that there is time or agree with the fact there is time. Or he resents the fact that there is time, and so he loses time, so he gets stuck on the time track.

It isn't energy that sticks anybody on the time track. It's this fact. Somebody told him to move, and he resented it, so he didn't move. What's he done? He has fallen out of agreement about the progress of particles.

Communication itself has been used to shift his consideration about considerations. Somebody demonstrates to him completely that these are time. They tell him to stay in one place. You can demonstrate that to an individual very easily with a bullet. He's going ahead, beautiful automaticity, just mocking up things flying here and things flying there, regiments of soldiers marching here and marching there, and in one way or another why he's just as much part of the enemy as he is part of himself, but he's got a new consideration that he is part of himself, and this bullet comes through space, and if he were able to see it—a Civil War cannonball for instance he could have seen very easily, they only travel about sixty miles an hour —and he would have done this space-particle-position, you know, space-cannonball-position, space-cannonball-position, space-cannonball-position, space . . . BOOM. He has just considered himself into a complete confusion, hasn't he? He's considered himself right on down the line to an impact, so he says, "Now look, the best thing to do—when you see anything that even faintly resembles a cannonball—you don't say 'space-particle-position, space-particle-position'. No you don't. You say, Nothing." The fellow's learned to keep his mouth shut.

"We don't see cannonballs." Nope. But he's in agreement with the man on the right and he's in agreement with the man on the left, and they're in agreement with the man on the right and the left, and he's standing on the ground and he's in agreement with the body, and all these things are thoroughly in agreement with the fellow who fired the cannonball, and so the cannonball will come across anyway. And boy, is he invalidated now! On his right and his left and behind him and below him he stayed in agreement with all other things which were in agreement on the subject of rate of change. He stayed in agreement with all these other things which were saying space-particle-position, so he's saying "space-particle-agreement", unwillingly, unwittingly. And this will leave him really hung. This will leave him with a certain unreality.

Well, he's postulated no time, and so he can get stuck on the time track. You see that? Only his mockup is kind of thin, because he depended for the solidity of mockups such as the material universe on all these other people mocking 'em up too. Everybody's mocking them up. He's just staying in agreement with everybody, and he doesn't quite have to mock them up, so what has he got now? He's got a dependency upon the agreement to keep time for him. So if he's done this then he's lost his power to completely unmock everything, hasn't he?

Time as you conceive it, the time that is running on your watch, is simply the motion of a bunch of little wheels and a couple of hands and a second hand. And that's just consecutive motions. Those are changes in space. And everywhere you look, mechanically you will find that time never amounts to anything else than a change of position of a particle in space. You see we have two conditions here. If something is postulating the change of position of a particle in space, and you're agreeing with that something, then *you* will get a change of position of particle in space. It's just a consecutive consideration, but that is all time ever is. The change of position of particle in space. To see anything you have to have space-particle-position.

Now in order to stay in good agreement it would be a very, very good thing to have a uniform rate of change, wouldn't it? "Let's all together now chant"—the universe is saying—let's all together chant space-particle-position, space-particle-position, space-particle-position, and we'll chant it together so that we are all uniformly saying this, and we will then have time because we're saying it and not for any other reason. We are postulating it. And so we've got space-particle-position, space-particle-position, space-particle-position as the hymn of time itself. And it goes right on running all the way down any years that are because those are the years.

Let's not get divided up again on the subject of, "Well, now there's *thought*". The old Theta-MEST theory is a terrifically interesting theory simply because it led into this. The idea that there was a universe and that there was thought—theta without wavelength, without mass, without time, without position in space: this was Life. And that was impinged upon something else called the physical universe, which was a mechanical entity which did things in a peculiar way, and these two things together, theta-MEST interacting, gave us life forms. But then we get a further refinement of that.

We find that the physical universe itself is simply this chanted space-particle-position, so MEST is coming from thought itself, so what do we get? We get the appearance of the physical universe having a seniority in mechanics. It appears to be above consideration, because of the agreements you have made with so many people concerning the continuation of it.

Continuation itself is another word which could be supplanted for time and so is survival. Now, what then would we say is the common denominator of time? Consideration.

Below this level, in the field of mechanics, what would we say is the common denominator of time? Change. That is the one thing we could say was the common denominator of all kinds of time anywhere, anyhow, in any universe.

Now let's not lose that one. A certain set of particles or a certain body of individualized life forms, or an automaticity postulated by such life forms, could go on saying that there are a certain set of particles, they're moving in a uniform rate of change, and they're postulating the same space over and over again—and we would get at that moment a uniform time continuum. And that is a condition which has to exist in a universe and it is that which makes a universe peculiar. It's the time continuum for that universe. In other words, it's this agreed upon chant. It's where we are chanting and with whom we are chanting, that makes the universe.

So we have the people of earth and this universe chanting or simply agreeing with something that *is* chanting space-particle-position. And so we've got time, time, time, time, time.

If all of a sudden the chant stopped, nothing would move. You might still have some space on a hangover of a past consideration or something, but you wouldn't have any new particles moving anywhere. The walls would simply vanish, the space go, to a very marked degree. Everything would kind of look like a Black V (*Black V*: a heavily occluded case characterized by mental pictures consisting of masses of blackness. This is a "Step V" in early procedures such as Standard Operating Procedure 8.) caving in on himself. That's the way things would look if this stopped. It would look just like that because that's what he's done.

Then in order for a person to have time, to be in present time, it is necessary to be in contact, at least in contact, with those particles which are being formed by this continuous hymn to time. It's at least necessary to be in contact with the particles. If we're not, we're out of time.

If we're simply agreeing, then we're out of time, and we get stuck on the time track, stuck in old facsimiles, all messed up—we're not postulating any time at all, and we're not looking at any time particles, not looking at any particles or their change, and as a result—where's anybody going to get any time?

He has to either himself start chanting space-particle-position, space-particle-position, space-particle-position, until he gets time going again for himself, or you have him feel the walls, and feeling the walls, he'll say, "Ah, what do you know!" He's getting into time.

Agreement is a very important thing because the thetan begins to depend upon the universe keeping its own chant and stops chanting himself.

What happens if he does things? He has to agree with something which is vibrating, doesn't he? So he himself becomes mass. And that's how a thetan becomes mass. He's not chanting any more, so he goes one hundred percent into agreement with something that is doing the chanting, and then he falls away from agreement with what he was depending on to keep on agreeing with him for.

He depends upon that wall, decides that wall is harmful to him, and he's no longer chanting. He's no longer now in contact with the wall because it's dangerous.

Where's he going to get any time?

He isn't going to get any. He may fish around and contact another time continuum in another universe and be to some vague degree in contact with that time continuum—another entire body of beings and automaticities chanting space-particle-position, space-particle-position, space-particle-position, space-particle-position. Another song going on.

A preclear gets out of time. He himself is sort of mocked up in agreement, therefore he gets to vibrating and he as a thetan vibrates *out of phase with.* He's vibrating bobobobobobop, and the walls are vibrating bap bap bap bap bap bap. *Oh,* he'd say, *what time is it?*

He'd have to get some kind of a *duplication* to run this out or straighten it out. Just by having him contact the walls of any universe by the Opening Procedure of S.O.P. 8C you get him straightened out on his vibrations and he stops being so much mass—simply by getting him into good agreement.

If the common denominator of time is change, then why do you think a preclear is so anxious to change? What is his anxiety about change? Well, he is doubly inverted—he finally depended on just agreement alone. He wasn't postulating time any more and he was just depending on this universe alone to say change change change change change—change of position of particle in space, change of position of particle in space, change, change, change.

He has (1) depended on that, (2) stopped depending on that, (3) fallen away from it, and (4) says:

"Look. Wait a minute. To have any survival or to go on with any of these items or any of these responsibilities or anything, something has got to change around here. So let's change, change. Let's change other things. Oh, I can't change those. People are easy to change, so let's try to change those. ... Well, I can't change those. I'll change myself, change myself, change myself, I'll change myself, change, change, change, change, change, chan, chan, cha, cha, cha, chachacha .... BOOM."

Totally-fixed-self-personal-time-track-with-no-agreement-any-place-else which looks like a solid mass, because it's changing so fast, and there's nobody agreeing with it—and he's gone out the bottom.

And that is why people get into compulsive change.

8-C Opening Procedure will get people out of that. Opening Procedure by Duplication will resolve this because you're changing at a uniform rate, and you, the auditor, are in agreement with him, and as a result he will be able to come on up out of it until he has re-timed.

A preclear who is having any difficulty at all, the first thing that would be wrong with him is that he'd be out of time as a car gets out of time and its motor doesn't run well. He's going off on his own time factor which to be aberrative to him would have to be totally automatic. He'd have to have set it up and now be unconscious of it. And he's out of time, and that's why he's obsessively changing, and why the individual who is worst off will want to change the fastest and the hardest and has the most compulsion and obsession about it.

So we see what this subject of time is all about, how it is possible to process it, and we see that we *have* been processing it all along.

CHAPTER THIRTEEN

AXIOMS

(*Part 1*)

The Axioms of Scientology are a list of usable or self evident truths and are a major part of the technical information of a Scientologist.

Having these we are now operating on just fifty axioms and definitions, where the Dianetic Axioms of 1951 were in excess of two hundred and ninety. We arrived at these fifty Axioms of Scientology through a great many changes, a great many major developments—all of them in the direction of higher workability and simplification.

A student in training in Scientology is not expected to read these Axioms. He is expected to *absorb* them, quote them verbatim and by number, understand and apply them.

Webster's says that an axiom is a self evident truth.

Comparing the Axioms of Scientology with axioms in another subject, these are certainly as self-evident as those of, for instance, geometry, which is actually a relatively crude subject in that it proves itself by itself, which is a limitation that Scientology does not have.

The Axioms of Scientology prove themselves by all of life.

In geometry we find the Aristotelian syllogism arbitrarily cutting across the whole subject. In Scientology we needed a better base than the syllogism and we have a better one. The platform on which we base our understanding is, if something doesn't work when applied we change what we are doing and find something which does work. We are certainly not bowed down to the great god No Change.

Well, true enough, these Axioms are self evident truths. But they are not so thoroughly self evident that they leap out of the page and introduce themselves to you. You have to introduce yourself to them.

The first of the Axioms is a bit of understanding which if you did not have and did not actually understand very well you would not be able to do anything with Scientology.

It's just as blunt as that.

AXIOM ONE: LIFE IS BASICALLY A STATIC.

And what is this static?

Definition : a Life Static has no mass, no motion, no wavelength, no location in space or in time. It has the ability to postulate and to perceive.

This is a peculiar and particular static, having these properties and a further peculiarity, which we find in the next Axiom.

AXIOM TWO: THE STATIC IS CAPABLE OF CONSIDERATIONS, POSTULATES, AND OPINIONS.

You can't measure this Static.

When you find something which has no mass, no location, no position in time and no wavelength—the very fact that it can't be measured tells you that you have your hands on Life itself.

You can't measure it, yet all things measurable extend from it. From this Static all phenomena extend.

You cannot measure a dog by his biscuits and you cannot measure this Static by the phenomena extending from it.

Space is one of these phenomena. You could say that Life is *a space-energy-object production and placement unit* because that is what it does. But when you measure these you do not measure Life.

A thetan is very, very close to being a pure Static. He has practically no wavelength. Actually a thetan is in a very, very small amount of mass. From some experiments conducted about fifteen or twenty years ago—a thetan weighed about 1.5 ounces! Who made these experiments? Well, a doctor made these experiments. He weighed people before and after death, retaining any mass. He weighed the person, bed and all, and he found that the weight dropped at the moment of death about 1.5 ounces and some of them 2 ounces. (Those were heavy thetans.)

So we have this thetan capable of considerations, postulates and opinions, and the most native qualities to him—in other words the things which he is most likely to postulate — are these qualities which you find in the top "buttons" of the Chart of Attitudes. "Trust", "Full Responsibility", etc.

So we have then actually described a thetan when we have gotten Axioms One and Two. Without these known well an auditor would have an awfully hard time exteriorizing (*Exteriorizing*: exteriorization: the state achieved in which the thetan can be outside his body with certainty) somebody—because if you thought that you reached in with a pair of forceps and dragged someone out of his head, well, this it not the way it is. You would not be thinking of a thetan. To exteriorize something that can't possibly be grabbed hold of, that's quite a trick.

A thetan has to postulate he's inside before you can have him postulate that he's outside. But if he heavily postulated that he's inside, now your trick as an auditor is to do what? Override this thetan's postulates? That would fit into the field of hypnotism, or maybe you could do it with a club, but the way we do it in Scientology is a little more delicate than these. We simply ask him to postulate that he's outside, and if he can and does, why, he's outside. And if he can't, why, he's still inside.

Thetans think of themselves as being in the MEST universe (*MEST universe*: the physical universe, from the initial letters of matter, energy, space, time). Of course, this is a joke, too. As the Static they can't possibly be *in* a universe.

But they can postulate a condition and then they can postulate that they cannot escape this condition.

AXIOM THREE: SPACE, ENERGY, OBJECTS, FORM AND TIME ARE THE RESULT OF CONSIDERATIONS MADE AND/OR AGREED UPON OR NOT BY THE STATIC, AND ARE PERCEIVED SOLELY BECAUSE THE STATIC CONSIDERS THAT IT CAN PERCEIVE THEM.

The whole secret of perception is right there. Do you believe that you can see. Well, all right, go ahead and believe that you can see but you'd certainly better believe that there's something there to see or you won't see. So there are two considerations to sight, and they are covered immediately here in that you have to believe there is something to see and then that you can see it. And so you have perception. All of the tremendous number of categories to perception come under this heading, and are covered by that Axiom. So that Axiom should be known very, very well.

AXIOM FOUR: SPACE IS A VIEWPOINT OF DIMENSION.

Do you know that physics has gone on since the time of Aristotle without knowing that! Yet we read in the Encyclopedia Britannica of many years ago (the Eleventh Edition, published in 1911) that space and time are not a problem of the physicist. They are the problem of one working in the field of the mind. And it says that when the field of psychology solves the existence of space and time why then physics will be able to do something with it. And all those fellows with their Ph.D.'s—not for centuries actually but a number of decades (it seems like centuries if you've ever listened to their lectures)—going back to the days of Wundt, The Only Wundt—about 1867—they didn't read the Encyclopedia Britannica and find out that they held the responsibility for identifying space and time so that physics could get on its way.

And because they avoided this responsibility we have to pitch in here and discover and develop Scientology —not to work in the field of physics, however, but to work in the field of the Humanities. But it so happened that I discovered very, very early while I was studying nuclear physics at George Washington University that physics did not have a definition for space, time and energy. It defined energy in terms of space and time. It defined space in terms of time and energy, and it defined time in terms of energy and space. It was going around in a circle. I first moved out of that circle by putting it into human behavior—*be, do* and *have,* which you'll find in *Scientology : 8-8008,** but the point is here that without a definition for space, physics was and is adrift. One of our auditors was recently talking to an engineer in an Atomic Energy Commission plant, and happened to remark, "Well, we have a definition for space." This engineer said, "Uh, you do?" and got instantly interested. Of course we didn't make this definition for nuclear physics, but they could certainly use one. The engineer asked, "What is the definition of space?" and the auditor said, "Space is a viewpoint of dimension." This fellow just sat there for

* *Scientology: 8-8008* by L. Ron Hubbard. See book list in back pages.

a moment, and he sat there, and then all of a sudden he rushed to the phone and dialled a number and he said, *"Close down number five!"* He had suddenly realized that an experiment in progress was about to explode and one of the reasons he knew it was about to explode is that he had found out what space was. This is of great interest to nuclear physicists, but they will get one of these definitions and then they will start to figure, figure, figure, figure, figure. They don't take the definition as such and use it as such. They figure-figure, and they lose it.

Using the process R2-40: *Conceiving a Static** gives an understanding of exactly why, every time they get hold of one of these definitions they lose it.

AXIOM FIVE: ENERGY CONSISTS OF POSTULATED PARTICLES IN SPACE.

Now, we've got space: a viewpoint of dimension.

You say: "I am here looking in a direction." We've actually got to have three points out there to look at, to have three dimensional space. If we only had linear space we would have only one dimension point. One point to view. And energy consists of postulated particles in space, so we'll demark these three points out there to have some three dimensional space and we'll have these particles which we will call Anchor Points, and we'll have energy.

And so we come to objects.

AXIOM SIX: OBJECTS CONSIST OF GROUPED PARTICLES.

If we just kept putting particles out there and pushing them together, or if we suddenly said, "There's a big group of particles out there," we'd have what is commonly called an *object.* When an object or particle moves across any part of a piece of space—in other

* In *The Creation of Human Ability* by L. Ron Hubbard. See book list in back pages.

words a viewpoint of dimension—we have motion.

And we come to the subject of time.

AXIOM SEVEN: TIME IS BASICALLY A POSTULATE THAT SPACE AND PARTICLES WILL PERSIST.

Time in its basic postulate is not even motion. The apparency of time—an agreed upon rate of change—becomes *agreed* upon time. But for an individual all by himself is simply a consideration. He says something will persist, and he has time. Now if he gets somebody *else* to agree on what is persisting, the two can then be in agreement. And if the items are motionless then they can't have agreements about how fast or how slow they're persisting, so they get them moving. And this gives them a clock or a watch. And so you carry a watch around on your wrist.

But time is not motion. Let's escape from that one right now. It is an error. We'll call that a heresy.

But this gives us another Axiom:

AXIOM EIGHT: THE APPARENCY OF TIME IS THE CHANGE OF POSITION OF PARTICLES IN SPACE. Now if we see particles changing in space we know time's passing, but if you had a piece of space and some particles, and you were simply sitting there looking at those particles and there was absolutely no change in them whatsoever, you would be very hard put to describe even to yourself whether any time was passing or not.

And so the apparency of time is the change of position of particles in space.

AXIOM NINE: CHANGE IS THE PRIMARY MANIFESTATION OF TIME.

If you were looking at motionless particles you would not be able to tell whether time was passing or not because you might be looking at one time or another. Then to prove time you could say they moved this far at such and such a speed or something of the sort. And you could say, "Therefore this much time has gone by." So we can say that change is the primary manifestation of time. Now, oddly enough you have your "Black Five", occluded case ("no pictures, only blackness") right there. A Black Five is trying to change himself simply because he's in agreement with particles in motion. That's all. He's simply acting on compulsion or obsession to change, and if you asked him very suddenly in which direction he's trying to change he would not be able to tell you. He has no real goal. He doesn't particularly want to be better, he doesn't particularly want to be worse, but he's got to change. He's frantically got to change. Well, *why* has he got to change? Because he has these particles all around him which are dictating change *to* him. They're saying, "Time . . . time . . . time . . . time . . . time . . . change . . . change . . . change."

In other words, he's in agreement with the apparency of time, and he has fallen far, far away from the mere *consideration* of time. So he doesn't conceive what time is. He becomes a nuclear physicist.

AXIOM TEN: THE HIGHEST PURPOSE IN THE UNIVERSE IS THE CREATION OF AN EFFECT.

We could do a tremendous amount with just that one Axiom, and in processing we would discover then good reason to have space and to have particles and how all these things get there. People want to create an effect, and they get into very interesting states of mind about this sort of thing. They say to themselves, well, let's see now—I caused that effect but that effect is horrible, Therefore I can't admit that I caused that effect, so I'll introduce a lie here and say I didn't cause that effect. And then—they become an effect. If they can't be at cause they become an effect. They are the effect of what they have caused without admitting they caused. But it can get even worse than that—worse than being at total effect. They get *way* down the line, to the point where they're *the cause of any effect.* They blame themselves, in other words. A man in Sandusky falls down and breaks a glass of pink lemonade and cuts his little pinky, and this person who is in San Diego at the time hears about that and knows he must be guilty. That's complete reversal.

A person can get into a state where he's cause and effect simultaneously. That is to say any effect he starts to cause he becomes that effect instantly. He says, I think I'll kill him, and he feels like he's dead. Just like that. Now we've got to have *time* in order to witness an effect. As an example of this one could observe that science is dedicated to observing an effect and does not have any other real goal. Once in a while you see a scientist who is also an idealist. He wants to use his materials to improve Man. But science at large, and particularly when it got over into the field of the mind. was simply a goal-less, soul-less pursuit, the totality of which is just to observe an effect. They are not really even causing an effect. They just go around observing effects. And they fill notebooks and notebooks and notebooks full of effects, effects, effects, effects, and you find they carry on experiments—not to prove anything, not to do anything, but just to observe an effect. They go around and put a pin in the tail of a rat, and the rat jumps and squeaks, and so they say "Ah," and they note it down carefully: "When you put a pin one inch from the end of the tail of a rat he moans". Actually the rat squeaked. Well this was observing an effect—the way it's recorded by science. This goes so far that a leading scientist of the day—an Einstein—says that all an observer has any right to do is look at a needle. If they were just going around observing effects, eventually they could build an atom bomb, and say "Well it isn't my fault. I'm not to blame." The few scientists who did feel badly about this and joined organizations to try to do something were promptly fired by the government. They had some responsibility.

AXIOM ELEVEN: THE CONSIDERATIONS RESULTING IN CONDITIONS OF EXISTENCE ARE FOURFOLD.

And here they are in exact axiom form:

(a) AS-IS-NESS is the condition of immediate creation without persistence, and is the condition of existence which exists at the moment of creation and the moment of destruction, and is different from other considerations in that it does not contain survival.

(b) ALTER-IS-NESS is the consideration which introduces change, and therefore time and persistence into an AS-IS-NESS to obtain persistency.

(c) IS-NESS is an apparency of existence brought about by the continuous alteration of an AS-IS-NESS. This is called, when agreed upon, Reality.

(d) NOT-IS-NESS is the effort to handle IS-NESS by reducing its condition through the use of force. It is an apparency and cannot entirely vanquish an IS-NESS.

AXIOM TWELVE: THE PRIMARY CONDITION OF ANY UNIVERSE IS THAT TWO SPACES, ENERGIES OR OBJECTS MUST NOT OCCUPY THE SAME SPACE. WHEN THIS CONDITION IS VIOLATED (PERFECT DUPLICATE) THE APPARENCY OF ANY UNIVERSE OR ANY PART THEREOF IS NULLED.

Alfred Korzybski in General Semantics was very careful to demonstrate that two objects could not occupy the same space. In other words, he was dramatizing "Preserve the universe, preserve the universe, preserve the universe". Now this statement tells you that if two objects can't occupy the same space you haven't got a universe, and sure enough if you just ask a preclear repetitively: "What object can occupy the same space you're occupying?" he'll work at it and he'll work at it and work at it, and the first thing you know, why, he's capable of doing many things which he was not able to do before. His space straightens out. He can create space again—merely because this MEST universe has been telling him so often that two objects cannot occupy the same space that he has begun to believe it. And he believes this is the most thorough law that he has. So he find a person perfectly contentedly being in a body believing he is a body. Why, he knows that he, a thetan, could not occupy the same space as a body. He knows this is impossible. Two objects can't occupy the same space. He's an object, and his body's an object, so the two can't occupy the same space.

This is very interesting because you'll find that two universes can occupy the same space and actually *do* occupy the same space. You'll find the universe of a thetan is occupying the same space as the physical universe, but once he declares that the both of them are occupying the same space, you get an interesting condition.

Now, I'm not going to try to take up at this point the perfect duplicate but it's enough just to say that two objects are occupying that space—identically occupying that space—and poof, it's gone. That's the way you make things vanish. That is to get its As-isness, and this is why As-is-ness works and why things disappear when you get their As-is-ness. This is an important Axiom.

Now here is the oldest thing that Man knows:

AXIOM THIRTEEN: THE CYCLE OF ACTION OF THE PHYSICAL UNIVERSE IS: CREATE, SURVIVE (PERSIST), DESTROY. Now, that's the oldest thing Man knows, but it went on the basis of death, birth, growth, decay, death, birth, growth, decay, death, birth, growth, decay and so on. He knew he had time involved here, on a linear line. The odd thing here is that you've got to postulate death to get a cycle of action, and you've got to postulate time to get a lineal line, so we're dealing here with one of the most intimate things of existence. We find this by the way in the Rig-Veda. It's been with Man about 10,000 years that I know of and we find that this is the cycle of action of the physical universe—create, survive, destroy.

In Dianetics, I isolated just one portion of this line as a common denominator of all existence, which was Survive, and sure enough any life form is surviving. It is trying to survive and that is its normal push forward. And that has, incidentally, terrific impact, but this has two other parts and those are create and destroy. Create, survive, destroy. And survive merely means persist. So all of these things are based on time, and we have underlying Axiom Thirteen this primary consideration that there is time.

Now we can go on and find that the conditions of existence fit these various portions of the survival curve. And this would be given as follows:

AXIOM FOURTEEN: SURVIVAL IS ACCOMPLISHED BY ALTER-IS-NESS AND NOT-IS-NESS, BY WHICH IS GAINED THE PERSISTENCY KNOWN AS TIME.

That's a mechanical persistency. In other words we keep changing things, saying they aren't, and changing them, and then pushing them out and reforming them and trying to vanish them. Using energy to fight energy, we'll certainly get survival. We'll get *persistency*.

AXIOM FIFTEEN: CREATION IS ACCOMPLISHED BY THE POSTULATION OF AN AS-IS-NESS.

Now all you have to say actually is: "Space, energy, time, As-is. That's the way it is, and, it's now going to persist." You've added time to it. If you immediately after that simply looked at it and got its As-is-ness again it would vanish. All you had to do is get it in the same instant of time with the same type of postulate and it would disappear. You could create it again and it would disappear. It would As-is.

AXIOM SIXTEEN: COMPLETE DESTRUCTION IS ACCOMPLISHED BY THE POSTULATION OF THE AS-IS-NESS OF ANY EXISTENCE AND THE PARTS THEREOF.

Complete destruction would simply be vanishment. You wouldn't have any rubble left. When you blow something up with guns you get rubble. Ask anybody who was in the last war. There were certainly an awful lot of broken bricks lying around. If anybody had really been working at this in a good sensible way, and he'd really meant total destruction, he would have simply gotten the As-is-ness of the situation and it would have been gone and that would have been the end of that. If he'd wanted to declare the whole As-is-ness of a country, if he'd been able to span that much attention and trace back that many particles that fast to their original points of creation, he would of course have a vanishment and that is complete destruction. So complete destruction is As-is-ness, and As-is-ness is simply a postulated existence.

What we're looking at most of the time in this universe is:

AXIOM SEVENTEEN: THE STATIC, HAVING POSTULATED AS-IS-NESS THEN PRACTICES ALTER-IS-NESS AND SO ACHIEVES THE APPARENCY OF IS-NESS, AND SO OBTAINS REALITY.

In other words we get a continuous alteration, and we get this apparency called Is-ness.

AXIOM EIGHTEEN: THE STATIC, IN PRACTICING NOT-IS-NESS, BRINGS ABOUT THE PERSISTENCE OF UNWANTED EXISTENCES, AND SO BRINGS ABOUT UNREALITY, WHICH INCLUDES FORGETFULNESS, UNCONSCIOUSNESS, AND OTHER UNDESIRABLE STATES.

Quite an important Axiom and very true one.

AXIOM NINETEEN: BRINGING THE STATIC TO VIEW AS-IS ANY CONDITION DEVALUATES THAT CONDITION.

CHAPTER FOURTEEN

AXIOMS

(*Part 2*)

It is a remarkable thing that life itself can be codified in terms of Axioms. It has not been done before. The first time it was even attempted was in 1951 when I wrote the *Logics and Axioms,* which I did simply to give an alignment to thought itself. And as a matter of fact copies of these Axioms were sent over to Europe and in 1953 I found them in Vienna *fully translated into German.* It's quite remarkable. Over there they were terribly impressed simply because it had not been done before. Nobody had before codified life to this degree and nobody had codified psychotherapy. And they were not impressed with whether the Axioms were right or wrong, it was only that nobody had done it before. In these Scientology Axioms we're not quite doing the same thing. Those 1951 Axioms of Dianetics were quite complicated and these fifty Axioms we now have are nowhere near as lengthy, but their reach is greater and they pack a great deal more punch.

We come here to the interesting subject of a proof of ultimate truth. If we have reached an ultimate truth, then we have reached an ultimate solution, and who would ever suspect, really, that an ultimate truth or an ultimate solution could be subjected to mechanical proof. We have done just that. We have discovered the phenomenon of a perfect duplicate.

AXIOM TWENTY: BRINGING THE STATIC TO CREATE A

PERFECT DUPLICATE CAUSES THE VANISHMENT OF ANY EXISTENCE OR PART THEREOF.

If you can bring someone to make a perfect duplicate of anything it will vanish. We have a perfect duplicate clearly defined:

A perfect duplicate is an additional creation of the object, its energy, and space, in its own space, in its own time, using its own energy. (And we could append to that "the considerations which go along with it", because it couldn't be anything *but* considerations.)

And: *This violates the condition that two objects must not occupy the same space, and causes vanishment of the object.*

If you ask somebody to simply make a perfect duplicate of, for instance, a vase, just exactly where it sits, it will begin to fade out on him, and he can do that to almost anything.

Why doesn't it fade for *somebody else*? This is quite remarkable. Everything in this universe is displaced or misplaced. When we talk about a lie, we really don't mean that simply changing the position of something is a lie. We have to *alter the consideration regarding it* to make a lie. It isn't really a lie that everything is so scrambled in this universe. It is scrambled. Just in the last moment or two several cosmic rays went through your body. Those were particles which emanated from somewhere and they arrived where you are—they had been *en route* for a hundred million years. To get one of those cosmic rays to vanish we would have to find its point of creation, and we would have to make a duplicate of that ray at the moment of its creation, and then we would have to make a duplicate of having done so. At that instant that cosmic ray would vanish.

This is very interesting to the physicist, it's very

interesting to almost anybody, and it is demonstrable. You can *do* this. I asked an auditor one afternoon simply to "look to the garage wall over there" and to choose a very small area, and "find the atoms and molecules in the wall there, and put an attention unit" —a remote viewpoint—"next to each one, and follow it immediately back to where it had been created." He was leaning on the fender of the car, and he did this —and he came off the fender of that car as though he had been shot. The object itself, this tiny portion of the object, had *started to disintegrate*. And he rushed over to it to hold it in place with his hands!

Why doesn't the whole universe vanish? Well, probably on the very site of this building there was another building once and that building has been broken up and the bricks have been moved and part of it is out there in the street, and part of it is still in the ground below and part of it—maybe some brick dust —got on somebody's suitcase who went to World War II, and part of it's in Germany and it's spread all over the place, and here are all these cosmic waves and rays going all over the universe—and to get each one of those at its moment of creation in the time and space, and to make a perfect duplicate of all this, would be quite a job. It's not an impossible job. It requires an ability to span attention. You would get a physical object to disappear so thoroughly that everybody else would know it was gone.

You see that it isn't true that an object sitting before you at this moment, or your chair, has always been in that position. Nor is it true that the materials in that chair have always been in that position, nor is it true that the atoms which made up the chair in raw material form were always in that particular ore bed or in that particular tree. So you see it's quite complex. This universe is scrambled.

That doesn't mean you can't make it vanish, however.

As we can produce this phenomenon, we know we have an ultimate solution. The perfect duplicate was the little latch string hanging out that opened the door to an ultimate truth. Well, what would an ultimate truth be? An ultimate truth is a Static, and an ultimate solution is a Static. In other words, an ultimate truth and an ultimate solution is *nothing.* Get the As-is-ness of any problem, make a perfect duplicate of any problem, and the problem will disappear. You can subject that easily to proof. So if you can make a problem disappear by simply getting its As-is-ness, then you've got the solution to all problems, or the ultimate solution. Well, the MEST universe itself is just a problem, and so if you could get its As-is-ness, it would disappear. It would disappear for everybody. Well, let's study that and get that very well and get what the definition is there, in the Axioms and Definitions. This is the total solution, by the way, to the vanishment of engrams—what we were handling in Dianetics. The vanishment of ridges, of all energy forms and manifestations, all these can simply be accomplished by making perfect duplicates of them. That doesn't mean that you should now make nothing out of everything or get your preclear to try to make nothing out of everything, but that it just can be done.

AXIOM TWENTY-ONE: UNDERSTANDING IS COMPOSED OF AFFINITY, REALITY AND COMMUNICATION.

We understand understanding a bit better when we see that it is simply the ability to get the As-is-ness of something. For example we could say "I don't quite understand this car. Don't quite understand what's wrong with it. It just won't start." And we walk around it and look at it and then we find out that we haven't turned on the key. And we turn on the key. We've understood it, in other words. We have unmocked the fact that the key was not turned on and we have turned on the key (which actually is practicing Alter-is-ness). If we walked around a car and said "I don't understand what this object is . . . I don't understand what this object is . . . AH! it's a *car*!" We would feel immediately relieved. We'd feel a lot better about the thing, but if we were to get its total As-is-ness there would just be a *hole* sitting there.

So understanding is As-is-ness and understanding in its entirety would be a Static and so we have the fact that Life knows basically everything there is to know before it gets complicated with lots of data, merely because it can postulate all the data it knows. All knowingness is inherent in the static itself. A thetan who is in good shape knows everything there is to know. He knows past, present and future. He knows everything. This doesn't mean he knows data. This merely means that he can As-is anything and if he can As-is anything believe me he can understand it.

Man's salvation I've said several times depends upon his recognition of his brotherhood with the universe. Well let's misinterpret that just a little bit and say Man's salvation—if you want to save him from the universe—would depend upon his ability to make an As-is-ness of the physical universe at which moment he wouldn't have a universe, and this would be total understanding.

Understanding has three parts: Affinity, Reality and Communication.

You can actually compose from ARC all the mathematics there are. You can combine ARC into mathematics. You can accomplish anything with ARC that you want to do. Symbolic Logic, even calculus, could be extrapolated from ARC.

Affinity depends upon reality and communication. Reality depends upon affinity and communication. Communication depends upon affinity and reality. If you don't believe this try to communicate sometime with somebody without any affinity at all. Get real mad at somebody, and then try to communicate with him. You won't. Try to get somebody to be reasonable when he is very angry and you'll find out that his reality is very poor. He cannot conceive of the situation. He'll give you some of the weirdest things. There is no liar lying like an angry man.

If you raise somebody's affinity you will raise his reality and communication. If you raise somebody's reality, you'll raise his affinity and communication. And the keynote of this triangle happens to be communication. Communication is more important than either affinity or reality.

AXIOM TWENTY-TWO: THE PRACTICE OF NOT-IS-NESS REDUCES UNDERSTANDING.

In other words, something is there, and we say it's not there.

Someone is driving down the road like mad and there's an enormous boulder lying in the middle of the road, and almost anybody, just before the crash, will say the boulder's not there. And by golly it's there. And this makes him feel he's a weak thetan. He failed. And the funny part of it is that if he were to immediately *As-is* the boulder down the road, instead of denying it's there, and if he could make this a perfect duplicate, the boulder would disappear.

He doesn't do it that way. He sort of puts some

energy up and pushes against the boulder, and says, "It's not there, it's not there. I deny it."

Well, he'll have a mighty thin understanding of the whole thing.

He doesn't want to communicate with it, so he says it's not there. He doesn't want to have any affinity for it at all, so he says it's not there. And believe me his reality cuts down. The practice of Not-is-ness reduces understanding, and that is what Man is doing constantly. He's trying to avow that something that isn't there is there, and he's trying to avow that something that is there isn't there, and between these two things, giving it no As-is-ness at all or new postulates of any kind, he's having quite a time of it.

AXIOM TWENTY-THREE: THE STATIC HAS THE CAPABILITY OF TOTAL KNOWINGNESS. TOTAL KNOWINGNESS WOULD CONSIST OF TOTAL ARC.

Here we have a condition of existence which is As-is. That would be total knowingness. Well, if we had somebody who could say "As-is" to everything, and trace all parts of everything back to their original time, location, and simply got them as they really were, we of course would have nothing left but a Static. We would have zero. We wouldn't even have space.

If you wanted, by the way, to make this whole universe vanish, you would have to be able to span this whole universe. You would have to be as big as the universe. You could drill somebody up to the point where he could do that.

AXIOM TWENTY-FOUR: TOTAL ARC WOULD BRING ABOUT THE VANISHMENT OF ALL MECHANICAL CONDITIONS OF EXISTENCE.

All *mechanical* conditions of existence. It wouldn't bring about the sudden death of everything. It would bring about the exteriorization of everything. It would mean the vanishment of all space and all form. Mechanics.

Differentiate between a consideration—a postulate—and a mechanic. Be sure to get the difference between a quality such as complete trust, a quality such as full responsibility, in other words the qualities along the top of the Chart of Attitudes—and the mechanics. A person who is all out for mechanics, and won't have anything to do with considerations, believes completely that considerations are of no worth and that mechanics are the thing ("You can put your hands on it, you can feel it, you can touch it")—this person would have to be made thoroughly acquainted with the existence of these mechanics before he could As-is them sufficiently to reach a level where he would have the ability to consider. He has sunk below the level of mechanics.

That's why 8C Opening Procedure, which acquaints the person with his immediate environment, works as it does.

Well, when we say mechanics, we mean space, energy, objects and time. And when something has those things in it we're talking about something mechanical. That's all that would vanish if you As-ised all of existence—just the mechanics—and you could turn right around and postulate them all back again too with great ease.

AXIOM TWENTY-FIVE: AFFINITY IS A SCALE OF ATTITUDES WHICH FALLS AWAY FROM THE CO-EXISTENCE OF STATIC, THROUGH THE INTERPOSITIONS OF DISTANCE AND ENERGY, TO CREATE IDENTITY, DOWN TO CLOSE PROXIMITY BUT MYSTERY.

Affinity, in terms of mechanics, is simply a matter of distance. Affinity is basically a consideration, but it does represent itself mechanically. For instance, *Total*

Knowingness goes down to *Lookingness.* You have to *look* to find out. Well that's different from simply knowing without looking. We go down to Looking, now we go just a little bit lower than that. (This Know-to-Mystery scale is by the way an Affinity scale.) We go into *Emotion,* and then we no longer have knowledge by looking. We have to have knowledge by emotion. Do we like it—do we dislike it. There are particles in emotion: "I don't like it"—in other words "I have some anger particles about it" or "I have some resentment particles"—and by the way a preclear has his reactive mind full of these emotion particles.

Now if I "have to feel it to know it is there", I've gone immediately into *Effort.* And my affinity for something would be good if I could feel it and it would be no good at all if I couldn't feel it. You get a Step V, a Black V, who is swearing by mechanics (and swearing *at* all life forms) and builds atom bombs and such things—and he tells you that he cannot contact life. He can't contact this thing called the Static, therefore he "can't believe in it". This is very interesting. You ask him why, and he says, "Well I can't feel it." He's twisting the snake around so it'll eat its tail. He's proving it all upside down and backwards. He says he can't get the existence of something he can't feel. And the odd part of it is that we can measure electronically the existence of life. There is a little meter on which we ran some tests, and we can actually demonstrate that one individual can turn on in another individual at some great distance from him a considerable electrical current, enough to make this little machine sit up and sing. And the other person can turn it on at will, and the person on whom it's being turned can't stop it. Here is a manifestation that can be measured. We've done the impossible there too. We've done the impossible in many places in Scientology. You can't measure a Static but we've done so by having a person, at a distance, bring a mechanic into being.

When a person gets down to Effort on this scale then he's into a level where he's "gotta work", *everything* has got to be work. He's got to touch everything and feel everything before he can know anything. A person in the Effort band, by the way, as he gets to the lower part of that band, has *facsimiles.* He's got mental image pictures. He'll even do weird things like this: he will get a *picture* to *know what's happening to him.* In other words, he'll get a mental image picture of a past incident in order to get an idea. He gets the picture and then he gets the idea, he doesn't get the idea and then get a picture. You want to watch that. Sometime you'll find a preclear who's doing this. You'll be saying, "All right, get the idea of being perfect." And your preclear will sit there and say, "I got it." You want to ask him, "How did you do that?" That's a wonderful question to ask a preclear at any time. "How did you do that?" And he'll say, "Why, of course, just like everybody else. I got this picture and this picture came up and I looked at it and the picture said, 'Be perfect,' and it showed me a circle, and a circle—well, that's perfect." That's how your preclear was doing that. He wasn't making the postulate at all. He was waiting for a picture to come and tell him what it was all about.

Now we go down from Effort into Thinking, and we get our "figure-figure" case. This case is hard to get along with—*he can't work.* Life is not composed of thought, particularly. It's composed of space and action and all sorts of things. The Static can do all these things and is not necessarily "all pure thought". Thinkingness comes in down the scale at the level *below*

Effort. And it comes in as figure-figure-figure-figure-figure. Now a person can *postulate* without *thinking about it,* and if that's what we mean by thought, that's fine. But usually what people mean by thought is figure-figure. "I'll just figure this out and I'll get a computation and a calculation and I'll add it up to . . . now let me see . . . can you go to the movies? I don't know," —the kind of answer a little kid gets. "Now let me see. I'll have to think it over. Give me a couple of days."

We don't know how all of this mechanic got into a postulate, but they've let it get in there. So that's the level, *Thinkingness.*

Now we go downstairs from Thinkingness on this scale and we get into *Symbolizingness. A symbol contains mass, meaning and mobility.* A symbol is something that's being handled from an orientation point—a point which is motionless in relationship to the symbol. It's motionless, and the symbol is in motion, and has mass, meaning and mobility. "Where are you from?" "I am from New Jersey." This fellow is telling you that he is *from* an orientation point called New Jersey. It's motionless and as he runs around the world, he is always from New Jersey. He has mass, meaning and mobility. He has a name. When a person drops down the scale below figure-figure, he is into a point where he *figures with symbols.* Now that's a condensation, isn't it. Each of these was a condensation.

The next one down the line, below Symbols, is *Eatingness.* Animals eat animals. Animals are symbols and they eat other symbols and they think they have to stay alive by eating other symbols. This is real cute and eating is quite important of course and it can be a lot of fun, but here you have a *real* condensation. In other words, Effort got so condensed that it turned into an inverted kind of Thought, and that became so condensed that it packaged thinking—that's what took place there—it became so condensed it became a Symbol. A word, for instance, is a whole package of thought. So packaged thinking is a symbol and packed symbols are a plate of beans.

Below that, when a person doesn't believe he can eat any more, when he thinks he is not going to survive, he will go into the *Sexingness* band. If you starve cattle for a while they'll start to breed, and if you feed them too well they'll stop breeding. Quite irrational, but then who said any of this was rational? Cattle who are starved or lacking certain food elements will decide, well, we'll live again in some other generation—and they'll breed up a lot of calves. Of course there's nothing to feed the calves on but they haven't paid much attention to that. In Arizona we have an interesting fact—we have some very beautiful cattle who have stopped breeding. They've just been too well fed. The way to get those cattle breeding again would be to simply start starving them. Freud by the way was so condensed he had to get way down there to that condensation level of Sex "in order to find out".

Below Sex we have a new level of knowingness, the level of *Mystery*.

Mystery of course is the complete displacement of everything, and everything in a terrific confusion. The anatomy of Mystery is unprediction, confusion and then total blackout. First he couldn't predict some particles, and then it all seemed awfully confusing to him and then he just shut it all off and said "I won't look at it anymore". That's what Mystery is, and your Step Fives by the way are very, very concerned about Mystery. They're very concerned about Thinkingness and trying to solve the Mystery. Well the Mystery is already solved in an ultimate truth. The ultimate solution of course is simply the As-is-ness of the problem. And the As-is-ness of a Mystery is simply the Mystery. That's really all there is to it. There really *is* nothing to know back of a Mystery, except the Mystery itself. It's just As-is-ness. But Mystery is the level of always pretending there's something to know earlier than the Mystery.

To sum this up we have, under Axiom Twenty-five:

By the practice of Is-ness (Beingness) and Not-is-ness (refusal to Be) individuation progresses from the Knowingness of complete identification down through the introduction of more and more distance and less and less duplication, through Lookingness, Emotingness, Effortingness, Thinkingness, Symbolizingness, Eatingness, Sexingness, and so through to not-Knowingness (Mystery). Until the point of Mystery is reached, some communication is possible, but even at Mystery an attempt to communicate continues. Here we have, in the case of an individual, a gradual falling away from the belief that one can assume a complete Affinity down to the conviction that all is a complete Mystery. Any individual is somewhere on this Know-to-Mystery scale. The original Chart of Human Evaluation was the Emotion section of this scale.

CHAPTER FIFTEEN

AXIOMS

(*Part 3*)

These Axioms of Affinity, Reality and Communication are inherent in everything we are dealing with in Scientology.

They are of extreme importance and usefulness. If you want to find where a break in a communication line is coming from, why, look for some affinity that is off, and if you want to audit somebody who is having a rather rough time, then you had better audit them with considerable affinity. If you demonstrate enough affinity one way or the other, you will be able to overcome their communication reluctance.

It's very important to understand that all these things are basically a consideration. We have to consider that they exist before they exist. We are covering on this track the considerations which Man has composited into an existence.

Man has decided that certain things exist and he has agreed upon them very thoroughly and so they exist for all of men. And if he had never decided upon these various existences, they wouldn't exist.

So we look at Affinity, Reality and Communication. We are looking at a long series of considerations which Man holds in common. These are not considerations simply because we in Scientology consider that they exist. We can do enormously important things with this information, this codification of the organization of this universe which has spanned a period of something on the order of magnitude of seventy-six trillion years, and to be able to bust it loose and knock it apart is quite an interesting feat.

In looking at the subject of affinity we see that the first thing to know about it is that it is a consideration, and then that in the ARC triangle the distance of communication is represented by affinity to a marked degree, and the type of particle.

They say that absence makes the heart grow fonder. That hapens to be a lie, but you could postulate it that way and make it come out. You could also say that if you get two people far enough apart, they're likely to get mad at each other. A country wars with another country as a result of being far enough apart to afford to get mad. Somebody very furious at you as long as they are on the other end of a telephone line—when you went around to see them they weren't mad at you any more. That's an inversion on the situation. You closed the distance, and so you achieved a better affinity. There are many ways that you could handle this but again basically it's a consideration.

AXIOM TWENTY-SIX: REALITY IS THE AGREED UPON APPARENCY OF EXISTENCE.

The whole subject of Reality is a baffling one to people who do not add into Reality Affinity and Communication. It's not "This is my reality and that's your reality".

The person can postulate anything he wants to postulate, and he does have a personal reality. He could simply say, "It's there", or "That's real". Or he can have a facsimile appear which is more real to him than the actual universe around him—the psychotic to whom facsimiles are far, far more real than anything else that exists. Well these are two conditions which we don't recognize as reality. On the one hand the person merely postulates a reality, and so that's his reality and other people don't agree upon it. The other is also a not-agreed-upon reality and that is an *other-determined* reality. Somebody's given him a facsimile and has really impressed him with it, and so this looks more real to him than reality. In other words, we have complete self-determined postulation, and complete other-determined postulations, neither one of which is what we consider to be *reality*. Those are extremes.

What we actually consider to be reality is *in the mean* of these. That is: *what do we agree is real*. You and I agree that there's a wall there—and there's a wall there. We agree there's a ceiling there, and there's a ceiling there. That's real simply because you and I safely have agreed that that's how it is. Now if somebody came into the room and looked at forty people sitting down and said, "What are you all standing up for?" why, you'd have rather a tendency to believe there was something wrong with this fellow. As a matter of fact, the society uses *natural selection* to take out of the line-up people who have too much personal reality and too much other-determined reality. If this person walked in and said, "What are all you people standing up for?"—if he did that consistently about a number of things and said, "What is that lion doing walking on the ceiling?" there would be a tendency for him to get locked up. In other words, he would be moved away from survival where he wouldn't procreate. In other words, we'd move these people actually out of at least the genetic line-up These are called the insane.

Now here we have in Reality a very embrasive subject, because Reality is actually *Is-ness*. And unreality is *Not-is-ness*. An effort of trying to make things disappear with energy. Trying to make things disappear with energy was talked about amusingly in such places as the Bible and they used to say "He who lives by the sword dies by the sword" and somebody said once "Turn the other cheek", and what these people were actually saying was: fighting force with force does not bring about anything like a perfect duplicate.

Maybe they didn't know they were saying that. But using force to fight force brings about an unreality. Oddly enough using force to *build* force brings about a reality.

Continuous alteration gives us an Is-ness. A Not-is-ness—saying it doesn't exist—gives us an unreality. So there we have Reality and Unreality defined.

Now how could you use this principle of Reality in auditing:

Reality is basically agreement. *A mechanical* agreement is: for two forms to be exactly similar. In other words, one's a copy of the other form. That's mimicry, and we learn by mimicry, which is the lowest level of entrance to ARC, and is a very good thing for an auditor to know in any case. What we know then as reality is: the agreed upon apparency of existence.

AXIOM TWENTY-SEVEN: AN ACTUALITY CAN EXIST FOR ONE INDIVIDUALLY, BUT WHEN IT IS AGREED WITH BY OTHERS IT CAN BE SAID TO BE A REALITY.

And we find that those things which have become solid to us, very fixed, must have been agreed upon by others.

The anatomy of Reality is contained in Is-ness, which is composed of As-is-ness and Alter-is-ness. Is-ness is an apparency, it is not an Actuality. The Actuality is As-is-ness altered so as to obtain a persistency. Unreality is the consequence and apparency of the practice of Not-is-ness.

This agreement is part of the total As-is-ness of this universe.

If you ask a preclear for "some things you wouldn't mind agreeing with," or "something that you could do that other people would agree with", and so on, you'll notice a change in the case. Why? We're improving his level of agreement. He is actually bound by certain considerations, and until he postulates otherwise, he will continue with those considerations. This is how somebody gets *fixed into* something.

The whole of existence in this universe actually is run very much like a hypnotic trance.

The worse off a group is, which is to say the less communication they have, actually the more communication can be forced on them, and you see a form of hypnotism there, but the interesting thing is that they must have been prepared by an enormous number of agreements before they got into that state. In other words somebody else prepared them, so they didn't care who they agreed with after a while. When someone of higher rank in a uniform walks up to a soldier and says do something, the soldier will do it. Well, this is a form of hypnotism. You could get a group to agree first that you were simply standing there, and then the next thing that you could get them to agree to is the fact that they were listening to you, and then you would give them a few little things on which they would agree, and at some point you could tell them that the world was on fire, and the audience would rush out to find out, or maybe they'd just sit there and burn.

Now what is this all about? Does that mean that anybody bringing about an agreement would bring about hypnotism? Oh, no.

The reason why, in Scientology, we do not bring

about a hypnotism even in Open Procedure by Duplication, is that we are *undoing* the agreements which people have been making for seventy-six trillion years. We're undoing these, thus auditing makes a person freer, and freer, and freer.

Now, this fellow on the stage who simply gets the audience to agree and agree and agree and agree, and then tells them the place is on fire, isn't really going in the direction of making them freer, is he? His intention for this is entirely different. It isn't that an intention is above agreement, it's that *consideration* is always above agreement, and he is trying to work them into a situation where they will accept what he says without question. In Scientology we're not interested in anybody accepting what we say without question. We ask them to question it. We ask them to please look at the physical universe around you, please look at people, at your own mind, and understand *thereby* that what we are talking about happens to be actual. This is the series of agreements. These *are*. I could get people to agree with me about a lot of things and every once in a while throw them a curve. I could quite imperceptibly introduce a false datum into the science, and people have done this sort of thing but one can trace back in this development and see that what we're doing here is laying out the map of what has happened in seventy-six trillion years of a universe.

Your agreements have finally mounted up to a point where you believe this universe is all here and what you're agreeing to fortunately are the very things which you agreed to. We aren't giving you new things, we're giving you old things, and by understanding these old things which we have re-discovered, you become free.

What is this feeling of unreality that people get—

this unconsciousness and upset and forgetfulness and so on down the list of discomforts of beings. Actually forgetfulness stems from an effort to make things disappear by pressing against them with energy. You can imagine that if we push against a thought hard enough and say it isn't there while it's still there, why, we will surely become forgetful. And if we push hard enough we will become unconscious. But remember we had to postulate that we could forget and we had to postulate that we could become unconscious before either of these things could happen. People toss around waiting to go to sleep, then they say "I am going to sleep." Well, inspect R2-40 and you'll understand why the proper thing to do is to simply say, "I'm asleep." "Well," they say, "that's a lie." No, it isn't a lie unless you consider that you're awake. Now, if you said, "I'm awake, and now I am going to sleep," why of course you wouldn't go to sleep. The point here is that you could make at any moment a prime postulate.

We come to the formula of communication.

AXIOM TWENTY-EIGHT: COMMUNICATION IS THE CONSIDERATION AND ACTION OF IMPELLING AN IMPULSE OR PARTICLE FROM SOURCE-POINT ACROSS A DISTANCE TO RECEIPT-POINT, WITH THE INTENTION OF BRINGING INTO BEING AT THE RECEIPT-POINT A DUPLICATION OF THAT WHICH EMANATED FROM THE SOURCE-POINT.

Now understand this word *duplicate* as *copy,* and we have *perfect duplicate* which means As-is. When we talk about a duplicate we merely mean a copy. Copy, facsimile, duplicate, are pretty much the same thing, and when we're saying perfect duplicate we mean the object created again in its place, in its time, with its own energy. So we send a telegram from New York City which says, "I love you" and it arrives in San Francisco saying "I loathe you". Something has happened there, that we don't get a duplication. Well the more mechanical an individual becomes the less he can duplicate and the less he can make perfect duplicates —so he can't As-is anything. He falls off to a point where he can't make a copy. You say, "Go around the corner and tell Betty I love her", and he goes around the corner and says, "Joe said, uh . . . to tell you he loathes you". In a line of soldiers we whisper a message, "H hour is at 10 o'clock," and when it goes through a dozen soldiers this way we find at the other end that "We had beans for supper". This is the inability to make copies. And this is a most disruptive thing, and the most important thing in communication. A workable statement of the formula of communication is simply: *cause, distance, effect with a good copy at effect of that which was at cause.* That's all you really need to know about communication.

AXIOM TWENTY-NINE: IN ORDER TO CAUSE AS-ISNESS TO PERSIST, ONE MUST ASSIGN OTHER AUTHORSHIP TO THE CREATION THAN HIS OWN. OTHERWISE, HIS VIEW OF IT WOULD CAUSE ITS VANISHMENT. *Any space, energy, form, object, individual, or physical universe condition can exist only when an alteration has occurred of the original As-is-ness so as to prevent a casual view from vanishing it. In other words, anything which is persisting must contain a "lie" so that the original consideration is not completely duplicated.*

If Joe created something and then said "Bill made it," that's a lie, so he gets persistence stemming out of a second postulate, the lie.

AXIOM THIRTY: THE GENERAL RULE OF AUDITING IS THAT ANYTHING WHICH IS UNWANTED AND YET PERSISTS MUST BE THOROUGHLY VIEWED, AT WHICH TIME IT WILL VANISH. *If only partially viewed, its intensity, at least, will decrease.*

AXIOM THIRTY-ONE: GOODNESS AND BADNESS, BEAUTIFULNESS AND UGLINESS, ARE ALIKE CONSIDERATIONS AND HAVE NO OTHER BASIS THAN OPINION.

AXIOM THIRTY-TWO: ANYTHING WHICH IS NOT DIRECTLY OBSERVED TENDS TO PERSIST.

It's true that if you don't As-is it and you've already said it's going to be there, why naturally it will be there. But this is worse than that. You find somebody working and paying some attention to the work but never paying any attention to his machine. And you'll find he has facsimiles of the machine just all stacked up everywhere. He's never As-ised the machine. Or you find somebody who has always looked at lighted objects in dark rooms and has never looked at the darkness eventually seeing nothing but darkness when he closed his eyes. He'll have a "black bank", in other words.

AXIOM THIRTY-THREE: ANY AS-IS-NESS WHICH IS ALTERED BY NOT-IS-NESS (BY FORCE) TENDS TO PERSIST.

AXIOM THIRTY-FOUR: ANY IS-NESS, WHEN ALTERED BY FORCE, TENDS TO PERSIST.

AXIOM THIRTY-FIVE: THE ULTIMATE TRUTH IS A STATIC.

A Static has no mass, meaning, mobility, no wavelength, no time, no location in space, no space.

This has the technical name of "Basic Truth".

AXIOM THIRTY-SIX: A LIE IS A SECOND POSTULATE, STATEMENT OR CONDITION DESIGNED TO MASK A PRIMARY POSTULATE WHICH IS PERMITTED TO REMAIN.

Examples:

Neither truth nor a lie is a motion or alteration of a particle from one position to another.

A lie is a statement that a particle having moved did not move, or a statement that a particle, not having moved, did move.

The basic lie is that a consideration which was made was not made or that it was different.

AXIOM THIRTY-SEVEN: WHEN A PRIMARY CONSIDERATION IS ALTERED BUT STILL EXISTS, PERSISTENCE IS ACHIEVED FOR THE ALTERING CONSIDERATION.

All persistence depends on the Basic Truth, but the persistence is of the altering consideration, for the Basic Truth has neither persistence nor impersistence.

Now we come to something which is tremendously interesting because it is the proof of the fact that we have reached an ultimate truth and an ultimate solution. And that ultimate truth is itself very, very important to an auditor because that tells you whether or not Scientology is a total subject.

We could show this by a line representing knowledge, going upward from no knowledge as follows:

ALL DATA KNOWN

ONE NEW DATUM KNOWN

NO DATA KNOWN

From no data to one new datum to eventually at top ALL data known.

But this is actually a circle. At the top is NO DATA KNOWN. Just before the top is ALL DATA KNOWN, and as we move to the top and then return to NO DATA we then move to the next point of ONE NEW DATUM KNOWN and so on around the circle to more and more, then ALL data, then again none:

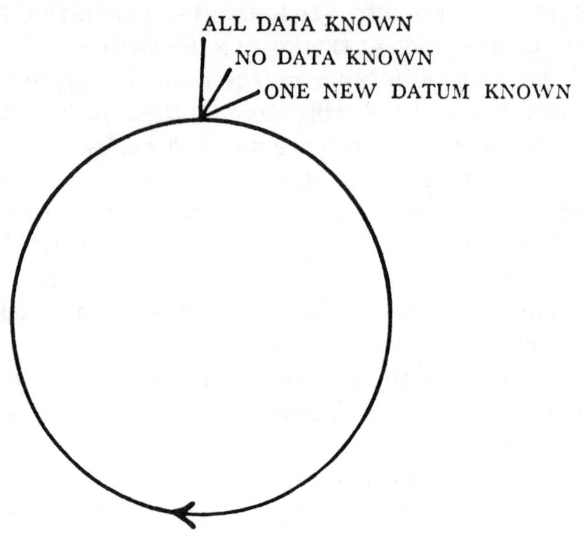

You see that on this circle everything known and nothing known are adjacent.

Well, we have reached that point in Scientology because we know that the ultimate truth, the ultimate solution, is the Static.

The solution to a problem is the As-is-ness of the problem, because by solution is meant: what will cause this problem to dissipate and disappear. With As-isness we have reached the solution to all problems. We have reached an ultimate truth. So that we know we have in Scientology a total subject.

AXIOM THIRTY-EIGHT:

1: STUPIDITY IS THE UNKNOWNESS OF CONSIDERATION.

2: MECHANICAL DEFINITION: STUPIDITY IS THE UNKNOWNESS OF TIME, PLACE, FORM, AND EVENT.

He knows something happened, but he doesn't know what happened. He can't add it up. He can't do anything with it. We call that stupidity.

1: TRUTH IS THE EXACT CONSIDERATION.

2: TRUTH IS THE EXACT TIME, PLACE, FORM, AND EVENT.

Thus we see that failure to discover Truth brings about stupidity.

Thus we see that the discovery of Truth would bring about an As-is-ness by actual experiment.

Thus we see that an ultimate truth would have no time, place, form or event.

Thus, then, we perceive that we can achieve a persistence only when we mask a truth.

Lying is an alteration of Time, Place, Event, or Form.

Lying becomes Alter-is-ness, becomes Stupidity.

(The Blackness of cases is an accumulation of the case's own or another lies.)

Anything which persists must avoid As-is-ness. Thus, anything, to persist, must contain a lie.

He says: "I am a man," so he's a man. That's the exact consideration. He is not telling a lie until he has said I am a man—and then has masked or hidden the fact that he is a man, and says, "I am a woman", Now the odd part of it is that he made a truth when he made the first postulate. And that which denied that truth then persisted. The *second postulate* always persists. I give you R2-40. The dissertation in R2-40 in the Handbook* makes this much clearer. The second postulate introduced time. Persist is time—that's all. Mortality,

* See *The Creation of Human Ability* by L. Ron Hubbard. Available as listed in back pages.

immortality—this is a matter of time. It's also a matter of Identity, but it's basically time. That which is persisting means that which is time-ing. And if you have assumed that after you made a postulate you then had something which permitted you to make another postulate, you'd have to postulate time there, wouldn't you? It's quite interesting. So that your second postulate then introduced time, merely because it's the second postulate. You had to introduce time. You see, there is no time in the Static, natively. Time is just a consideration. All right. So you introduce time. You get a lie. Now any time the first postulate is masked (this is mechanical by the way, this is the way it works) and you put a second postulate in front of the first postulate, it's the second postulate which persists, but it derives its strength from the first postulate.

Entered into the solution of this subject of Scientology and life was this datum, that stupidity is the unknowness of consideration. Well, then truth is the *knowness* of the consideration, isn't it? Right back there we have that perfect duplicate. We found out that when you got the As-is-ness of anything, if you made a perfect duplicate of it it would disappear. So truth is a perfect duplicate. But that's a disappearance. Well, if that's a disappearance then all you've got left is the Static. So that truth is the Static. And it follows through just as clearly as that. It's a mechanical proof. It's as mechanical as any kind of proof you ever wanted in any field of mathematics. It's totally mechanical.

Now again a problem is a solution only when you get the As-is-ness of the problem. We get the As-is-ness of the problem, therefore what have we got left? We've got the As-is-ness of the problem and we have nothing left. Oh, but we *don't* have nothing—we have a Static. So we find out that the ultimate truth is also the basic truth, contains no time, no motion, no mass, no wavelength, and we find also that the ultimate solution contains no time, no motion, no mass, no wavelength. So we come back to something which is not an imponderable: does and can one of these Statics exist? Yes, that too we can subject to proof, and we can subject it to proof immediately, instantly and easily. Nothing to it.

You just ask somebody who's in not too bad condition to "Be three feet back of your head." You can ask him to be anywhere, to appear anywhere in the universe, and he can. You ask him to manufacture space and energy, and he can. You can inspect actually whether or not this is taking place. And you'll find out that it is taking place, and you'll find out that Man is basically a Static. So he doesn't move. He *appears*. Therefore we have this thing called the Static. We have the perfect duplicate—the As-is-ness. We have an ultimate truth and we have an ultimate solution. At this point in Scientology we have wrapped it up. There are a great many strong points on the track where there's a lot of data hidden, and chaos and confusions and that sort of thing which we've by-passed, a lot of things which we haven't described adequately—for instance I'm not even satisfied at this moment completely with our description of Affinity, but I can tell you this, that they are knowingly by-passed points.

The other evening (at two o'clock in the morning) I suddenly found that I had arrived at the edge of a cliff, looking at End of Track. There isn't any more road out there, that's all, because we've come back to the Static, and we have found out what this Static is, we can demonstrate its existence, we can demonstrate what it does, we can prove it and we can all agree upon that proof, and we can do wonderful and miraculous things with it. The forty processes contained in the Auditor's Handbook* can do those things *just like that.*

When you know well this material and can apply it in the first few of these processes, you will be doing very, very well.

* *Auditor's Handbook*: 1954 edition of the book which, greatly expanded, became *The Creation of Human Ability* by L. Ron Hubbard. See book list in back pages.

CHAPTER SIXTEEN

AXIOMS

(*Part 4*)

Having these Axioms we are now particularly interested in this whole subject of truth and its actual use in auditing. We see immediately that any problem of any character or scope is the basic business of a Scientologist. If you have someone who wants to know about solutions, you had certainly better give him not *a* solution to a problem but *the solution to problems,* and that of course would be a basic and ultimate truth. Well, if you can describe a basic and ultimate truth, and describe it exactly, you have no problem at all in solving problems.

We see that failure to discover truth brings about stupidity. A person begins to believe he's stupid if he can't As-is.

We see that the discovery of truth would bring about an As-is-ness, by actual experiment, and thus we see that an ultimate truth would have no time, place or form. Whatever we had there would simply disappear if we discovered an ultimate truth. The ultimate truth is a perfect duplicate and therefore a Static. And, operationally, to achieve a Static would be to make a perfect duplicate.

We see that a lie as we understand it is an alteration of time, place, event or form, and that only lies persist.

We have to have a basic postulate, and then another postulate, before we get time. Two postulates. We can't have time with one postulate unless it is the postulate that there will be time. That could be one postulate. But normally in operation we find that two postulates are necessary to achieve time.

Now which one of these postulates is going to persist if the two postulates deny each other: the second one is going to persist, because it is the time postulate.

Lying becomes an Alter-is-ness, and becomes stupidity. In other words, we don't discover where the thing is, we don't discover exactly how it is, so we can't unmock it, and there we are. The only thing that we can do with it possibly is to Not-is it or Alter-is it some more or do what a Black V does—just stir it around and hope it will disappear. He doesn't As-is it. It doesn't disappear.

Oddly enough, lying will develop into a stupidity. It also develops into a mystery—into this blackness which individuals are so upset about. It's just an alteration of time, place, event or form after the fact of its having been created.

There would be two kinds of lie here. A *mechanical* lie does not lead to blackness. Mechanical lie: we mock up some space, and we put an object in that space and then we move it. The moment we've moved it we've lied about it. We've said it's over there when as a matter of fact it was created in the first location. Now in view of the fact that there is only consideration this of course would bring about mechanically a lie. It doesn't disappear, it doesn't do anything peculiar simply by moving it around. The mere handling of energy does not bring about a stupidity. It takes another consideration than simply moving something to bring about an occlusion.

Now, anything to persist must avoid As-is-ness, and

thus anything to persist, really to *persist,* must contain a lie. And we get the next Axiom:

AXIOM THIRTY-NINE: LIFE POSES PROBLEMS FOR ITS OWN SOLUTION.

Now what do we find here, in a problem? We find something which is persisting, the As-is-ness of which cannot readily be obtained, and would be the definition of a problem. Now to solve that problem it would be necessary to get its As-is-ness. Well, how do we prevent something from being As-ised, in other words vanished? We introduce a lie into it.

AXIOM FORTY: ANY PROBLEM, TO BE A PROBLEM, MUST CONTAIN A LIE. IF IT WERE TRUTH, IT WOULD UNMOCK.

When the preclear is *being a problem,* we know very well that there's a lie somewhere on the track that he's trying to obtain the As-is-ness of. It's not necessarily his lie, but it certainly is a lie. And under Axiom Forty we get:

An "unsolvable problem" would have the greatest persistence.

It would also contain the greatest number of altered facts. To make a problem, one must introduce Alter-is-ness.

In other words, this problem must have been moved and shifted and shoved around considerably to be unsolvable.

AXIOM FORTY-ONE: THAT INTO WHICH ALTER-IS-NESS IS INTRODUCED BECOMES A PROBLEM.

Any time you Alter-is something you've got a problem on your hands.

This whole universe, then, is a problem. Therefore this whole universe must contain a lie to go on persisting the way it does. It certainly does contain Alter-is. It certainly does contain a lie. It contains a variety of lies about its creation, and there are all sorts of things about this universe which cause its persistence, and all of those things boil down to the one fact that it must be based upon a lie and it must be very definitely altered.

Axiom Forty-one tells us that it was alteration which brought the preclear into a problem, thus we find any child who has moved extensively, who has had his home changed, who has been shoved around to various parts of the world, eventually becomes a problem, first to the environment and then to himself.

AXIOM FORTY-TWO: MEST (MATTER, ENERGY, SPACE, TIME) PERSISTS BECAUSE IT IS A PROBLEM.

It is a problem because it contains Alter-is-ness.

Your physicist is busily at work trying to unmock it but he is unmocking it by Not-is-ness. He's using force to alter force, and because he keeps altering it, it all naturally just gets worse and worse. He will solve nothing with an atom bomb. He will simply make things go worse, more complicated, more confused, more dispersed. The atom bomb is a dead-end track and is folly, it is great folly.

If an atom bomb were introduced into a war the number of particles and the amount of MEST which would be altered, we would discover immediately, would have introduced a great number of lies into the situation, it would have deteriorated the society and everything else. If we were foolish enough, for instance, to atom bomb Russia, or if Russia were foolish enough to atom bomb the United States, enough confusion would have been introduced into the cultures of earth so that probably there would be no other choice but to sink into a barbarism, in the absence of an understanding of life itself.

AXIOM FORTY-THREE: TIME IS THE PRIMARY SOURCE

OF UNTRUTH. *Time states the untruth of consecutive considerations.*

I call your attention to *interest,* as an interesting thing to observe. There are two classes of interest, and we want to know why we're thinking about this in terms of time, and this is because time is the basic lie behind all lies. We believe there are consecutive moments. We see consecutive motions and this all very pleasant—we agree to this—and it's only when we have masked them with some vicious intent that we really get a kick-back from the progress of time.

But we discover here in the matter of interest that we have two facets: one is "interest*ed*", and the other is "interest*ing*".

A thetan is *interested,* and an object is *interesting.* A thetan is not interesting. He is interested. And when a person becomes terribly interesting he has lots of problems, believe me. That is the chasm that is crossed. That is the chasm which is crossed by all of your celebrities, anybody who is foolish enough to become famous. He crosses over from being interested in life to being interesting, and people who are interesting are really no longer interested in life. It's very baffling to some young fellow why he can't make some beautiful girl interested in him. Well, she is not interested, she is interesting.

AXIOM FORTY-FOUR: THETA (THE STATIC) HAS NO LOCATION IN MATTER, ENERGY, SPACE, OR TIME. IT IS CAPABLE OF CONSIDERATION.

We have put it right in there again just to drive it home well. There's no time in this Static. Time is a lie.

Time can be postulated by the Static but is only a consideration and thereafter a thetan gets the idea that he is persisting across a span of time, and he is not.

He is not persisting. Objects are going across time, and energies and spaces are changing, but he is not. At no time does he actually change. He has to *consider* he is out of his head before he can be out of his head.

A Step V, or Black Five, is quite interesting in this regard. He is always thinking the auditor's going to reach in and pull him out of his head. He's waiting for something else to do it! Of course you could probably hypnotize him and tell him that he was, and he'd probably react in various ways, but *he* has to say, "I am now out of my head," and then he will be out of his head. But "waiting to see" whether or not he's out of his head is complete nonsense. The only way that he can get *anything* done, is to *consider* that it is done, or consider that that is the condition which exists.

AXIOM FORTY-FIVE: THETA CAN CONSIDER ITSELF TO BE PLACED, AT WHICH MOMENT IT BECOMES PLACED, AND TO THAT DEGREE A PROBLEM.

Any time we fall away from Axiom One, which is repeated as Axiom Forty-four, we discover that we have less of a Static than before. In other words we just *place* this Static, and it's less of a Static. A thetan, then, can have a problem, just by being placed. Quite in addition to that he ceases to be quite as interested.

He himself, placing himself, can get away with it. This isn't very hard for him to do. And he can perceive from this new place, and so forth, but as long as he is placed, he will be less than the Static. Just remember that. He is to that degree a problem.

AXIOM FORTY-SIX: THETA CAN BECOME A PROBLEM BY ITS CONSIDERATIONS BUT THEN BECOMES MEST.

A problem is to some degree MEST, MEST IS a problem.

What is this MEST? We find that an interested

thetan is a thetan, but an interesting thetan has become MEST. What is MEST? Well, it's actually simply a composite of energies and particles and spaces which are agreed upon and which are looked at.

We have the difference between inflow and outflow. A thetan who is being interested is simply outflowing. Interested — outflowing. Interesting — inflowing. He wants the attention of others to flow in to him: interesting. That's MEST. Attention of others flows to it. That doesn't tell you that all MEST is is a series of trapped Thetans.

It says that it is a type of life which is being interesting, as opposed to something which is being interested in it.

Now, Number Forty-six: *Theta can become a problem by its considerations, but then becomes MEST,* is followed by this, that MEST is a problem, and will always be considered a problem, and is nothing else but a problem. *MEST is that form of theta which is a problem.* That's all. Therefore, it is that form of theta which has a lie introduced into it. And so, of course, it is a problem.

AXIOM FORTY-SEVEN: THETA CAN RESOLVE PROBLEMS.

AXIOM FORTY-EIGHT: LIFE IS A GAME WHEREIN THETA AS THE STATIC SOLVES THE PROBLEMS OF THETA AS MEST.

Now that means that theta is the Static, and theta is the object? Yes, indeed. It can be both ways.

It all depends on which one is being interested and which one is being interesting. And we find that a preclear gets more and more solid the more interesting he becomes, and the more problem he becomes, the more problems he has and the more figuring he does on his problems, the more solid he is going to get.

AXIOM FORTY-NINE: TO SOLVE ANY PROBLEM IT IS ONLY NECESSARY TO BECOME THETA, THE SOLVER, RATHER THAN THETA, THE PROBLEM.

That is a very, very important Axiom. That tells you why SOP 8C Opening Procedure works. It works because the main form of theta which we find desirable, which has mobility, which has freedom which is happy, which is cheerful, which has all those qualities on the top of the Chart of Attitudes *is an observer of problems and a solver of problems.* So if you get somebody to simply look around the environment, he will cease to *be* a problem and will become the solver of problems. That's all. Just looking.

Get him to look around and recognize a few problems and he will feel better. Somebody then who is worrying about himself constantly well he's all mixed up in a problem and his affinity is at a closure with this problem. He's having an awful time. Well let's take this and turn it around the other way and let's have him observe himself as a problem, and we get that part of the process which is "Problems and Solutions". And naturally, if we asked a thetan to be a solution often enough, he would eventually become a Static. That's all. If we asked him to *observe* problems long enough he would simply become a Static. In other words he would go out of it both ways.

A Thetan could become a problem, more of a problem, more of a problem, more of a problem, more and more and more and more and more and more—static. You see he could go "out the bottom".

Or, he could go: less of a problem, less of a problem, less, less—static. He could go either way. So there's no avoiding it, you're going to survive anyway, and so are your preclears, but we're going to have a better world doing it.

AXIOM FIFTY: THETA AS MEST MUST CONTAIN CONSIDERATIONS WHICH ARE LIES.

In other words, there isn't a single piece of MEST in the world which isn't to some degree lying.

Looking at that, then, we find that the only crime that you could possibly commit in this universe is being there. It doesn't matter *where*. This is the only crime that you could commit. And this is all your parents objected to, and this is all the preclear objects to when you're auditing him and he growls at you. They add tremendous significances into this, but all they object to is being there. Now if you ran SOP 8C, Opening Procedure, and you ran it very, very definitely with that postulate: to get the fact that the wall is there. Get the fact that the chair is there, that something else is there, etc., you'd be likely to knock your preclear flat at some point. I am not advising you to use this form of Opening Procedure. It's a violent process. If you get almost any preclear and just have him stand in the middle of the room, and say "get the idea", to that empty space out in front of you there, "that it's there", it's there, it's there—his mother will show up and eight or nine of his wives and all sorts of other things will show up all the way down the line. He'll have all kinds of people standing in front of him. They're all "there". But that's the only crime a thetan can commit. It's a lie, you see. That theta can be THERE is a lie, and that's the only bad thing that anybody has ever done is to *be* there. Now, that's all, actually, that the body is doing. He's got a body and he's *visible*. He is being there. And we must have introduced a lie. And the basic lie which is introduced is Time.

It is interesting to note that it is the second postulate which persists, because persist means time, and it's the second postulate which introduces time, and this becomes elementary. Now let's look at this one: let's take this fellow who's awfully sick. He's terribly sick. Boy, is he a problem. He's a problem to himself, a problem to his family, and a problem to his auditor. He is a problem. He's terrific.

You know that he must have had an original postulate that he was well before he could make the second postulate that he was sick. And you know the postulate that he was sick must have denied the postulate that he was well, and so his original sickness was a falsity and he knew it at the time he made it—he actually knew it well. He knew—when he said he was sick that day to keep from going to school—that it was a lie. He knew it was a lie and he got a persistence of the sickness and now here he is eighty-nine years of age and all crippled up and we find out that the basic postulate was the fact that he was well. How could sickness ever get any power except through wellness?

Now we look underneath every lie to find out that it was the truth—the Static itself—which gave it power. The lie has no power itself because it is a perversion. Persistence has no power that is not based on the Static itself. So we have the basic lineup at all times and in all places, that the lie is empowered by truth. Truth must have existed and a good condition or quality must have existed prior to a bad condition or quality.

As we study the problem of goodness and badness in the world, we find out that we must be studying the second postulate, because that is all that persists.

Now let's take a situation where something is persisting—and it's *good*. We could say that that looks as if it must have been based upon a prior postulate which was *bad*. But you can't make a prime postulate which is a lie. If you'll just get the idea that there are no postulates, that you've made no postulates of any kind, that there are no postulates which have been made—now make a postulate. That would be a prime postulate. That postulate *can't* be a lie. Now make a second postulate denying the one you just made. That's a lie. Now which one of these two is going to persist? Of course the second one. And it is going to get its power from the first postulate.

It would not matter what the prime postulate was. That is not the point, here. We're not going on the basis of badness or goodness. A consideration is a consideration.

Now, do we mean reach back on the track, and find these postulates?—reach back and run it out with straight-wire? No, because there is no time, and all address to the past—every address to the past and every address to the future actually is validating a lie. There's only *now*. There's never been anything else but now. There's a consistent change, and a consistent series of postulates going on which give us a continuance of now, but the continuance of now is a lie.

You can move objects around, and that's quite honest, that's not bad. But we're looking at two kinds of lie here, and we discover that when we are trying to make a condition change we simply have to postulate, as though it exists in present time, the opposite condition. So somebody who hates the human race—he must have loved them desperately by prior postulate. There's no hatred like that which can exist between two brothers or a nation torn asunder in war. Well, that's because they loved each other so well, you see. And so they can hate with violence. But what is their hatred depending on but the fact that they loved each other? So if we have somebody hating madly somebody named Bill—we would say, "Now, get the idea of loving Bill." Grrrrr, he'd go. "Now, get the idea of loving Bill." Grrrr. "Get the idea of loving Bill." Grr. "Get the idea of loving Bill." "Well, he's not too bad a guy." We wouldn't necessarily restore love, but we'd certainly run out the hatred for Bill.

EDITOR'S NOTE

The description of actual processes given in this book are not published here as final, or current standard textbook procedure, but rather as valuable background in the development and understanding of modern Scientology technology. Though not greatly changed in themselves, these processes are now used only in the exact ways and levels indicated on the *Classification, Gradation and Awareness Chart of Levels and Certificates*. They belong to the auditor specifically trained for their proper levels.

Standard technology is contained in the course materials compiled from the technical Bulletins of L. Ron Hubbard as issued and used in the Academies of Scientology around the world and in the Saint Hill Special Briefing Course at Hubbard College of Scientology, Saint Hill Manor, East Grinstead, Sussex, England.

CHAPTER SEVENTEEN

TWO-WAY COMMUNICATION AND PRESENT TIME PROBLEM

Although you discover in examining existence that consideration is senior to all other things, you have in any preclear who is living in the physical universe, who is still associating with a body, an *enforced mechanic*. In other words, the mechanics of existence are enforced upon him consistently and continually. Therefore mechanics are much more important to this individual than considerations. He goes on an inversion. He is found not really considering—he is not making a postulate and having something come true —he is trying to figure out who's to blame—that's one of the main things he's trying to do. He's trying to figure out when that ridge in front of his face is going to go away. He's waiting until the auditor does something spectacular.

He's doing a lot of things, but first and foremost he is contactable in the field of mechanics, not in the field of considerations. Considerations are prior to mechanics. This is obvious. But your preclear has gotten to a point where he is inverted on the subject and by his day-to-day living he is closer into contact with mechanics than he is considerations and yet there he is considering.

Well, he's never going to recover from anything *considering*. He might figure he's way out of the trap. He might think he's way out of it, but as long as we approach the problem as really a purely mechanical problem of a set of convictions rather than considerations we'll be successful with the preclear.

And the first and foremost of his convictions is that it is very aberrative to communicate. This he's certain of. He may have lots of other certainties, but that one he's actually very certain of and we discover that the only thing that is punishable in this universe is communication—non-communication is not punishable.

We discover that the inanimate object is not guilty. It was the animate object which was guilty. We discover that the driver who was going faster than the other driver was always to blame.

This, by the way, is not even vaguely true. It's just the way people look at things to keep them turned around so that they don't have to take responsibility and make everything disappear.

So we discover, as we look over this problem, that our preclear is certain that if he communicates he will be punished. He has communicated in the past. He has tried to talk to people. And he has met with the greatest contribution of psychiatry, for instance, the pre-frontal lobotomy. It would do just as much good to cut up some calves' brains lying in the butcher's window, as it would to cut up someone's brain and psychiatry knows this. They know it very well. They have never made anybody well with pre-frontal lobotomies or transorbital leucotomies.

They go on doing it because a psychotic's condition is desperate, and they compute that they of course have to be desperate in treating it. They have therefore nothing but solid failures behind them. That is not a condemnation. That is just the truth of the matter.

By the way, the only reason they do a pre-frontal lobotomy is—because people can often *survive* it. That is what is stated in the original case history on this.

Just as long as I've mentioned that subject, I might give you a little data on it. The first and original case history of this, and the only case history that's quoted in psychiatry, is of an idiot blacksmith's helper who approached the forge, and the forge exploded, and a crowbar flew through the air and drove into his right temple and came out at his left temple. And he survived this. You look in vain in that case history to discover whether anything happened to his idiocy. We find that no change occurred with regard to his idiocy. But a part of his brain had been removed and he did survive, and this is the sole authority to this day for doing pre-frontal lobotomies.

In another case they did a pre-frontal lobotomy on a fellow, and they put him on display, and somebody asked him whether he noticed any change in himself as a result of the pre-frontal lobotomy. And he looked very solemnly and somewhat covertly around and he said, "Yes. I've learned to keep my mouth shut."

So that is the basic lesson anybody learns in this universe. They learn to keep their mouths shut, and it's the wrong lesson. When in doubt, talk. When in doubt communicate. When in doubt, shoot. And you'll be very successful all the way along the line if you just remember that.

There's no compromising with this. A thetan is as well off as he can communicate, and he's no better off than that. And when a restraint comes upon his communication, then he starts to wind up and finish up and that is the end of him. So, our preclear sits there, and he is sure that if he communicates he'll be punished. Anything he says will be used against him. They've told him so for many lives. Anything that he cares to bring up—he knows that the person he brings it up to is going to make fun of it, going to dive on it, going to challenge him with it and so on. He's certain of this, and that if he happens to impart any immediate secret of his existence he knows it will undoubtedly be on the radio by four o'clock that afternoon. So he will approach a session with considerable diffidence. He will not be sure what he should say. As an extremity of human duress which can be used to illustrate this, let's take the case of a psychotic. This person had a terrible obsession. It was just a fantastic obsession. He would not talk because he knew that if he said anything, the person he said it to would carefully store it up and wait for the right time to use it against him. And this was all this person would tell you! This person would utter that sentiment in one way or another—it was a one hundred percent psychotic dramatization—but it lay straight across his communication line. This person was utterly insane, could not take care of the body or perform menial tasks or anything else, and yet this person would just go over and over that record—"Well, if I said anything you would store it up and you'd wait for the right time and you'd use it against me." And then the person would clam up. Try to get him into communication again—he'd go through this same routine.

Well, let me assure you of something, a person doesn't have to be psychotic to have that basic manifestation in this universe. They're not even vaguely psychotic and they have it. They adjudicated their own sanity by knowing when to talk and when not to talk, and it starts to peel down to a point where they know. They know when not to talk, and when to talk. And then they know WHEN NOT TO TALK, you see, and when to talk. And then—silence. And that's the way the cycle goes.

So don't for a moment suppose that Step 1 (Get into two-way communication with the preclear) is included as just a handy way to start a session. It's processing.

Your preclear is accessible ordinarily on the Third Dynamic—groups. This is probably the last dynamic to fold up. They carry a social dynamic all the way through. Processing itself is a Third Dynamic situation, and so is aberration. It's the thetan *plus* the body that can bring about an aberrative state. It's the thetan *plus* the Sixth Dynamic, the physical universe, that causes a difficulty, and so on.

All right, we have then Two-Way Communication as Step 1 simply because it is the most difficult step. It is the most arduous step. And it is the step which was missed by everybody from the Aesculapians (Roman medicos) to the most recent psychiatry out of Wundt, Leipzig, 1869.

Around that time in Germany they got started on the first idea that the mind could be approached on a scientific basis. That was the original premise of psychology, and a good one brought up by a fellow by the name of Wundt. There was nothing wrong with this. It was a good hunch.

It has never been followed up by that particular field.

Scientific methodology was actually not, there and then, immediately classified, and if he had sat down and classified scientific methodology at that moment he would have been all right. But what they did was unregulated, uncontrolled, wildcat experiments, fuddling around collecting enormous quantities of data, which data was supposed to amount to something one day. But that field was never able to do anything in the field of a two-way communication, never knew the parts of communication, and doesn't to this day. They are more and more "The Only One". They never solved communication, so they don't go into communication. They don't have Step 1.

When we come to psychoanalysis we find that in that field they used various methods—originally Breuer and Freud did—to produce a two-way communication, and then they went all out, and they decided, Gee, if you could just get somebody talking—but their first approach to it was the hypnotist's and that is a very poor approach and not only a very poor approach, it's a very inhibitive approach.

If you have ever had anybody as a preclear who had been hypnotized you would appreciate this, for instance, running 8D (*8D*: Standard Operating Procedure 8D, 1954. Primarily for heavy cases, the goal of this procedure was "to bring the preclear to tolerate any viewpoint." See *The Creation of Human Ability* by L. Ron Hubbard.) Running this on "Where would a . . . be safe?" you could put in "hypnotist". You'd get some idea of the aberrative nature of hypnotism.

In psychoanalysis they actually didn't solve two-way communication. They got a system by which somebody simply talked endlessly, and talked, and talked, and talked, and there was no communication from the analyst. You may have seen the cartoon where one analyst is cheerful and he had been so every afternoon at quitting time, and the other analyst said, "My goodness. How can you be so cheerful sitting there all day long listening to those patients?" and the other said, "Who listens?" Psychoanalysis had this idea that if they could just make the person outflow, outflow, outflow, outflow, outflow, this would solve it. It doesn't solve it.

It's TWO-WAY communication. What success psychoanalysis did have was just due to the fact that they did specialize in trying to get somebody into communication one way or the other. But they again didn't have any idea of the anatomy of communication.

And we move on forward to various thoughts and philosophic endeavors on this subject and we discover that an individual very rarely is found in a good state of communication when he sits down on the couch and I don't care who this person is, they're just not in a good state of communication. They're either obsessively communicating, or they're inhibited—they haven't got a good balance on this subject. And you take the most average preclear in the world, he'll give you ordinarily just social responses. You say "How are you?" and he'll say, "I am fine", Forty-five minutes later the oddity is this person says to you, "I feel terrible". You first got a social response, and then the preclear answered the question. The question sometimes, if you'll notice it carefully, will come up as non-sequitur entirely, and, for instance, forty-five minutes after you ask him how he is he *tells* you. And the gap in between is filled with social responses. It's just trained social response—a little machine. So that isn't two-way communication with the preclear at all, is it? You're talking to social machinery.

Well, you've done this all too often, much longer than you should have, in plain social activities. You went around to ask somebody about a loan or ask him about something or other, and you went on talking, and this person went on talking, and actually you were not talking to anybody, and then you wake up with a great shock to discover that you have just been arguing with somebody, or been trying to make somebody be better, be nicer to you, be kinder to their neighbors or something of the sort, and after a long dissertation on the subject, and you think you've had a two-way communication with this person, he comes up with some completely disrelated remark, although he seems to have been agreeing with you. He seemed to have said "Yes, that's fine, I'll be a better boy," or something of the sort. You just never reached an agreement, because the actual truth of the matter is if you'd reached an agreement with him he would have been a better person. You weren't talking to anybody. You were talking to some social machinery. Well, that's just in the social world.

How about an auditor? Should he be able to spot this? Well he should, but he would never spot it if he didn't recognize that there was something very definitely there to spot, and that is: who's talking? Are we talking to the preclear? Or are we talking to an education from Harvard? Are we talking to the preclear, or are we talking to Mama? It's a nice thing to have a very, very high on the Tone Scale attitude toward preclears, but there's one point there where the column (Chart of Attitudes) reverses, and that's where it's Trust at the top and Distrust at the bottom. When you're working preclears, you keep with all the top buttons of the Chart of Attitudes except that one—you just reverse that column. It goes right straight across—Distrust is the top for an auditor as far as a preclear's concerned, and it's a remarkable thing how many times you can actually crack a case if you'll just simply say, "How are you doing that?" or "What are you doing?" "Who is talking?" "Did you do that?" "Who touched the wall?" "How did you do that?" Once in a while you'll find there's a File Clerk (*File Clerk*: Dianetic auditor's slang for the mechanism of the mind which acts as a data monitor. Auditors could get instant or "flash" answers direct from the "file clerk" to aid in contacting incidents) or something of the sort and he's taking every response he gives you as a flash answer from the File Clerk. If he's been trained in Dianetics he will sometimes do this to the exclusion of any answer *himself*. Well, these are social responses, and that is not a two-way communication. That's two-way communication between you and a circuit maybe, or between you and a machine, but it's not a two-way communication between you and the preclear, and it says specifically in Step 1 that we begin a two-way communication with the preclear. Well, how many ways could there be to start a two-way communication with the preclear?

One of the ways to do it is to talk about his problems. He's fairly interested in these, and you get away from the social responses.

And he's there because he's being a problem, so we get step 2 as an assist to Step 1. Step 2: PRESENT TIME PROBLEM. But of course Step 2 is more important than that. You sometimes miss on a preclear by processing him when he's dog tired or he's emotionally upset or something very bad has just occurred, and he wants to be processed so that he can run away from it, and if you don't ask whether or not he has any Present Time Problems, you'll miss sometimes, and have a whole session, or two or three sessions, wasted. I remember processing somebody who seemed to be rather frantic, and he finally came up with an astonishing fact. The case was not making progress, you see, and I got very interested in this and the person would not, just would not give me any clue. And I just kept pounding it and pounding it and talking about it

—any upset the person had in his current life—you know, yesterday, or today, or something that's going to happen tomorrow—I just kept talking about it, you see, and saying, "Is there anything that is occurring that I should know about," and so on, because the behavior of the case just simply said that this case is so restive and so upset that he just doesn't seem to listen to my auditing orders and he seems to be distracted all the time by something, and certainly this person is either completely off his base, or he's really a psycho, or he has some very bedevilling Present Time Problem. And finally the guy got the communication and gave me an answer. That processing session series was being very badly interrupted because he was being sued for divorce. He was being sued for divorce over the period I'd been processing him. And he would leave there and go down and talk to his lawyers and he wanted to keep this very secret, and he thought there was something very horrible about this, and so he wouldn't even tell his auditor about it. Now, you see, he's punished for communicating, and thus we get right back to that. He doesn't impart the data about what's going on because he'd be punished for communicating.

Occasionally you will run into someone for whom medicine could do something. The person has an acute illness of one sort or another and is so afraid of any possible treatment that would be offered to him medically, because medical treatment may not be particularly kind, that he has not told anybody about it.

This again will be giving him sufficient Present Time Problem that he would not gain well in auditing, and is the most important reason why you do not audit a person who should be getting a condition handled medically which can so be handled. But it is the fact that in this universe he is punished for communicating that makes this something to watch for and to see to it that a medical situation is handled medically before you do any auditing.

In order for any gain or release to take place by reason of communication alone on any kind of subject there has to be a *two-way* communication, not one-way communication.

Therefore, the neatest trick in the whole book of tricks of auditing is knowing how to start and continue a two-way communication.

It is dependent in its skill on the auditor's ability to grant beingness and actually talk on both sides of the conversation.

Communication is opened first and foremost by any sensory perception. *Any* sensory perception. Get the preclear to *touch* something—you have opened communication with the preclear. If you could take his hand and he could register the pressure of your hand on his hand, and this in the case of a semi-conscious person is very workable, you would be communicating with the preclear. A two-way communication doesn't have anything to do with—and quite incidentally when it does—with words. It's a *communication*. You're there. He's there. His trouble is inhibited communication, and the trouble you're going to run into is getting a two-way communication started. Any perception can be used in a two-way communication. Just *sight* is enough. If he simply registers the fact that you are there in the room with him—if he'll just look at you—that is a communication. If we define communication by: *awareness across a distance,* no matter how minute that distance is between the preclear and the auditor, we discover that starting a two-way communication is actually much easier.

Continuing with examples—"the worst it gets" type of situations—not that these are what you'll be auditing —if you want to start a fairly perfect communication, of course, you would simply physically duplicate what the preclear's doing. He's lying still—you just lie down and lie still. You'd be surprised how odd this will seem to him after a little while. He'll get real curious about you. He'll go into communication with you. He picks up the stool and he heaves it at the door with a terrific crash. You pick up the stool and heave it at the door with a terrific crash. That's a bottom-scale level of entrance into communication—mimicry—because of course duplication enters into the formula.

But if your preclear is sitting there in complete silence, do you think that if you pour out a great flow of words you're going into communication with this preclear? No, because he's putting out a communication already—*silence*. If you suddenly admit that as a communication, it will disturb him a little bit, and it's likely to stir him up into a communication. If you will sit there silent while he sits there silent, sooner or later you're going to go into communication. You can make a preclear enter into communication with you simply by doing whatever the preclear is doing.

Now it's necessary for you to turn around and have the preclear register a communication *back*. It's just as important for the auditor to go into communication with the preclear as it is for the preclear to go into communication with the auditor, and the auditor can do it by mimicry because he knows how. It's harder for the preclear to do it. Time spent at the beginning of a session just getting a two-way communication going until you really know you're talking to the preclear and he's talking to you is some of the best time you ever spent.

Opening Procedure 8-C is a considerable assist to this.

Improvement of communication is the key-note of all auditing.

CHAPTER EIGHTEEN

OPENING PROCEDURE OF 8-C

It is utterly fascinating what you can do with a process which is apparently as permissive as the Opening Procedure of SOP 8-C. The exact details of the process are given in Issue 24G of the *Journal of Scientology*.*

The number of case factors which are handled in 8-C is fascinating, because here you are processing straight toward simplicity.

We know that what is wrong with a person is his subjective universe. That has gotten into trouble. Now, in view of the fact that he could mock up a tremendous amount of space if he had to, he could mock up lots of energy, he could mock up objects, and he could do this any number of times, then why he's lugging around something called "his universe" is a little bit difficult for a reasonable man to understand, and yet that is what people are doing. You get a sort of idea of somebody walking around with a great many clanking chains, old tin cans, old cigar butts, and so forth and calling these possessions. "His universe" looks like a kid's toy box. If you've ever looked into a three year old's choicest possessions, that's about the order of havingness the thetan pulls along with him.

He gives these things up with the greatest of reluctance, yet his total health, you might say, is dependent

* This issue of the *Journal* is included in its entirety in *The Creation of Human Ability* by L. Ron Hubbard. See book list in back pages.

upon his ability to make, to have, new fresh things, and to do almost anything he wants to with them.

But, remember, it was always very, very difficult for him to get an object into such a circumstance that it was actually somebody else's object. To procure an object which was somebody else's is what he has to do in order to have that object. If we look at the four conditions of existence, the "Ises", we discover just exactly why these things are so very valuable to him. They are so valuable because they mean to him a period when he was actually in communication with thetans as such, and he could blame *them,* and if he could blame them then he could have something. And if he couldn't blame them then he couldn't have anything—unless he duplicated himself, and so had another thetan to blame. This way he would get a persistence, he would get survival in terms of motion. Otherwise it would all seem completely motionless to him.

Now again all of these things are simply considerations, and in view of the fact that they are all considerations, we can get enormously baffled as to how considerations could be so important.

Remember they are only important because of the considerations which one held in common with others.

It would be one thing simply to change one's own considerations all over the place, and it would be quite another thing to do this when one has a series of considerations which have been thoroughly agreed upon with others.

So the thetan, with his old cigar butts, torn playing cards, and clanking chains—you see he's been in communication one time or another and the system of communication was all established and therefore he could have an other-determinism so true and so convincing that even he, would not be able to question its convincingness. Nobody could possibly question the validity of these objects he was carrying around.

It's simply, then: he will have some way of blaming somebody else for having put that mass of energy there, and then that energy mass will persist. If he can't blame anybody else why it can too easily be As-ised and so disappear. Other-determinism becomes vital.

Now, when we look over this problem we discover that an individual can go just so far down this line, and then he becomes himself disabled. He begins to count on other-determinism more and more and more heavily to produce his own survival. We can see this in terms of attention—an individual in this society without any attention from anybody else would not have much chance of surviving. An individual, just on the basis of food alone, would have great difficulty, but he's gotten down to where those objects really have to be solid, and so we get this physical universe, and the particles of this physical universe are so beautifully lost, so completely confused, so misplaced away from point of origin that they can be subjected to a law in physics known as the *conservation of energy*: that energy cannot be destroyed, can only be converted. Anything that's lost, misplaced, confused, can only be converted, unless you discover the point where it was actually manufactured.

This universe thus becomes valuable. It becomes valuable because we've gone to so much trouble to lose enough things that we then have a continuance of objects.

A thetan who has become upset about the various agreements in existence believes that he no longer can communicate with something. He is a nothingness, therefore he has to communicate with a nothingness, he thinks. The communication formula places him at fault.

Here we have an individual who is living by the communication formula and yet cannot recover his own ability easily to follow the basic of communication, which is *all things are on the same point*. When you consider a consideration you find out it doesn't have any dimension whatsoever. And a thetan has no dimension. So he's gone to a lot of work, to make a universe that's as heavy as this one. And he's blamed it all on God, and he's blamed it all in various directions, and he has made what amounts to a considerable investment. He has a big investment. And now he has gone so far that having made this investment he can no longer look at it, because he has to follow the communication formula. He cannot occupy the same space as an object. Two objects cannot occupy the same space. Therefore he is not a thetan-plus-body. He is a body.

And once in a while we run into some materialist, in processing, and just the barest thought that he is something other than a body is completely, completely contradictory to him. It's utterly assaulting. You'd think that you'd held a gun on the man and asked him for his money. He'll become very excited. "I am a body. I know I am a body. That is all I am. I am one," exclamation point, exclamation point. He gets real worried about it.

This person at the same time is likely to be the one who is most concerned with God. This is curious isn't it? Well, he has to have an other-determinism. He has to avoid responsibility. His field of awareness will be relatively black, by the way.

That's not a criticism of the individual. That is just the state he is in. Why is he in it? He knows two things can't occupy the same space. Obviously if he is there, and the body is there, then he must be the body. That's the most elementary thing we could possibly put together. This individual has himself mocked up as something, and is being something so thoroughly that he cannot disassociate himself from it. So you tell him to be three feet back of his head—and he can't be three feet back of his head.

Now, we're processing something which has four parts: (1) the thetan, (2) his machinery, (3) the body, and (4) the reactive bank. The reactive bank is a stimulus-response machine of some magnitude.

The body actually is something capable of collecting an enormous number of molecules and electrons and converting energy and doing all sorts of interesting things.

An auditor occasionally makes a gross error in that he processes any one of these things other than the thetan.

So there are that many engrams?—well, does this so assault our sensibilities, that these things exist, that we must vanquish and make every one of them, one by one, disappear? Actually what we want to do is improve the thetan's ability to handle reactive banks.

Or an auditor comes along and he starts processing "the body". The body, the body, the body. What kind of auditor would this be?

It would be an auditor who had to have *something*. This auditor can't possibly have nothing, yet if he's auditing he's actually auditing a nothing. He's trying to free a nothingness. And if he can't conceive of a nothingness and has to go in the direction of a somethingness he will not actually audit the preclear.

Every once in a while some preclear has such an observable surplus of thetan machinery, that an auditor just can't stand leaving that machinery alone. He just can't stand it. He's got to get in there and get all these mechanisms out of the road, get 'em all mopped up and wiped out, and the next thing you know the thetan is very, very sad indeed. Look at all the years he's spent blaming this machinery on somebody else. But when you've gotten through processing all this machinery, what've you done anyway? You've just processed some machinery. And *it* wasn't sick!

So we have these four major parts, but we are processing the thetan. He doesn't have any mass, he can make space, he can make energy, and he can locate objects in space. He has very definite capabilities. Very positive, definite capabilities. And by the improvement of these capabilities we improve his ability to communicate, and so, improving his ability to communicate, we make him able to handle not just the reactive bank he's mixed up with at the moment, not just the body he happens to be inhabiting or hanging around at the moment, and certainly not his bank of machinery. We make it possible for him to handle large quantities of things—other people's machinery and anything. It's very interesting what he can do. But he cannot possibly be hung up on the basis of "two things can't occupy the same space". He couldn't be hung up on that one. Another thing he couldn't be hung up on, if you're going to separate him easily, is that *it's all other-determined.* You see, if it's all other-determined, then he would depend on other things to place him in space, and if he's depending on other things to place him in space, he will sit there and "wait for the auditor to exteriorize him". So our point of approach here is *the thetan.* Now, the easiest way to approach this is simply *to make and break communication with the immediate environment.*

Environment is the physical universe, security, it's right there, it's solid. This is the space of the room, the floor, the ceiling, the walls, the objects there, and if we happen to be looking *through* these things, then it's the walls in the next room, and up through the roof, the air about the house and down through, it's the earth underneath the house. And environment means how far can this individual perceive with great certainty in the physical universe. And that's what we're interested in when we say environment. We don't have the preclear in Chicago, for instance, and then, because he is an inhabitant of Iowa, process him in the environment of Iowa. Now this sounds, this sounds too utterly stupid, that anybody could do this, but believe me, it has happened. And what would they be processing? They'd be processing a set of facsimiles.

There is a immense ratio between the amount of facsimiles or energy masses a person has, and his ability to communicate. The more energy masses and more facsimiles which a person has, whether white, or green, or purple, or whether they're black curtains or actual apparent solid objects—we don't care what these are—the more energy mass the individual has, the less he is capable of communication. A fellow runs a concept—and gets a flow past his face. He feels something moving past his face. Ah, we've got a case of energy masses. How did they get there? They got there by the thetan directing his attention in various directions, manufacturing energy the while—and you're going to process this case as a preclear, this thetan in such a way that he sprays out new energy masses around his body? That would be a curious thing wouldn't it? And you know there are processes that you could run—not any listed in Intensive Procedure—which would lead an individual to immediately mock up more, and more, and more and more energy masses in the vicinity of his body. You could actually artificialize his condition.

He's as well off as he doesn't have to have energy masses.

A preclear has to have energy masses to the degree that he believes he cannot create space and energy. That's a direct index. So we find somebody who has large floating ridges and that sort of thing and this individual is having just that much difficulty. No question about it and no exceptions. It doesn't matter what manifestation he's exhibiting at this particular moment, a person is as bad off as he has these energy masses which are not placed but are floating. You could say they are "floating" energy masses because—everywhere he walks he's got them. Now he's as well off as he can simply take or leave the walls and other items of the physical universe wherever he finds himself. He can take them or leave them, see them or not see them at will. He's *well* off when he can do that.

What process would you tailor up in order to accomplish this? Well, you could simply have a preclear sitting in a chair and looking around the room spotting spots in one location after another. It's a fantastic technique. It'll do quite a bit for a preclear, just to have him do this. And actually you are applying this further when you have him get up and walk around and PICK OUT the spots, and TOUCH them, and then at will, BREAK COMMUNICATION with them. And SOP 8-C is actually a gradient scale, and 8-C's Opening Procedure is a gradient scale of getting this done.

There is an additional process that could go along with this. You could have him close his eyes and start checking off spots in the environment.

The case that has had his perception turn on very fully, and then promptly turn off and it has never been on since, has simply practically scared himself out of his wits. His perception turned on and that was too much Is-ness. It was too steep a gradient, he could see everything too clearly, and this made him nervous, it upset him, it has disturbed his thetan digestion, and made him very unhappy—and what *is* this? This is just simply a case of too much, and instantly he said "It isn't". He said "Not-is". He took a look at all this environment and said, "Dull down. Get real dull. It better be unreal around here, it's just too bright, it's too loud," and so on.

Well, what happens if we have this person sitting there in the chair with his eyes shut and we just have him look around and spot spots in the room, and a facsimile shows up? We just have him go on spotting spots in whatever he can see. We don't suddenly stop and say, "Oh, you've got a lot of blackness. Let's spot some spots in the blackness". No, you just keep hounding him for some sort of perception of the room. That's what you want. And he keeps spotting spots in the room and spotting them and spotting them and spotting them and spotting them. Just that and no more. Spotting them behind him, above him, below him. If you don't watch him a little bit he'll spot them all in front of him. You've got to direct his attention behind. A thetan has a 360° periphery of vision. There is no "behind", or get thee behind me thetan.

Now, here we have in a thetan, then, a possibility that the moment he really saw the room he'd turn it off again. He'd flinch. And then you keep right on processing in the direction of the room. You see what this would be. They'd flinch, their perception would go off, and you just take it from there and have him spot spots in the room. So he says his perception's all turned off—well, you just have him find something he can perceive. He says, "I think it's a facsimile. I don't know what it is, really. It doesn't seem to me to be terribly real . . ." You just say, "Close your eyes. Now spot some spots in the room." The preclear says, "I . . . what d'you mean close my eyes and spot . . ."

"Well, can you see anything when you've got your eyes shut there?"

"No . . . of course not."

"Well, why don't you look around. Get an impression of anything?"

"Mmmm. Well, what do you know. It's all black." He never noticed this before.

You say, "Well, all right. How about this now—you say it's all black—well, is there any place where the black is thinner?" Behind you, for instance, or above you or below you? Do you make out anything at all about this room?"

"No."

"Well, as you're sitting there with your eyes closed, do you know the location of anything in this room?"

"Yea, well, I know where my body is."

In course a case like this will probably assert to you violently, if he wasn't prepared otherwise, that he was a body, had always been a body, would always be a body, had never been anything else but a body, and that you live but once. And he would also tell you that during his study of Korzybski's *Science and Sanity* he agreed with him entirely that two things could not occupy the same space. He'll tell you all these things. It would be a *very* informative conversation if you let him proceed. You only let him proceed on such a conversation, by the way, long enough to keep two-way communication going, then you get him *doing* something.

"All right," you'd say, "Well, do you know of the location of any object in this room?" And the fellow says, "Well, there's a table right over there, I know that."

"All right. Look at that table."

Probably his eyes will pop open and he will stare at it—but you have him keep his eyes closed. You'd get an exchange something like this: He knows there's a table over there, and you say "Spot some spots in it."

He says, "I can't possibly spot any spots in the table if I can't see it."

"Do you know it's there?"

"Yes, I know it's there. I saw it when I came in."

"Well, all right. Spot some spots on it."

"But I'll have to open my eyes."

"Go ahead and spot some spots on that table."

He finally does. And the blackness starts to get a tattle-tale grey around him, and then it flickers on and flickers off, and perception comes on and all of a sudden he's aware of the fact that it's all real, and then he convulsively shuts off all of his perception, and then he lets it turn on again, and then he shuts it off again, and then he flinches this way and flinches that way. Why? He knows it's dangerous to look at things. He *knows* that. He knows, again, that it is dangerous to communicate. And he shuts it off before something else shuts it off. He's there ahead of 'em. But after it goes on and off and on and off a few times, it's likely to be more and more upsetting to him for the time, because it's likely to be getting more and more real. The room is likely to be getting more and more real, more and more solid.

Now you don't let him completely fly out through the doors and the walls on this process, and let him spot at unreal distances—spotting at a thousand yards, when a thousand millimeters would be much too great and three millimeters is about what he can tolerate. So we keep him in the immediate environment, and we mean the physical universe when we say environment, and we mean objects that he's fairly sure are there, and we just work him on that basis, and then, the first thing you know, the walls will start to disappear on him and then they'll flicker on again and then they'll flicker off, and it gets more and more real, and he gets upset about it and then he becomes calm about it and he goes through a lot of variations—and doing what? Just sitting right where he's sitting and you don't care where that is, spotting spots in the room whether the room is black, green, purple, or whether he's got facsimiles that he's really spotting or not. We don't care what this preclear's doing as long as he continues to spot spots. If he's got a facsimile sitting there, and he shifts his attention on the facsimile he'll let go of it. He gets rid of some of this mass.

If he's really just spotting into blackness, really changing his perception direction, you see, then *Boooom,* he'll start looking *through* the blackness. If you have him look at the blackness and spot spots *in* the blackness you are validating these masses of energy which a thetan is as bad off as he has. What he's witnessing with all these possessions and masses of energy is his own inability to really mock up something and have it belong to somebody else. That's what he's witnessing.

So there is that process. And out of this basic you get Opening Procedure of 8-C. But you can also do Opening Procedure of 8-C with the *thetan, without* moving the body. You could have the thetan touch things in the room. But actually you don't have him touch things and let go, you have him look at and look away. And you can carry through all the steps by more or less drilling the thetan in the room—preclear sitting there with eyes closed, and this becomes a tremendously workable procedure.

Actually its most simply form is to just tell him to close his eyes, and if he knows of any object in the room at all while he has his eyes closed, spot spots in it.

Now the classic Group Processing example of this is a very simple one and that is "Three spots in the body, three spots in the room". Have them spot three spots in the body, three spots in the room, three spots in the body, three spots in the room, back and forth and at the end of this time, at the end of an hour's group processing on perfectly green people, you'll have four or five out of the twenty of them exteriorized—the usual run of people you run into.

8-C done with the body, however, and with no further tricks, its most elementary auditing commands as given in Intensive Procedure, is the only process—please mark this one down, please remember this—it's the only process to use on the very, very low or difficult case. Let's put that down, and recognize that when a very low level preclear comes in he has already determined exactly the processing he's going to get. It's down below Two on the Tone Scale, and what it takes to handle this case is Opening Procedure of 8-C, because in essence it is a purity of communication and is a very simple process to use, but that doesn't mean that you don't have to be an artist to use it.

CHAPTER NINETEEN

OPENING PROCEDURE BY DUPLICATION

This will take any case that has hung up and is having difficulty and will move him up through successive tone levels swiftly. One should not suppose that a case will not move on the scale. Auditors have been known to have had the goal, in an auditing session, of a good, quiet, orderly preclear. I never have had that goal particularly, but on the other hand I have scrupulously avoided techniques which merely produced an effect and did not produce a result.

Well, here we have a technique which produces an effect *and* produces a result, because when you get through with this, somebody's communication level has been *raised*. When you've done Opening Procedure by Duplication for any length of time above a half an hour you will see a change of tone in the case. Now this can be the change of tone of the G.E. (*Genetic Entity*: A composite of all the cellular experience recorded along the genetic line of the organism to the present body. It has the manifestation of a single identity. It is not the theta being or "I".) The G.E. can change tone, the thetan can change tone. But where we have a G.E. changing tone we can then be prepared to have a little bit of a skid in tone when we've been doing Opening Procedure by Duplication. Let's say we did it for one hour with considerable pyrotechnics. We laid off at that time and did not do it further. We did something else. The fellow seemed to be in fairly good shape. We can expect a few days later to have some semblance of all of this in view again, because the G.E. is in revolt, at which time we would simply do it again. This does not mean that a preclear slumps because he's run on this. He never returns to the same state he was in, but the condition deteriorates slightly which you attained if you did nothing else in the session but Opening Procedure by Duplication. So we shouldn't consider Opening Procedure by Duplication a finished and final thing with a case until we've done it several times.

It goes this way. We get into communication with the preclear. Naturally if your preclear is extremely low scale, getting into communication will require mimicry and other such activities on your part—anything that would be communication. We get into a two-way communication with this preclear, and we talk to him enough to keep up the communication and to get some idea of some sort of a present time problem—we see whether he has any. That is mostly in the interest of: you're interested in him and you are in communication now about something which is real to him.

Having proceeded that far, we would then tackle this problem bluntly and head-on. We would tackle *any possibility that this individual was unable to duplicate a command many times*. And we would go into Opening Procedure and we would do Opening Procedure just as such very lightly for a very short time. We would have him go over and put his hand on the desk, and locate something that's real in the room and go over and take hold of it, and withdraw from it, and we'd march him around the room for a very short time. I do mean a *short* space of time, because what we're getting down to is the reason he won't be able to perform Opening Procedure very easily.

THE PROCESS

We're going to find two locations in the room, and we'll have an object in that location. We will have a book on the table, and on another side table or window-sill or something of the sort we will have another object, preferably a dissimilar object. We might have a hat, or an ashtray—any kind of object. One object on the table, one object in some other location in the room—dissimilar. Don't use two books, for instance.

Now we ask the preclear to go to the first object, and we ask him to pick it up, and we ask him to describe it. We ask him its color, its temperature, its weight. Then we have him put it down. Of course a repetition of "*put it down*" looks possibly not good, being a sort of repeater technique in itself (*Repeater Technique*: This refers to the Dianetic technique using repetition by the preclear of a word or phrase in order to produce movement on the time track into an engram containing that word or phrase), but the fact is that that command will work out in this process as the case proceeds.

So we have him put it down, and then have him go over to the window and pick up object two, and have him look at it, describe it—we have him describe it to keep him in two-way communication. We have him describe it verbally and have him feel the weight of it, and have him get its temperature, and then we have him put it down right where he picked it up. And then we have him go to object one, and we have him pick it up and describe it and feel its weight and feel its temperature and have him really ascertain this. We want to make certain that he did ascertain this, and that's the one thing we hound him about through this process is make sure that he really feels the weight of it you see, that he really gets what temperature it is, that he really tells you what the colors are and the appearance of the object is. And put it down, and go over to position two and pick up that second object and get what its weight, its color, and its temperature is, and we have him put it down in the same place he picked it up from—be very insistent on that—and then have him go back to position one.

How long do we do this? We do this until he can do it happy as a jaybird for about ten minutes without a single upset, until he can do this time after time and be just that cheerful about it.

How long is it going to take you to do this? Fifteen hours? Well, of course you realize that an individual knows he would die if he were asked to do this for fifteen hours, and that the auditor would shoot himself long before that time! You realize this to be the case, and then go right ahead and do it for fifteen hours if necessary. The shortest time in which I have been able to do it effectively has been one hour. I got the preclear all the way from apathy, tears—real tears (real apathy too by the way), a horrible stomach ache, feet fell off at one point—preclear was absolutely sure of this—through rage, antagonism, contempt, boredom, apathy again, fear, anger, antagonism, contempt, apathy, grief, fear, antagonism, enthusiasm, apathy, and so on up again to the first time the guy had ever been on the first level of the Know to Sex Scale, to sexual excitement, to symbols, to anger, to laughter, to apathy, to sex again, and eatingness showed up there just as plain as could be. "Well I suppose I could *eat* the book. I suppose that's what you want me to do now. Eat it. Well I won't eat it, so there." And another time—the other object, "I suppose I'm supposed to use this for sexual purposes now. That's what you want. Isn't it!" These various manifestations—until finally the case simply booted right up on the tone scale and stayed up there. He went through sex, and he went into effort, and then he said "Well, I don't know, it's *exercise* walking back and forth," and went up to emotion. He began to very interested in the fact that he had had *emotions* regarding this process, that this process would make him emotional was now curious to him. He became rather curious about the process, the first time we'd gotten into curiosity even vaguely, and went on up to—all of a sudden—tremendously brilliant visio (*Visio*: the ability to see in facsimile form something one has seen earlier so that one sees it again in the same color, dimension scale, brightness and detail as it was originally viewed) turned on, and then went on further until his sonic (*Sonic*: the ability to recall a sound so that one can hear it again as he originally heard it—in full tone and volume) picked up, and became intolerable, and then shut down again to a tolerable level.

And the longest I myself have done this on a case is five and one half hours. That's a long time. Actually, I didn't ever while I was running this have any real tendency to get awfully bored. It's enormously interesting how many kinds of reaction this simple process produces.

One of the things they ascertain immediately is that you are trying to get them under complete control. They're sure of this. They become sure of various things—all of them bad—concerning you as an auditor, if they're having a bad time of it. A case that is under good control may do this for half an hour well-controlled, emotionally stable, doing it just fine, and then go to pieces, just can't stand it any more, that's all.

And so you can expect, I suppose, that the entrance to many cases would be that you've got a very well behaved preclear for a little while, he was being social, and then boy did he go *anti*-social.

Now this procedure, of course, utilizes duplication to an arduous, wicked extent. Duplication is an essential part of any communication, and if you want to get in communication with your preclear, you'd better get him so he can duplicate. This process does two things. It produces an effect, you can be sure of that, but it also produces a result, which is the only reason we're using it, and produces that result faster than any other process I know of.

Now we've all known that Opening Procedure was pretty good, but what part of Opening Procedure was really hot, since you could run *anything* in 8-C, any step of SOP 8-C could be run by Opening Procedure. You could make a fellow move around and do whatever that step was. It would take a little figuring on the part of the auditor to get this done, but that's a fact. Well, duplication is tremendously important. It just can't be over-emphasized in a case. And when Opening Procedure ran into Duplication we got an enormous effectiveness and where it was not used to level out duplication, but was used to produce random activity, it was not as effective, anywhere near. So we have this procedure built up this far now. We have: Two-Way Communication, find out if there's a Present Time Problem, then we could do just a little bit of common ordinary Opening Procedure of 8-C, you know, just to get them used to the idea of moving around and not being embarrassed because they're doing something kind of silly—they often think that—moves around the room, puts his hand on the table—and so on into Duplication by Opening Procedure with two objects, picking them up, feeling them, describing them, putting them down in the same place, picking up the second object, describing it, putting it down in the same place, and so on.

What happens to a body when you run too much Opening Procedure on it? You're bringing the body up scale as an entity. How long will it come upscale as an entity? Until it's very restless. Well, there's our point. There's where your Opening Procedure collapses a little bit, or drops back, therefore it isn't an end-all process, is it? You could probably run Opening Procedure long enough on a body to finally exteriorize the G.E. from the body—if you see that kind of a complexity. But, however you run it, everything the body's been revolting against is likely to come to the surface immediately and intimately and abruptly. It's likely to be quite violent. What's the body doing? The body has been threatening these revolts for a long time. The thetan quite ordinarily has the body in indifferent control, and the body, of course, runs up through these things, blasts through some of his ridges and the thetan discovers that he can handle the body regardless of what it is doing. That is what the thetan discovers and that's why your Opening Procedure by Duplication is effective. It is more effective with the thetan exteriorized than interiorized—much more effective. But if we ran it long enough on the body itself, and if we addressed the body itself to run it, we would probably get some weird manifestation, some new phenomena showing up—something weird happening. We wouldn't quite be prepared to say exactly what would happen. In the first place it's not a possibility to audit this straight on the body. The body itself is an animal. On a stimulus-response level it has some intelligence, but if you started to drill that intelligence in any way it would have to come up through too many strata.

But the point is: (1) Opening Procedure by Duplication is violent. (2) The condition attained after an hour and a half or so of Opening Procedure by Duplication can be expected in the next day or so to deteriorate, but not to the level where the preclear's body tone was originally, and would have to be done again to that degree in order to pick up and stabilize the tone. I have done it three sessions running, each one about five days apart, and on the last session there was a stability attained simply by this processing.

But this is not an end-all process. This process gets the case into shape so that he will do a good job of following your instructions and will do a good job of communicating, and it picks up the communication tone of the individual. Therefore the length of time you care to run this as an auditor is markedly shortened.

If it were an end-all process, which itself went for broke, this would be the way you would run it. You would run it an hour and a half or something like that, or two hours, you would wait a day, two days, three days, something like that, you would run it for another hour or two, and you would go three or four days, and you would run it again on the preclear for fifteen minutes or a half an hour. And then you would have attained a stable state and you would have improved his condition. Run in that fashion it *is* an end-all process, but not run really in the fashion in which you would run it as an Opening Procedure.

But let's look now at how it is combined in a procedure to get the preclear out of his incipient explosion, so that it won't get in your way as an auditor. And just consider Opening Procedure by Duplication, although it in itself is very beneficial, as something by which you, the auditor, are going to monitor the preclear so that he really will be able to do what you say.

If a case were to find it consistently difficult to communicate with you, if a case were consistently seeing everything black, if a case were consistently occluded and consistently twisted your orders and so forth, you would simply have to, you would have no other choice but to, sit down and grind with Opening Procedure by Duplication on this case until he was actually out of the woods on it. Now how about the necessity for lapsed time between sessions? Well, actually it isn't absolutely necessary. I'm talking now about professional auditing. This is how you would schedule these things optimumly. You would make just a little less progress by doing it a couple of hours a day for two or three days. You would invest perhaps thirty percent more auditing time because the case hadn't had a chance to settle out, but you would get there. Two or three days, a couple or three hours a day. Letting the fellow settle out gets him matched back against his environment and saves you time in the long run. He goes back into his environment, he gets restimulated, then he comes back for an auditing session and he blows that. He goes into the environment again, and you actually, day by day, are getting another type of environment which you're running out of the preclear. It would be an end-all process if you did it this way. It would be an answer in itself, just Opening Procedure by Duplication. That's all you'd do with the preclear.

Well, it's a fantastic process in the way it will blow a case. If a case explodes or blows under this—there is no other process known which will break loose a covert communication line which is twisting a process. If a case blows that means the case had a tendency to twist a process, because he can't duplicate entirely, and so he was sliding out of your hands, and as long as he can slide out of your hands as an auditor, he then will alter a process every time that process gets him into going which is too rough for him and he's got to go through that rough going.

And you won't be able to drive him through with a concept. So you have Opening Procedure by Duplication standing there as the only thing known at this time which will push a case all the way through into a good communication and an ability to duplicate your auditing commands. If you just did this for a little while with a case, you would still get an improved communication line. If you did it for many, many hours with a case on consecutive days or consecutive weeks, you would get a total improvement in communication on the part of the case. This is a certainty. But where your case blows, gets upset or excited, you can look at this fact, that you must have invested—if you audited this case by other processes earlier—you must have invested a great deal of time trying to get the case "to break through the sound barrier". The case didn't. Now why does this require a little violence? One of the things that happens is that the individual knows that he mustn't display any violence, and this technique brings him up to the point where he displays it, and he finds out nothing happened to him. This in itself gives him a tremendous confidence. Did you ever see somebody who got mad and then found out that nobody objected, and then was cocky evermore? Well, Opening Procedure by Duplication gets you there and saves you an enormous amount of time. The amount of time saved in this is probably in terms of scores of hours, if not hundreds. If you have a case that is hanging up, it might very well go right on hanging up unless you get as violent as Opening Procedure by Duplication. And if the case is hanging up to any degree, why you remedy of course his Opening Procedure by Duplication. It has its own role. It is in itself its own remedy, but what you're trying to do as an auditor is blast through places where he would hang up and which it might take you years to get him through entirely.

So it isn't just a passing thought, this process. It seems to contain in it all those elements which go to make a case stable, and therefore is quite important to the auditor. But if an auditor works this without expecting violence, if he works this without expecting he's going to have an awful time every few preclears, why he's even more of an optimist than I am, which is impossible.

CHAPTER TWENTY

THE IMPORTANCE OF TWO-WAY COMMUNICATION DURING OPENING PROCEDURE BY DUPLICATION

When we say thetan we're talking about an emanation point. We're talking about a person. He writes letters, he greets you in a silly fashion, he does this, he does that. Let's examine, for a change, the Cause end of this line. All too often one examines only the Effect end of the line, because that's where interest gets centred. When we examine the Cause end of the line we discover something of tremendous interest about it: Cause, if it desires to get anything like an ARC effect at the Effect point, must take into consideration the fact that the Effect point is often quite incapable of mocking itself up as Cause.

Here is CAUSE—DISTANCE—EFFECT. Now, to get perfect duplication it is necessary that Effect *mock itself up* in some fashion or other in order to get in the duplication of this Cause—in order to receive the communication at all.

To give you an example of that: you're an American in France. Now a Frenchman comes up and he says, "Blotheree zomberfiel, ello blfthblorerup." And you say, "Huh." You weren't an effect at all, really, not the kind of effect he intended. He wanted you to put your baggage on the van or something. And you sure get a kind of an only-one feeling when you wander around doing this a lot, and people come up to you who don't speak English, don't speak deaf and dumb, don't speak

Boy Scout Semaphore. But they throw a lot of verbalization in your face which is supposed to mean something, and you don't comprehend it. Furthermore, you are actutely aware of the fact that their customs are probably unfathomably strange. For instance, in France, if you're an American, your idea of plumbing and the French idea of plumbing are two entirely different things. Two *entirely* different things. The whole problem of trying to walk into any civilization is actually the problem of being able to mock yourself up. You don't willingly mock yourself up as a Frenchman. You don't willingly mock yourself up as part and parcel of all these strange and outrageous customs. You could understand this quite easily on the Effect point, but how about the Cause point? The Cause point has, much more so than the Effect point, to mock itself up, because the Effect point mockup is being assisted by Cause, but the Cause point mockup is not being assisted, and it's this fact—that it's not being assisted—which causes people to think they need help.

They get used to being on the Effect side, and when they get over on the Cause side they say, "Where's all the help?" So they invent an analyzer and a computer and a Reactive Bank and all kinds of things in order to be over here at Cause point, because the Cause point has to mock itself up just like the Effect point or subordinate Effect points which are not really capable of any great change, which are not capable of mocking themselves up, and will never be communicated to, unless Cause mocks itself up.

So in order to deliver an effect, Cause has to be able to mock himself up on a much higher self determinism than Effect because Effect is assisted in the mockup by Cause.

The ability to be at Cause point is necessary for

good communication. You have to be able to *be*. In other words you have to be able to mock yourself up. If you, instantly, addressed by this Frenchman, were to mock yourself up as a French official, were you able to do this, you see, you would find suddenly that it was "all on the house". Actually something would come out of an interchange of this character—you say suddenly, "What are you doing without your identification papers?" or something of the sort, and he would say, "Oui, Oui, merci, thank you very much, no checkee . . . uh . . . adios . . ." or whatever. You have to mock yourself up as something he recognizes as Cause, but what kind of a second sight would this take? What does this Effect recognize as Cause? You mock yourself up as what this Effect point normally recognizes as Cause, and that puts you on the Cause end of the line. It is therefore the Cause end of the line which you should examine, because that's where, as an auditor, you're trying to put the preclear. You're not really trying to put the preclear at the Effect end of the line. Now if you understand that thoroughly—you're getting what is meant by the increase of self determinism. We mean we're increasing this preclear's ability to be at the Cause end of the line.

If the preclear came into the auditing room, and all he said was "Hehehehehe", why, you would recognize that he is not quite at the Cause end of the line. In fact, he's probably not at the Effect end either, he's probably half way between the two points, *being a communication particle*.

An individual can drift away from Cause point, get on the line itself, and become a particle on the line. If you walked up to him on the street and wrote an address on his chest and put a stamp on his forehead and put him into a mail box he'd be perfectly happy about it. Such cases have become communication particles. They are a message. They don't even *have* a message, they *are* one. The exhausted messenger throwing himself off his horse and dying at the king's feet as he announces the defeat is being his message. There isn't any reason why anybody should kill horses or messengers just to tell some king that he lost a couple of chunks of real estate, but they used to do it all the time. In other words these people could very easily be communication particles. Not cause or effect at all.

The decline is simply from able Cause to fixed Cause—and then they start riding out on the line. From an Effect which can receive, to an Effect which has to receive, to an Effect which won't receive. *Desire, enforce, inhibit.* Eventually somebody would be found avoiding all causes, avoiding being Cause, avoiding anything else which was Cause. Whatever they'd do they'd finally get on the line as a particle or symbol. They go from Cause into the state of Symbol, they go from Effect into the state of No Symbol, but they get on the line, they slide around, and they get mass, meaning, mobility. Now there's nothing totally bad about this. But let's restore this preclear's ability.

When you encounter a person who is incapable of addressing you physically or verbally in any acceptable way that makes an easy communication it is because he *cannot change*. He is fixed. If you, or the warden of a prison, or the soda jerk down at the corner drugstore, or the President of the United States walked in, he would be found in the same fixed state of address.

Well, if he can't change he is expecting continually that he's going to be the Effect. So we have a preclear sitting there and it's: "Well, you go on and audit. I'll be effect." They sit there in "can't change", unwilling to be Cause. So it's up to you to get the preclear to the point where he is at least conscious that he is moving something, that he is not being moved. That's why you get him to go around touching walls and objects.

But the essence of this is contained in duplication. This person cannot duplicate blitherarerup, therefore he can't talk with you, but that's true of him and all life. He recognizes his inability to duplicate life and he recognizes that he can't get on a two-way communication basis with it in such a way that it then is assisted in its receipt. Life will receive your messages, if it recognizes that you are a communication source. How does it do that? Well you have to be like it. You have to assist its duplication.

This does not mean that an auditor has to get down on the floor and grovel and duplicate all possible weird and bizarre things that a case could do, because actually all you're duplicating there is the circuit (*Circuit*: a part of an individual's bank that behaves as though it were someone or something separate from him and either dictates or takes over his actions. Circuits are the result of engramic commands.) but certainly an auditor could be called upon to duplicate any average motion. The person folds his hands, the auditor folds his hands. He sees then a physical gesture being duplicated.

The common denominator of this inability is the duplication factor. In all this communication difficulty, there is basically this inability to duplicate—so much so that reality could be called and rephrased and redefined as: *the degree of duplication.* Affinity is actually *the distance and the particle size.* Communication of course is *Cause-Distance-Effect.* And the degree of duplication is what makes reality. You are as real to those around you as they can *receive* you. Did you ever get some kind of an inkling around your family that they weren't receiving what you were talking about? Well, that's because they fixed in their minds a long time ago the fact that they were duplicating you *little*. You were different in size. This all by itself would be sufficient to make the family incapable of receiving information from you. Grandpop's a fairly successful manufacturer, and he's seen this grandson who's been running around while grandpop was in his middle years, and the kid goes off and studies sales promotion, with all the verve of youth and a good background and a good inheritance on this whole line and boy he could give Grandpop cards and spades on the subject of promotion. He moves into Grandpop's sphere of activity and he's on the job. He puts a suggestion memo on Grandpop's desk. Do you think it ever gets read? Ha ha, that's just from Jimmy. And Jimmy goes out and starts to work for another company, and it starts selling the whole field and wipes out Grandpop. "He didn't know what he was talking about." Grandpop has already conceived the idea, you see, that the smallness of Jimmy is not a duplication. And that being his primary idea connected with this individual, he then knows that all he can receive really from this individual is "Ga-ga-ga-ga", "Gimme a lolly pop" and "Gimme a nickel". Something on this order would be within his basic communication line with this child, so afterwards he could not then take the child's communication line seriously. But the child changes, grows up. The main impatience that you ever had with parents or anybody like that around you is their fixed idea that you are small. Then you come around later and your parents are getting on in years and they're ailing and you say, "Why don't you"—and give them some sensible suggestion—you're going to help them. And you find out that almost anything you suggest is unacceptable, because they know they can't duplicate someone your size. They know, if they know anything, that you're about a foot tall, or two feet tall—wherever they're stuck on the track as far as you're concerned. Mama very often gets stuck on the track at birth with the child, the first view of the child, and after that the child just doesn't ever have a sensible solution to anything. But the child is actually better adapted to the modern environment than Mama is.

Thus an odd thing could happen, if an auditor were not fully aware of this duplication factor in the beingness of the preclear. He could be under the delusion that the preclear is improving—when the preclear is actually simply getting *more like the auditor.* Well, that is what the entire field of psycho-analysis is built upon: if we could just get the patient to be just like the analyst, why then we'd be all set. They apparently go through some magic rites, as I was taught—in order to accomplish what?—the patient's shifting into the valence of the analyst. Well, the assumption by the preclear of a beingness other than his own—a valence—is not the goal of an auditor. The goal of an auditor is to return to the preclear more and more self-determinism. It is to make him capable of being at Cause point and at Effect point by his own self-determined choice.

How many dozen ways could you run Duplication? You could run it the basic way. Highly stylized, very pure technique, and simply run it like that. That is the most effective of all processes we know on duplication.

If an auditor failed with this process it would be because he didn't maintain two-way communication. He lets the preclear go on to an automatic endurance run without actually finding out what the preclear really feels, really experiences, what it's all about, what the sensations are. This doesn't mean that the auditor even vaguely varies his auditing commands. The auditing commands are always the same. They're given in the exact order in which they're given in R2-17: Opening Procedure by Duplication. But let the preclear talk to you! That *is* the difference. If you don't get him at the Cause point of the communication line, you've failed. So we make the preclear talk.

How do we do this? We give the exact command. This is one thing an auditor must learn—to keep continually in two-way communication while you're running any process without actually varying the process or coming an inch off the process, while you throw in on the communication line what is known as "dunnage", the stuff you put around the cargo to keep it straight in a ship.

The preclear goes over woozily and picks up the book. You say, "Look at it." You ask him to describe it.

He says, "Book?" Something's wrong with this bloke's communication! No, there's nothing wrong at all. You see you've got to get those commands in there just exactly in the order in which they are given. You've got to get him to the book, to the bottle, to the book, to the bottle, to the book, to the bottle. Just exactly. And then if you failed to demand to be answered, by failing to insist that the action be knowingly accomplished, and by failing to listen when the preclear says something—you would lose. He's picked up the book for the 565th time and all of a sudden the whole room goes purple, and he says, "My God!"

And you say "What is its weight?" Well, cut your throat—you've just cut the preclear's! Then, when he says "Ooohhhh," and you say "What happened?" it's not going to do any good. You've missed it.

When you see something happen to him, *find out what it is.* If you see that he's really going through it like an automaton, for heaven's sake pick him out of it. He's told you for the 55th time, "It's cool." I'm not above putting some two-way communication in there, getting him to say something. For fifty-five times, automatically, he was saying "Cool", "Cool", "Cool". He wasn't feeling it any more. He was still running the command you gave fifty-five times ago. Now if you don't make him communicate, if you don't make him describe, and if you don't listen to him, it all goes on an automaticity. It just goes on, and on, and on . . . and I swear if he ran it on a total automaticity, you could run it for 250 hours with no change in the preclear except that he'd get tired legs.

Now the key to this thing is that each moment must be a new moment. Each action must be a new action. And gradually he peels apart these actions so they are different actions, so that each moment is new, and that is the primary manifestation of Opening Procedure by Duplication. The newness of each moment.

So when he just gets repetitive, repetitive, you get suspicious. You say "What color *is* that book?" I've even gone so far as to say to a preclear who has been describing the object as "a book", "a book", etc.,— "Will you please describe it as an *object.*" New frame of reference. "Well . . . it's a . . . it's . . . it's a . . . r e c t a n g u l a r . . . it's a rectangular object . . . made out of paper . . . cloth . . . cloth on the outside. How about that! You know, *books,* they're *cloth* on the outside." He's back into an interest in the process. I've seen this process run, by the way, with two typewriters!

That's incorrect. They have to be two dissimilar objects. The preclear did get a lot stronger.

You could even get *that* on automatic. But the second these responses become monotonous you'll know that your preclear has simply settled down to being an Effect. You're trying to get your preclear to be Cause. So let's make him originate communications to you concerning the object. That doesn't mean that each new communication has got to be new and original, but it does have to tell you that he is experiencing that instant and not some other instant.

Opening Procedure by Duplication pulls apart all the moments of a time track. It pulls them apart because of the duplication. Unless each moment is a new moment you don't have that occurring. Book, bottle, book, bottle, book bottle, boooo—it's a book! It's not a word! Very difficult realizations come through to a preclear.

You've got to know that your preclear can talk, and he must talk, and he must describe what is happening to him. When something happens he's expected to call it to your attention, you're expected then to pay some attention to it.

That doesn't mean you go off the process. But let him tell you about it.

A preclear will exteriorize on Opening Procedure by Duplication. And when he's just about ready to exteriorize and wants to tell the auditor about the fact that he's just about to do this—that is not the time to give the next auditing command, or not be interested. The moment the auditor's not interested there is no auditing going on. I've seen preclears who've just gone "dead in their heads" through not being permitted to communicate.

The auditor is not there to suppress communication on the part of the preclear.

Remember that an obsessive overflow is not a communication. You have to know that. But actual communication on the part of the preclear must not be suppressed by the auditor. So there's the trick, and it shows up in Opening Procedure by Duplication because you do have to keep to the exact process commands. He does have to go repetitively through these exact motions. But you have to make sure that he's experiencing these things. You do that by communicating and you'll find Opening Procedure by Duplication working for you much more speedily than it ever has before. You are not looking out the window when a preclear has an enormous piece of news to impart. You don't sit there looking out of the window, auditing on a sort of prank basis—"Go over to the book, now touch that wall," or something of this sort, and without letting the preclear communicate, because the preclear gets a very sudden tone drop as a result of this. It'll actually stick him in his head. It has turned off perception. It will do all kinds of things.

Letting the preclear talk, demanding the thing really be described, keeping it out of the automatic machine category, making each moment new and fresh in Opening Procedure by Duplication, and never varying its auditing commands—that's how you win on this process. You can say other things than the auditing commands, but that doesn't give you any license to vary the process.

You just make sure that a communication is going on.

CHAPTER TWENTY-ONE

VIEWPOINT STRAIGHTWIRE

This is a process which is very simple, very easy to use, and makes continuous advances. This process is not mixed with other processes, it is not part of any Standard Operating Procedure. It is not part of anything you would do ordinarily. It doesn't particularly apply to one case level or another case level. It is an independent process which in itself is very simple to administer.

The formula of this process is: *All the definitions and Axioms, arrangements and scales of Scientology should be used in such a way as to bring about a greater tolerance of such viewpoints on the part of the preclear.* That means that any scale there is, any arrangement of fundamentals in thinkingness, beingness, could be so given in a straightwire process that it would bring about a higher state of tolerance on the part of the preclear.

To make this more intelligible you should understand what a great many preclears are doing, and why an auditor occasionally has trouble with one preclear more than another. A great many preclears are being processed solely and entirely because they are unable to bring themselves to tolerate an enormous number of viewpoints, and being unable to tolerate these viewpoints they desire processing so that they can fall away from them and not have to observe them, and the auditor is auditing somebody who is in full retreat, and Scientology is being asked to aid and abet the retreat by, for instance, taking the charge off an engram. The auditor at the same time, if he does this, gives the preclear something in the way of a change of viewpoint in that he erases something so that the preclear doesn't have to view it any more.

Well, as you can see, this is a weak direction. What the auditor then is doing is to some degree holding in question the ability of the preclear to tolerate viewpoints. *Time itself* may very well be caused by an intolerance of past viewpoints—a person doesn't want viewpoints in the past, and so at a uniform rate he abandons past viewpoints, and when he no longer is following this uniform rate but is abandoning them faster than the uniform rate, he starts to jam up in terms of time, and becomes obsessed about time, becomes very hectic, begins to rush time, push hard against the events of the day, feels that he doesn't have enough time to accomplish everything he is supposed to accomplish, and this falls off on a very rapid curve to a point where an individual will simply sit around idle, fully cognizant of the fact that he doesn't have enough time to do anything. And so doesn't do anything, but knows he should be doing something but can't do anything because he doesn't have enough time. This is idiocy itself, but is the state in which you find a very great many people.

Time is the single arbitrary entered into life and is well worth investigating on the part of an auditor. An unwillingness to tolerate viewpoints will cause a jam in time. The fewer viewpoints which an individual will tolerate, the greater his occlusion and the worse his general state of beingness is. As I said, an auditor can remedy this in various ways. He can erase locks, secondaries and engrams (*Lock, Secondary, Engram*: A *lock* is a mental image picture of a non-painful but disturbing experience the person has experienced and which depends for its force on an earlier secondary and engram which the experience has restimulated. A *secondary* is a mental image picture containing misemotion [encysted grief, anger, apathy, etc.] and a real or imagined loss. These contain no physical pain—they are moments of shock and stress and depending for their force on earlier engrams which have been restimulated by the circumstances of the secondary. An *engram* is a mental picture of an experience containing pain, unconsciousness, and a real or fancied threat to survival; it is a recording in the reactive mind of something which actually happened to an individual in the past and which contained pain and unconsciousness, both of which are recorded in the mental image picture called an engram). And by erasing these, he can make it possible for the individual to "tolerate the view", as he finds it in his own bank. Or, an individual can be so processed, as in exteriorization, that he can be caused to go around and look at various things and find out that they are not so bad.

Now, let's just take the mean between these two, and realize that a person who doesn't exteriorize is a person who does not want an exteriorized viewpoint. He does not feel he can tolerate an exteriorized viewpoint. He may have many reasons for this and one of the main reasons he will give is the consideration that someone may steal his body. In other words here you have a tremendously valuable viewpoint which he's likely to lose if he exteriorizes. Viewpoints then must be scarce, viewpoints are all obviously too valuable to be used. And this comes about by viewpoints becoming intolerable. Let's take somebody standing and watching his family being butchered by soldiers or something of this sort, Indians or other wild people. He would go along afterwards so intolerant of this viewpoint that he would fixate on it. It's the fact that he refuses to tolerate the viewpoint which makes him fixate on it. Now the reason for this lies in the various Agree-Disagree scales in the Philadelphia Doctorate Course lectures—the fact that if you want anything, in this universe, you can't have it, and that if you don't want it, you're going to get it. This is an inversion, and when this inversion comes about, an individual finds himself overwhelmed each time on whatever his own determinism is. If he starts to desire something he will find out immediately that he can't have it. Actually, *he himself* will take steps to make sure that he can't have it. When he wants something to flow in, it flows out, when he wants something to flow out, it flows in. There is nothing more pathetic, for instance, than watching a psychotic try to give up any material object—trying to make them hand over or give up, or throw away one possession, such as an old Kleenex, almost anything—just *try* to make them give it up. No, no, they just won't do it. They clutch it to them and I swear that if you handed them an adder, wide-mouthed and fully fanged, they would clutch it to their bosom. Anything that comes in they immediately seize and that's that.

Now you as an auditor, every time you are trying to get someone to give up something, are asking them to give up a compulsive viewpoint. You will see that every time you ask someone to give up something he is likely to hold it closer.

Now there are many processes. There are a great many processes, there are all the Standard Operating Procedures, and in good hands they all work. There's Universe Processing, there's Advanced Course Procedure, there's Creative Processing, on and on and on and on, a tremendous number of techniques, which can be applied with good sense to preclears. There are an enormous number of Straightwire processes, there's old-time Straightwire. The earliest Straightwire we had, which, by the way, was a marked advance on Freudian analysis, went like this: say we noticed that the preclear is afraid of cats. We would say: "Recall a time when you were afraid of cats", then: "Recall somebody who was afraid of cats", and then: "Find a time when somebody said you were like this person". That was approximately its formula—just Straightwire, and you sprung apart these valences very gently. However, it required a great deal of good sense on the part of the auditor.

An auditor now and then would become a Straightwire expert, and by just asking searching questions and causing the individual to recall certain things he would bring about a great deal of relief on the case. Why did the relief take place? The individual has been going along in the full belief that he could not tolerate a certain viewpoint and the auditor has come along and demonstrated to him that that viewpoint was in the past and therefore is tolerable. There, in essence, are the fundamentals of such Straightwire. You get key-outs (*Key-out*: Release or separation from one's reactive mind or some portion of it) on this—the individual comes up to *present time* so that he isn't looking *in the past*—assuming a past viewpoint. That is a goal of a great many processes, and is quite different from "wipe out the past so he won't have to look at it or experience it".

We have in Viewpoint Straightwire a very, very, new type of thinking. This is not to be confused with what we have been doing for all these many years. It hasn't any connection with it. It has an entirely different goal from that of any process you've ever done on a preclear. It takes the benefit of exteriorization, and reduces it to Straightwire. We get an individual to race around the universe to look at things, observe things, experience things. That's a Grand Tour (*Grand Tour*: The process R1-9, in *The Creation of Human Ability* by L. Ron Hubbard.)—that sort of drill—and here we reduce it right down to a Straightwire which is done interiorized *or* exteriorized.

One simply goes on the basis that the preclear is in the state he's in because he's not tolerating many viewpoints, and the entire goal of the process is to bring him to a point where he will tolerate viewpoints. That's all there is to the process.

The key wording of the process is "*you wouldn't mind*". Why do I announce this as something important, something new, something that is very useful to you? There are many varieties of viewpoint. If we were to take Full Knowingness, and squash it, we would find we were first getting into *space,* which would be perception. We have to perceive to know. This is the level of Lookingness. Now if we condense *that* we find out that we have to get Emote to know. A person has to emote. We squash perception, and we go into Emotion to know. Now, if we squash down and condense even further, we get Effortingness, and if we condense Effort even further, we get Thinkingness, and if we condense and package Thinkingness, we get Symbols. As an example of this, what is a word but a package of thought, and if we were to condense Symbols, we would get actually the wider definition of the symbol—we would get animals. You are probably thinking of it in terms of a viewpoint of a body, if you don't see that clearly, but the definition of a symbol is a mass with meaning, which is mobile. That is a symbol, and of course that is an animal, too. An animal has certain form which gives him certain meaning and he is mobile, and if you see that the Thinkingness condenses, then, into form, you will understand art. Just in so many words, a very simple thing.

We have Thinkingness condensing into Symbolizingness, ideas condensing into actually solid objects, and when these are mobile, we have symbols, and when these symbols are observed, they are found to wind themselves up with other symbols and take an associate, they associate with one and another, and take things from one and another, and you get Eatingness. That's a big, big band we're covering in there, that's the whole business of: "I have an idea about a form in this space and matter, and I'm going to get it all together, and I'm going to make this all mass together." Well, the second we've done that, something has been created. Now don't expect that thing which has been created to create anything. This is a thing which isn't creating, and therefore must subsist on an interchange of energy, and we get eating. Now we take eating and condense it down, that is to say, let's make food scarce, and let's make it very hard to get, and we get a *condensation* which completely escapes time itself, and you go outside of time and you get Sexingness.

That is to say that outside of present time, you get future time, which is sex.

An individual is right straight off the time track between Eating and Sex, and there's nothing will float on a time track like a sexual engram. They just float all over the time track. They don't nail down at all. They are very mobile. The individual, in Eatingness, starts to slide out of present time by this token alone, and people are terribly worried about how are they going to eat tomorrow, and when they have reduced this down to the *reductio ad gastronomy* you get to a point where "I can't solve this problem of eating tomorrow, therefore I'd better just leave it all up to somebody else," and slide in on the genetic protoplasm line and go up the line a little bit, and get another form, and be that.

That's the best way to solve eating—just to live tomorrow and maybe tomorrow there will be more food.

A very readily available test will demonstrate this. Notice those countries of the world which breed faster and harder than other countries of the world. We find India and China doing this. And we find that these are two countries which have extreme, chronic food scarcity. Now we can say, well look, they have the greatest food scarcity because they keep breeding people, and that eats up all their food. No, it's the other way around. They eat up all their food, and so they breed like mad. This can be tested also with animals. If you starve an animal, an animal will procreate faster. If you were, for instance, to give any family of homo sapiens a carbohydrate diet with a very, very low protein content—by the way this would be, you'd say, terribly unconducive to the production of estrogen, androgen. It's proven to be very unproductive of it—but if you give them a high carbohydrate, very low protein diet, the next thing you know they'll start to get very anxious about breeding. That's because you're telling them in essence right where they can understand it in their stomachs that they are unable to obtain enough food today, and so must eat tomorrow. Therefore you get countries of the Western hemisphere, which are very heavily starch dieted, and you find out that these countries are the most anxious about breeding and about tomorrow. There is no reason to stand around and prove this for hours. It's just the Know-to-Sex scale. Condensed knowingness.

"I don't know how I'm going to get along today therefore I'd better breed like mad and appear tomorrow and maybe I'll know then," is about the last ditch. Well, if you notice this, death must come, in this band, above sex. A person pre-supposes his own death to indulge in the protoplasm line. And so we get people like Schopenhauer and *The Will and the Idea* closely associating sex and death, and we get certain animals and insects, which so closely associate sex and death that they have accomplished death when they have accomplished sex. Fear Merchants (*Fear Merchants*: The aberrative personality. This was an early description of what is known as a Suppressive Person, or the Anti-Social Personality) like to tell you about the black widow spider. I don't know why the black widow spider is such an attractive beast to some people, but it is apparently so. I noticed that it exists mainly in California—Southern California. Lots of black widow spiders down there, and most California girls, if you get into any kind of discussion on the second dynamic at all, will sooner or later inform you that the female black widow spider eats its mate after consummation of the sexual act. Anyway, the main thing here is that actually when you go down this scale, although it doesn't belong on the scale, you'll find death just before sex. Know, Look, Emote, Effort, Think, Symbol, Eat, Death, Sex. Death doesn't belong there, but this shows you where this mechanism comes in.

Now, *beingness* might also be on this scale somewhere. Beingness might be on this scale, and if it were, you would have a tendency to look for it up toward the top, but the truth of the matter is, it's all up and down the scale, and there is no beingness like that beingness at Symbols. You find the human race having been made into a form—a mass, meaning, mobility. A mass with meaning which is mobile—that's a body, that's a word in a dictionary, that's a flag above a building, it can be moved around and it has meaning. You'll find that human beings indulge very, very heavily in being symbols. Well, you'll find people around being sexual objects too. So that this scale sort of interlocks on beingness. A fellow could be some effort—and actually we don't find beingness at the top of the scale at all, we find it down there pretty low on the scale, so when an individual has gotten to a point where he has to be something, he's practically at bottom. A further examination would have to put beingness at least at Symbols. A person *becomes* things at that level, and you will frequently find a preclear mainly being his name.

Looking further, we find that there are different kinds of viewpoints. There is something you might call a *know*-point. That would be senior to a viewpoint. An individual would not have dependency on space or mass or anything else. He'd simply know where he was. There would be a viewpoint, which is a perception point, which would consist of look, and smell, and talk, and hear, and all sorts of things could be thrown in under this category, viewpoint. Ordinarily we simply mean at that level of the scale, *looking,* but you can throw all the rest of the perceptions in at that level of the scale.

Going down a little bit from there we get something we could call an *emotion*-point. It would be that point from which a person emotes, and at which he emoted, and then there would be something else called an *effort*-point, and the effort-point would be that area from which a person exerted effort, and that area into which that person received effort. And as we went down a little bit from that, we'd find we had a *thinking*-point, and there of course we get the "figure-figure-figure". The person is thinking there, not looking. And if we go down a little bit further than this from a thinking-point, we get a *symbol*-point, and there, really properly, we get *words*. And below that we get an *eating*-point, and below that we get a *sex*-point.

If you considered each one of these points below known as *an effort to make space*, a great deal of human behavior would make sense. Let's take an individual who is simply trying to make space with words. Words don't make good space. So an individual who tries to make space with words sooner or later gets into bad condition. Much lower than that would be a person who is trying to make space with eating. Of course that's inverted, isn't it? And then there's the person who is trying to make space with sex, and that is really inverted. That goes both ways from the middle. The lowest part of the eating scale is excreta and urine. People will try and make space with that. Dogs, for instance, are always trying to make space that way.

There are people who are trying to make space with effort. This is the use of force, this is Ghengis Khan riding out and slaughtering villages. He's trying to make space. You notice that the space had to exist *before* he could ride out any place.

And we go up a little higher, and maybe you've known somebody who's tried to make space with emotion. And we go up a little higher and we get to the way you *do* make space which is by *looking*. And actually you get to *make* space by knowing. If you just knew there was some space, there would be some space, and that would be all there was to that. Just that simple. That's an effective way to go about it, and looking is another effective way to go about it, and when we get down to emotion, that is getting ineffective. People who try to make space with emotion don't get very far. That's literally, actually, figuratively, or any other way you want to look at it. It's too condensed, and it kicks back. Yet that is above the individual who makes space by working hard or by pushing hard or by exerting force.

In other words we see that there is quite a little bit of band there, at effort, and you'll see that they get less far than people who try to make space with emotion. And now we get into the thinking band, and people who try to make space with thinking, which is about the most unworkable activity that anybody could engage in.

When we get down to making space with symbols, here is a nation trying to fly its flag over all the world, which doesn't make much space, and then we go into eating, and an individual trying to make space by offering things to be eaten. A cattleman, for instance, is doing this. He's making space with cattle. And a fat man is trying to make space with food, and so on. Now when we get down into sex, of course, if an individual could breed fast enough and far enough he would wind up with all sorts of space, he thinks. Of course, he winds up with no space. This is the most condensed activity you can get into: sex. You can see somebody's bank all short-circuited—jammed on sex. But remember, we are looking at a gradient scale that runs from Sexingness right on up through the levels to Knowingness.

And if anybody comes along and tells you that sex is the only aberration, please laugh. You could answer, Yes, that was how we entered the problem, we found out that people were loopy on the subject of sex. So then we examined the problem further, and having examined the problem for many years, it was discovered that sex was part of a gradient scale of human experience which is basically an activity of trying to make space, and people try to make space in various ways. And when they get down too low on the scale they are abandoning present-time life and at that point they have sunk to the level of Sexingness. They are trying in this way to get some future up there on the track and it is a chaos. It is an attempt to derive experience from external sources, and to pull experience in.

Operation at the level of Sexingness is really a cave-in.

When you examine this band and its inversions up and down the scale you see that it gives us an enormous number of Straightwire questions.

The basic question would reduce this first from the stand-point of *viewpoint of the whole scale,* and that is where you catch your preclear most ably. You just take viewpoint of the scale, viewpoint of sex, viewpoint of effort, and so forth.

The systematic questions that go into this line would be as follows: you ask the preclear to give:

"Something you wouldn't mind knowing."

"Something you wouldn't mind looking at."

"An emotion you wouldn't mind observing."

"Some effort you wouldn't mind observing."

"Some thinking which you wouldn't mind observing."

"Some symbols which you wouldn't mind seeing."

"Some eating which you wouldn't mind inspecting."

"Some sex which you wouldn't mind looking at."

Just as mildly and quietly as that. And that's Viewpoint Straightwire.

CHAPTER TWENTY-TWO

REMEDY OF HAVINGNESS AND SPOTTING SPOTS IN SPACE

Spotting Spots in Space and the Remedy of Havingness is itself a total process. It has many ramifications. It is, you might say, a family of processes. There are many such families of processes, but actually it belongs to the family that we would call Opening Procedure of 8-C or the Opening Procedure family. This is actually a low order of Change of Space so it belongs also to another family, it belongs to a Duplication family, since Change of Space is actually a dramatization of the formula of communication. In Change of Space you dramatize the communication formula with the preclear exteriorized. (You have him be at one point then be at another point, then be at the first point and be at the second point, etc.)

That first point is the *source* point of something, usually, and so he—by being the cause and then being the effect and finding out there is a vast distance between them—becomes rather relaxed about the whole thing. But Spotting Spots and Remedying Havingness could then be said to be cousins to two families—to Change of Space and to Opening Procedure.

The reason why we relate it to Opening Procedure is that that is the way you are going to produce the most effect with it. As though it were Opening Procedure.

The first contest is to get the preclear to find the

spot in space. That is the first contest. The preclear will go around and he will find large spots, two or three feet in diameter. He'll go around and find only spots which come out so far from the walls. He can't find a spot independent of the room itself. His spots have energy in them, they have masses, they have color, they have size. In other words he runs into a lot of trouble. If he does locate a spot it's likely to be "suspended four or five feet above the floor on something that looks like a microphone stand".

The various manifestations which occur are quite fascinating, but all of them are completely useless. You want to get the preclear over these as fast as possible.

You get him over them simply by having him spot some more spots in space. That's all. Space where? In the space of the room. And you have him locate these spots in such a wise that he can go over and put his finger on them. Now, when you have him capable of spotting two or three spots, you've usually shot his havingness to ribbons. So you have to remedy havingness right away. If he starts to get queasy, sick, upset in any way remedy his havingness.

There's nothing more destructive to havingness than spotting some spots in space.

This is a precision action—you want him to spot a spot in space and then be able to spot it again. That spot is only a location. It doesn't have mass, and you want him to be able to put his finger on it and take his finger off of it, and put the finger of his other hand on it, and take it off, and move his body into it and move his body out of it and so forth. This is a location, and the more certain he becomes of these locations the better he is, and the next thing you know—why, he's able to tolerate space. And you accomplish this by remedying havingness all the way along.

Now let's suppose you had an individual who had an enormous struggle in spotting some spots in space, and the first spots he spotted were fairly large, and you just kept on nagging him until he finally got actually a location in space—and he started to get sort of upset. Remedy of Havingness had not been done yet, and he feels rather queasy about the whole thing. Then you say, "All right, mock up something that's acceptable to you and pull it in," and he says, "*What* mock-up?" And you say, "Well, just put something out there—a dead body." "*What* dead body?" "What are you looking at?" "Nothing." "What are you actually looking at?"

An interesting contest will come in at this point—getting him to tell you what he is looking at. What he's looking at in this case is usually blackness, and he won't tell you he's looking at blackness. This is "nothing" as far as he is concerned, but he's looking at blackness, and to get him to finally tell you what he actually is looking at is part of your first contest. "What are you looking at?" Well, it doesn't do you very much good with an individual who can't get any facsimiles, mockups, anything of the sort whatsoever, to mock something up and pull it in, because he's going to have too hard a time.

But supposing he can get a vague or indistinct image out there. Is that good enough? Yessir, that's good enough. Have him mock up several of those and pull them in on the body, and then go on spotting spots in space.

But supposing he couldn't get any. None.

Then enters upon the scene this interesting single straightwire question. The agreement between the MEST Universe and the preclear gets down to a point where the preclear has agreed entirely that two things cannot occupy the same space, and after that he is not able to pull anything in, which is the biggest trap you have, because the way a preclear makes something disappear, makes it vanish utterly is to pull it all the way in, and if he can't pull anything all the way in it continues to persist. How would someone fix up a being so that he's packed in energy masses? By getting him to agree that two things could not occupy the same space, and after that he couldn't destroy any energy mass that was around him. Quite Machiavellian. Well, Count Alfred Korzyski devoted a book to this called, "Science and Sanity", and there are others who have written on this subject, but they go back to Korzybski, and: "*It is utterly impossible for two things to occupy the same space.*" And if that book has any message, it says, *Differentiate amongst your words and statements and thoughts,* and, *two things can't occupy the same space.* You nearly summate General Semantics when you say those two things. Now, there is a lot to this, you understand. He examined the mechanics of this, but he examined them in complete agreement with the physical universe. With somebody who has studied General Semantics, you've got a picnic on your hands in doing a Remedy of Havingness. You wouldn't have realized it or recognized it but you have. He can't pull anything in. He can't remedy havingness and therefore can't destroy energy. Why can't he? Well, two things can't occupy the same space, so if he wanted to mockup a car out there to pull it in and remedy his own mass, he of course couldn't do it because he is already occupying the spot where the car would come into, therefore he couldn't remedy his havingness. The mockup disappears just before it gets to him, and the underlying agreement back of that is two things cannot occupy the same space. This is of course an utter falsity.

It happens to be a condition which when imposed resulted in this physical universe. That law is what keeps the parts and parcels and spaces and planets of this universe apart. It is an enforced differentiation in this universe which makes space for this universe. That is the law which keeps the space stretched in this universe. So of course Korzybski would get all involved with differentiation. Differentiation on the basis of the MEST universe holding itself apart. *Well, that isn't differentiation.* So as a result you'll have trouble at this point with anybody who has been in General Semantics. Here is this mockup disappearing just before it gets to him—in other words he isn't remedying havingness. Now, how do you know he isn't remedying havingness? Because he stays upset, of course. That's all.

He's spotted some spots in space, and "these aren't anything you can feel". It just made him feel kind of frantic, and made him feel kind of upset, and made him feel sick at his stomach—these are common manifestations—and then you said, "Mock up an acceptable . . .", and he says, All right. And you say, "Well, have you got a dead body there, or what have you got mocked up there?" and he says, "Well, I don't know —I've got a wrecked car," and you say, "Well, okay. Pull that wrecked car into your body. Now pull another one into your body, and pull another one into your body, and pull another one into your body". And you say, "How do you feel?" "I feel . . . just as frantic as I did," and so on. He isn't pulling anything into his body. It's disappearing before it gets to him, it's dissipating and other things are occuring there, so that his havingness isn't being remedied.

By the way there's a total process on this. You just simply have the fellow mock up things and pull them into his body, and the more massive the better, until you get planets and stars and black suns and all kinds of things being pulled into his body, and you'll start something called an avalanche after a while, and the planets start coming in with a roar, and it's quite an interesting phenomenon. I've seen one run for three or four days. They blow up every facsimile that gets in their road, they'll blow up the entire energy behavior pattern of the preclear if you keep on remedying havingness.

But if remedying havingness doesn't straighten him out it's because he has agreed to this single agreement which doesn't happen to be true, that two things cannot occupy the same space. He's agreed to that so thoroughly that he can't remedy his havingness.

The reason I'm stressing this is so that you will remember why you ask the preclear this question (and that this *is* the question, and that there isn't any other question) and that question is simply this—*"What wouldn't you mind having occupy the same space as you're occupying?"*

Well, he's got to change his mind immediately, and two things *can* occupy the same space, in order to fulfill this condition, and without your explaining to him how, he had to change his mind.

Sometimes it takes them five minutes, sometimes it takes them five hours, but the roughest case I know of at this time had to be given this for two hours before he could finally accept something in his own space. That is to say, until he could find something that he wasn't unwilling to have occupy the same space as himself. And this question was asked this case over and over and over and over. This case had never been able to remedy havingness, never been able to get mockups, never been able to do this, never been able to do that. Well, he remedied his havingness, and he got into fine fettle and doing very well indeed. This changed his case. If you're doing a lot of Change of Space you remedy havingness on the thetan. Have him put up eight anchor points and have him pull them in on himself, and eight more and pull them in on himself, eight more and pull them in on himself. When his body gets upset and restive, we simply do this. If he really pulls them all the way in they will disappear. That is how you make things disappear. All space is an illusion, therefore if you pull in all anchor points of course there's no space, so what happened to the anchor points? Well, they didn't exist in the first place, so if you make them occupy the same space as you they'll vanish, and actually recognition simply depends on *occupying the same space with.* That's why Beingness Processing works.

On this factor of recognition and knowingness in terms of beingness and facsimiles, etc., we simply get this: is he willing to occupy the same space as it? And if he is, it will blow, and if he isn't it won't. So if we get a case who can't remedy his havingness being therefore unable to destroy a concept, a lock, a secondary, and an engram. If he can't remedy havingness, he can't *occupy the same space with.* If he can't occupy the same space with, he naturally conceives that *it's* making space, so therefore *it* has validity. *And* it won't pull all the way in.

This process is very elementary but it could be hashed up most gloriously by over-running the preclear on spotting spots in space until he was good and groggy, upset and quite ill, and then expecting him to work in some fashion or another. Well, you would have driven him down tone scale to the point where he can hardly hold onto anything long enough to do anything about it. So, you're *now* going to remedy his havingness and do the rest of this? No, you do this *early*. Remedy his havingness *long* before he needs to have it remedied. You don't wait for signs. You could make them appear if you wanted to, but you just do this as a routine process. Whenever you spot a spot in space you remedy havingness, that's all.

The process we're interested in is this one: Spotting Spots in Space. We're not really interested in remedying havingness because this is only dramatizing his dependency on it, so we're just giving priority to the important thing here, and the priority is the spot in space, that's what's important. The remedy of havingness is incidental.

Why does his havingness chew up? There must be something awfully wrong with the way this fellow's handling energy for his havingness to chew up simply by trying to remedy it. All right, what do we do here specifically? We ask him what could occupy the same space as he's occupying. If we had any doubt about this, and here's where we get the answer to your question about that, if we had any doubt about this we would take up this problem *before* we fooled around with any spots in space. We would look at this fellow and there he is gaunt and emaciated or bloated, or anything strange with his physiology—and we would say "Oh, this guy has a little bit of trouble with havingness." You know, he's a banker or something. We could tell professionally. He's a commissar, a banker or a general? There's something wrong with this guy's havingness, otherwise he wouldn't be where he is, that's obvious, if he has to have in some other fashion than simply having. Using a system like "becoming a general". That's a method of having, you see. You go to West Point, and don't talk back, and graduate, and don't talk back, and get into a War Department post, and don't talk back, and coast along, and don't talk back, and then you have to, of course, get more and more suppressed about how famous you've got to be and the next thing you know, why, you will start to accumulate *troops* to remedy your havingness . . . and you've got a U.S. General. You don't do anything with the troops, just accumulate them. That's not just being snide about generals. You can look at somebody and tell whether or not he's having a lot of trouble with havingness. If he's having trouble with havingness, then it might be very wise for you to just sail in on that basis. Let's fix it up quick before we render him liable to anything. That would be a good idea.

But what's important about this process is Spotting Spots in Space. What do we do with all these spots in space? We just spot them, that's what. Well, I know, but what do you do with them after you spot them? Well, you spot them. Well, after you've spotted them then what do you do with all these spots in space? Well, you spot some more of 'em. That's what you do.

Don't look for any deeper significance in the technique than that except this: the preclear is sitting on three kingpin significances, (1) that he's there but he's gotta leave, (2) that he's there and fixed there forever —being fixed against his will, and (3) that "it was there in that spot but now it is gone". Three considerations there that are very aberrative on the track. Well, you could run these with this process. You spot a spot in the room and have him move the spot into his body. Have him stand there. You tell him: "Now get the idea that you can't remain there. All right. Find another spot. Okay. Now move out of the spot you're in and move this next spot into your body. You got that? All right. Now get the idea that you can't stay there."

You just do this in sequence. He's in the spot, "Now get the idea that . . ." and you are making him dramatize the basic formula of self-determinism, the location of objects in space. And if you make him locate objects in space one after the other he'll make considerable gains. Put this consideration onto it, that he can't stay there, and have him move to the next spot. You just spot the spot and have him move to it, and you can run the consideration that he can't stay there.

And we have him move onto a spot and then get the idea that he's fixed there and can't move, then we have him change his mind, not just break or disobey his postulate, we have him *change his mind,* and pick out a new spot, and move into it, and get the idea he's got to stay *there* forever, and then have him change his mind about staying there forever and get a new spot and move it into his body and get the idea he's going to stay there forever. You'd be surprised at the agony and weariness and tiredness that this one runs.

The next level is to have him spot the spot and get the idea that something very precious has just left there that he will never see again. You have him do this: just walk around and spot these spots and get the idea each one has just been vacated. There is the manifestation of the fellow trying to fill in the spots with energy—the mechanism that he's undergoing, and it has a tendency to blow this.

So there are three conditions—there are probably others, but those are certainly important conditions. Why? Well, what is the manifestation of *facsimile*? The manifestation of facsimile is not being able to remain in a spot, having to get out, and cussedly taking along a picture of it so that one can say he's still there. That's the rationale behind the facsimile. The facsimile is the solution to the problem.

So then, what is this thing called unreality? Unreality is that activity the preclear has engaged upon whenever he was forced to stay in a place where he did not want to be. His answer to this was to make it all unreal, so that he wouldn't really know he was there. He's trying to be self-determined anyhow, and the way he's being self-determined is to make it all unreal. He could say, "Although I am forced to stay here in prison, stone walls do not a birdcage make." That's why they put psychotics in cells. (Well, that didn't quite add up to a solution. That's just a reason as reasonable as anything else in that field, which has to do with nuttiness, so don't expect it to be reasonable.)

All right, he'll make things unreal then, if forced to stay in the same place. He'll dim down his perceptions on things. That merely says that he's unwilling to *be* there.

Now what's this thing called occlusion? Occlusion comes about as the consequences of loss. Something precious has disappeared from the person, and if he could still see, he'd notice it was gone, and this would be more than he could bear, so the best thing to do would be to cover it all up with blackness and that'd be that. That would be a good solution, wouldn't it? Let's just hide the whole thing. Let's just hide the problem and then let's just abandon the whole idea, and then, you see, *we could still pretend that it's still there.*

This is the basis of "it's too good to use", also. People will get to the point where if you give them something extremely valuable they will not wear it or use it. They promptly hide it. Well, that's because they know, if they know anything, that they lose things like that. I remember giving a very dear lady, my grandmother, a present one day because she was going around wearing a watch that was a shame—very disreputable—and I gave her a new watch, and she kept right on wearing this old disreputable watch. And later on I was going around looking for something and opened up a drawer, and there hidden in the bottom of the drawer was this brand new, very nice, rather indestructible, by the way, good watch. And I asked her why she wasn't wearing it and she said, "Oh, that's much too nice to use." And so I began to wonder about this a little, and went back and just glanced through some of her things there, and do you know she had more things that were too nice to use! It was a tremendous abundance. She couldn't use it, though, it was all too nice.

Well, people do this in another way. When they've lost something they turn everything black. They just hide it and they hide the fact that they've lost it. Also this is "no responsibility" and other factors. And occlusion adds up to *too many considerations*. Actually the basic occlusion is mystery. Unpredictability. "It's gone and I didn't predict it would went, and so . . . it's all black." Well, here you're making the preclear *predict* that something is going to disappear.

So there are these methods of handling spots in space, and these are the main considerations. Now, don't for a moment believe that there are eighty-five other considerations that can be added into that type of processing. The basic Pre-logic on which this is based is a very precise thing. It says: *Theta locates things in time and space and creates time and space and things to locate in them*. Self-determinism is *one's ability to locate things in time and space,* and this is directly processing self-determinism, so it doesn't go out in all directions. It's right there and it's on those three considerations: the consideration of loss, the consideration of "I got to stay here so I'll make it all unreal," and the consideration of "Well, I can't have that place any more so I'll carry a picture of it." Most of your preclears whether they know it or not are walking around with a childhood home over their heads. They can't have that spot any more—the orientation place —so they think, to see at all they'd better carry it around with them.

Now Spotting Spots and Remedy of Havingness—between the two of them the more important is Spotting Spots—and the consequence of Spotting Spots is having to Remedy Havingness. But why does he have to remedy havingness? Because he can't create energy.

There are obviously lots of methods one way or another which would get somebody out of creating energy. For example, after something had been discovered which the preclear was perfectly willing to have occupy the same space, the next thought was, "Well, let's see now. If there's that . . . that's energy . . . I think I'll . . . I'll mock up a *machine* of some kind or another to remedy my havingness," and mocked up a generator and then it went on to a power station and then on to suns. In other words the preclear went right on and remedied all of his considerations that he was dependent on anything else of any kind whatsoever for energy, and he started producing it himself. So that is the product of remedy of havingness. In other words, he would be saying that that is a very good procedure if you just change the considerations on it all the way on up. This is obviously a finite procedure. You don't go on remedying havingness forever. So—why don't you remedy the condition that makes you remedy havingness? There is, then, an indicated process. This will turn on mockups and perception and everything else: *"What wouldn't you mind occupying the same space as you?"*

And so we have the Remedy of Havingness and Spotting Spots in Space.

CHAPTER TWENTY-THREE

DESCRIPTION PROCESSING

This happens to be the most important subject that you will cover in auditing. It may not be the most important subject in the universe, but it is the most important subject in auditing. This is a Step One, Two-Way Communication procedure. And this is the relatively advanced procedure of conducting a two-way communication, and someone who would have no concept of the four conditions of existence would not be remotely capable of running this process, therefore this would not come at the very early part of one's study, although Step One itself comes early in training.

This requires *two-way communication*—every iron you can throw into the fire.

It requires all of your knowledge of Scientology and its theory and practice, to conduct an adequate two-way communication with the preclear, because if you do that you can, just by that and with no further process, resolve his case in a relatively short time. So this must be an extremely important process we are talking about here. It requires all of the knowingness you have of Scientology in order to do it. It is done by a clever auditor. It is not a process which is done by a fellow who, as his furthest effort of cognition toward the preclear, reads off a series of commands. It requires a continuous communication with the preclear—a two-way communication with the preclear. It requires that you establish it and that you maintain it and that you conduct it in such a fashion that the elements which compose the preclear's difficulty are vanished. Just by carrying on a two-way communication with the preclear, you can cause any difficulty he is having, such as non-exteriorization, such as a failure to take responsibility in other Dynamics, and so on, whatever his difficulties, you can conduct a two-way communication in such a way as to make those difficulties vanish. You will have just as much good fortune with this process as you are willing to be a clever auditor and to follow the exact rules of this.

The primary difficulty with this process Two-Way Communication is that it apparently is entirely permissive, it apparently can wander into any field, topic, subject, address anything—thereby an individual who is not cognizant of its very, very precise fundamentals would go immediately astray. He would go as far astray as men have gone far astray. It's a process which you can easily get entangled about. It's a process which you can be argued with about.

A two-way communication could be a very broad field, but it has a particular precision area where you as an auditor can concentrate. If you know the exact mechanics of what you are doing, used cleverly, this becomes the best process you ever had. When you don't know its mechanics, and you don't use it cleverly, it becomes the gummiest, most misunderstood, non-advancing sort of a process you ever ran into. So again here is a process that requires judgement yet is very easy to do.

The part of Two-Way Communication we are taking up here could be given a name all of its own, and we would call it DESCRIPTION PROCESSING. It could be given this name, but it's likely to get entirely lost if we always refer to it by this name. In the first place Description Processing would not be its entire description name. It would have to be DESCRIPTION RIGHT NOW Processing. But we had better call it a process known as Two-Way Communication, which is just exactly what it is labelled under Step One of Intensive Procedure, (*Intensive Procedure*: The Standard Operating Procedure, 1954, given in *The Creation of Human Ability* by L. Ron Hubbard.) and this comes at this distance into this material because it uses every single thing that you know about Scientology. And the main thing that it uses is this factor: *If you establish the As-is-ness of your preclear's condition to his satisfaction it will vanish.* And you *don't* establish its As-is-ness by tracing its consequences, by tracing its basics, by tracing its significances, by discovering what lies under the thing that lies under the thing that lies under the back of beyond the other side of, or "Let's change it all, change it all, change it all," because what will happen? The process will *persist* won't it? This is a tricky one, then. It is a process which actually and overtly processes and achieves Alter-is-ness, by using nothing but As-is-ness. You can get a change of case with the preclear very simply, solely by taking his case *as it is right now*. We want right now, no place else, we want to know how it is right now.

The key question of this process can be codified. The process is not sloppy, it's not all over the place, it is highly precise, and the key question is:

How does it seem to you now?

You could just go on asking this question. That is all you want the preclear to give you. How does it actually seem to him right now. If he tells you about the room, or a manifestation of some sort, or something he likes, or something he dislikes, or something he knows or doesn't know—whatever it is—what you want, and *all* that you want from the preclear about it in this process is how actually does it seem to him *right now.*

And by doing exactly that, you get change, change, change in the preclear, at a very fast rate—by doing what?—by asking for nothing but an As-is-ness. What is the condition as it is right this instant.

If you were a very, very clever auditor, all you would have to do is to take this basic question, How does it seem to you now, and couch it in a thousand different guises, always, always pointing straight at this one, that we want this individual to discuss exactly how it is. We want to know about it. And we don't want any romance, we don't want any embroidery, we don't want any alteration so as to get our sympathy. We don't want any super-pressure on us so that we will do something. All we want to know is how it is. That takes clever auditing.

It's quite a fascinating thing to watch a preclear come into cognition—not recognition, because he probably never knew it before (re-cognition would be "I knew it but I forgot it"). Conditions exist through him, around him, above him, below him—considerations exist of which he has no cognition. These have come into beingness without any understanding whatsoever on his part. He's never seen them before and yet they're right there, so what we're interested in is cognition—*looking* at it—and we want the As-is-ness of any and every condition which this fellow has.

The preclear begins to change very rapidly. The first thing you know he is saying, "Well, there's nothing wrong with my throat!" . . . "The back of my head's perfectly alive." If he doesn't know the formula of what you're doing, and he doesn't track with it at all, and he doesn't know Scientology, you have ceased at that moment to be entirely human as far as he's concerned.

Now I have run this process on preclears who were intensely resistive to auditing, who knew nothing could happen, who generally finished up sessions saying nothing happened, and I received the most amazing sort of result. The person knew something had happened. Cognition had occurred. And it had occurred with considerable action. The person knew this extremely well, that something had happened. You can't run this on *anybody* without changing his condition. It's impossible to do so. Even if you ran it poorly you'd change his condition.

Running this process you could do this occasionally. You could throw in *where and when*. Not often or repetitively. *Once in a while.* (Let's not stick him back on the time track.) And recognize well that if he spots this thing even vaguely in the time and place where it began, you are likely to get a whole chain of things blowing, but we are not primarily interested in that, because *where,* and *what,* is *present time*. Time is not just beginningless and endless. It would seem so, but time is a continuing postulate. It is a postulate which continues to be postulated. All time is now. What we call the future, which is entirely hypothetical, is *what will be,* and that is not an As-is-ness. You could have an As-is-ness *about* the future, such as "I am worried about the future," but you don't actually have a future in that preclear. And as far as the past is concerned, it has no more actual validity than the future. All that exists of the past is what is in the present. And if it's not in the present, so what? You could say, well, it might come *into* the present. No, it won't. Not if you've got the present straightened out. If you have a preclear in a continuous state of beingness, in this present, which is rising and getting better, and his cognition is better and better and better—you're turning on his knowingness. And if you turn on his knowingness in the present, his knowingness about the past will increase markedly.

I've had a preclear start out with a statement like, "I am a body, I know I am a body and nothing but a body", and tell me he has "heard things about Scientology and exteriorization" and so forth, and he recites all kinds of things he has picked up from the materialistic practitioners. Well, I read in a psychiatric text once upon a time (this is their knowingness level on this) that people occasionally had the delusion that they were not in their bodies, and that psychiatry used electric shock to move them back into their bodies. This would be more or less the level of practice of monkeys hanging from their tails—they really shouldn't be fooling around with such things as the spirit. These practitioners sat in their chairs for fifty years and for, I'd say, several million if not several billion hours, *and they didn't notice this?* Well they were starting out on the basic premise that man is mud is mud is mud, he's a body, and there's nothing you can do about it anyway—and going at it from this angle they were not likely to find out much of anything but the fact that there does happen to be some mud around.

The As-is-ness of the preclear was what was in the road of all the materialistic approaches to the field of healing. This is not to imply that a medical doctor is out of order in practicing on broken bones, obstetrics and such things—in other words mechanical structure—but when it comes over to his doing something about the mind, he has to deal with the spirit, because there isn't any mind. That was the thing they never learned about. They didn't find out that what they were studying didn't exist. They were studying a lump of computing machine made out of neurons and cyclotrons or something of the sort. Well, they could have studied it forever and never found out anything about it, because it has no As-is-ness. They could go on describing it forever, and of course it would continue to persist because it is itself an Alter-is-ness.

Well, don't you make the same mistake with a preclear. Don't go chasing after all the endless significances and symptoms—in other words, Alter-is-ness, Alter-is-ness, Alter-is-ness—don't make the mistake of addressing this, because all you will do is perpetuate the condition. Just don't make that mistake. What you want to do is quite something else.

You want to find out how it seems right now. You don't want any action on the part of this preclear who wants to go chasing after significances. He is so fixed on the idea of being an observer that let's let him observe. So there's a *white* area. He says, "Uh . . . I don't know . . . the back of the leg's kind of white and the front of the leg's kind of dark. And there seems to be something shooting up through the leg." "Well, how does it seem to you now?" Keep him looking at it, keep him looking at it *now*. You just want him to describe it and describe it and describe it. And then communicate and communicate and communicate and communicate, and we don't care if we seem to waste some time with it. So he goes off into some wild excursion, something like, "Well, it seems to me like . . . I don't know, I can't quite look at the room when that pain is on. I *try* to look at the room. I wonder why that is. I wonder why that is. I've had a lot of speculation as to why this is." You can let him talk for a while. It's burning time, but remember you're preserving a two-way communication, and throughout this process you're preserving a two-way communication, and that is its keynote and that is why it continues to work so easily. Your preclear does not seem to be under duress at any time. Believe me, is he *interested* in his conditions! And in Description Processing you simply use that overtly to get him to describe them as they are.

But this requires a certain sensitivity on the part of an auditor. He's got to know when the preclear starts weaving the fancy tales.

How is he going to know this? *The condition does not alter.* That's an interesting one, isn't it? He's describing how horrible it is. He goes on and describes this, and describes it and describes it and describes it for three or four minutes, and there's no change at all. He describes it for a few more minutes and there's no change at all.

Don't shoot him.

You could ask him *how his feet* seem to him. Get him off that subject, because you hit a *lying machine*, and if you'll just get his attention off of it, why, maybe you'll get some straight answers.

This is where you learn about people. But in what framework are you learning about people? You're going entirely on the very, very basic material of the four conditions of existence. You will see a person run this cycle over and over and over as he does Description Processing. People become so fantastically patterned, they are so predictable when they start this sort of thing—and they become very easy to process. This is not restimulative, because you're not trying to change the preclear. You're trying to find out how he is. You can do this for hours. Cognitions will occur, such as, that he's actually had a migraine headache for years and he didn't even know it, except that all of a sudden it stopped. All of a sudden, he said, "Wait a minute. What's happened to this pain? I didn't ever know I had a pain here." That sort of things happens in this type of processing.

"Description Right Now" Processing—Two-way Communication: Step One. This is how you get them into communication, how you keep them in communication and why you keep them in communication along this particular line. You could perform this in 8-C Opening Procedure, but you're simply maintaining a two-way communication. "How does this (part of the room) seem to you now?" You're trying to get the exact condition at that moment which he is observing. You will get continuous change. You are undoing all the change he has put into the condition. But it undoes with great rapidity, so there is some hope after all.

CHAPTER TWENTY-FOUR

GROUP PROCESSING

There is a subject of considerable interest to us, which is quite a remarkable subject, and that is group auditing. There are a number of things to be known about this.

A group auditor is one who stands in front of, sits in front of, or relays by loudspeaker system to a group (and a group consists of two or more people), auditing, so as to improve their condition of beingness as thetans. That is a full, complete definition of a group auditor.

If he's there to improve their condition, he will of course do his group auditing well. If he is simply standing there giving rote commands, he might do something too, because the mechanics of auditing will carry forward a great distance. But if he really wants to make people more cheerful, better, put them up into an operative band, change their condition, make the able more able, then he recognizes as he audits a group that he is auditing a number of preclears and he is auditing them collectively and individually all at one time, and a good group auditor recognizes that this is not unlike driving a twenty-mule team—it's a trick. So, some people are good group auditors. They recognize what it takes to do it, they don't flinch, and they can do it. And there are some who stand up at the front of a room and give auditing commands, but whom you'd hardly call group auditors. Now what are the conditions under which group auditing is best done:

First, the atmosphere should be quiet. And the

methods of ingress into the group auditing room, such as doors, windows, chimneys, and skylights, should be to some degree policed so that we don't get people walking into the session. And this would include, under a sub-heading, the fact that people don't come late to a group auditing session. A group auditor who knows his business simply follows that as a rule. He doesn't let people come late. They just don't come. When they get there they will find the next group auditing session is next Thursday, which fact might be announced on the door. He impresses this upon his people and upon his group, that people mustn't come stumbling in fifteen or twenty minutes after the group auditing starts, fall over a couple of chairs, fall over a couple of preclears, drop a couple of ashtrays, step on a couple of ashtrays, and then drop their pocketbook, upset the chair, nudge the fellow in front of them so they can say "excuse me", and, in other words, interrupt the session. That is because of the things that can happen by reason of that. You might have somebody sitting there in the back of the room where these people came in and sat down, who was just at that moment getting into something that was pretty darned hard to handle, and was having to wrestle it with himself. You were there helping him as a group auditor, true, and your next command would have a tendency to straighten this up, but this individual has started to flounder, and all of a sudden somebody comes in and helps him out by falling all over him. This introduces a randomity of unpredicted motion into the environment which is not conducive to that person's case improvement.

So the Group Auditor has a Code all of his own which happens to be the Auditor's Code, but the Group Auditor's Code has some more things to it. And amongst those things is: *People don't ever come late to a Group Auditing Session.*

Just to give a few other little items on this Code—*he doesn't audit with processes which establish long comm lags.* He avoids processes which do this on individual preclears. If he knows that a certain process produces a long communication lag on individual preclears here and there, he certainly avoids it in auditing a group. He audits primarily with techniques which will discover every person in the group alert at the end of an hour's processing. And that certainly doesn't include anything that will give somebody a twenty-two hours' comm lag.

Another part of his Code is: *He must be willing to grant beingness to the Group.* He isn't a lion tamer sitting up there with a bunch of lions about to pounce on him. He is somebody who is standing up in front of a group willing to grant beingness to that group. And as he grants beingness to the group, so the group recovers. If he is willing to grant beingness to a group, a great many things immediately fall into line. And these things follow: He gives his commands in a clear, distinct voice, and if he notices that people in one part of the room or another look at him suddenly after he has given the command, or look at him questioningly, he simply repeats the command for the whole group. In other words his mission is to get that command through and registered.

He recognizes and must recognize, that the people to whom he is talking in this group are not an *audience.* They are a number of people who are in a greater or lesser degree involved in recognizing, looking at or resolving problems relating to their beingness, and as such, of course, are slightly out of communication with him. He must recognize this just as in an individual session he has to give his commands clearly, distinctly and get them answered. In a group auditing session he doesn't have the answer. He doesn't get that answer that says, "Yes, I've got that." Yes, I've finished that, and so forth. Therefore he must do all of his auditing on such a basis that it obviates those answers. You see, he gives a command, and he's not going to get a reply from his preclear, and so *he must therefore take enormous precautions, actually very exaggerated precautions, to make sure that every word he says is clearly registered to the most anaten* (*Anaten*: an abbreviation of "analytical attenuation", meaning a diminution or weakening of the analytical awareness of an individual for a brief or extensive period of time) *person in the entire group*. His words must register. He must also be careful *to give his commands in such a way as not to give a number of failures to one or more individuals in the group*. For instance he says, "Now get a place, get a place where you are not. . . . Just contact that place." And he shouldn't give another, contradictory command until he's sure that everybody in the group has *found* at least one location. Let's take an example of that. He says, "Get a place where you are not." And he waits for a moment, and several people in the group already have spotted this place with accuracy, and so he says "Get one place certainly, and then some more." Now, what he has done is to take those five, six, eight people in the group who did not find that one place right now right away, and he let it be all right for them to go on and comm lag on it. And he still made it all right for the remainder of the group to go on and get other places.

One does not need to have a stylized patter in order to do this, but that does happen to be a very stylized patter. "Get one place, one place for sure . . . and when you've got that one place, get some more, and get some more places."

Now, if the auditor is willing to grant beingness to the group, he'll be heard all the way through the group, and if he's not willing to grant beingness to the group, he won't be heard all the way through the group.

Furthermore, if he's not willing to grant beingness to the group, he'll find himself, willy-nilly, shifting processes half way through. He suddenly decides he'd better run something else. He'd better run something tricky. He'd better run something that's very stunty. We were doing all right, we were spotting the walls of the room, we were doing Group Opening Procedure which, given in the Group Auditor's Handbook (*Group Auditor's Handbook*: This was a 1954 compilation of group auditing sessions resulting from the Advanced Clinical Courses of that year), is a very precise process. The auditor got that going fairly well, had just gotten that well started—and he decides—Well, let's shift off to some . . . Ah! Duplication by Attention! All right. Look at the right wall, look at the left wall, look at the right wall, look at the left wall, look at the right wall, look at the left wall . . . uh . . . I don't know, that doesn't seem to be getting very far. Let's see—what really should we do. And he switches to another process and another.

The group by this time is getting sort of restless. What's basically the trouble here? Is it the fact that the man doesn't know what he's doing? Well, it could be to some slight degree. But why doesn't he know what he's doing? Every single one of those commands and theory behind it can be found in the publications of Scientology. *What's he doing not knowing what he's doing?* Well I'll tell you what he's doing. He's trying not to grant beingness to that group. And there will be people *in* that group who are worried about granting beingness to the group and all these people getting bright and improving and becoming thetans and flying around and demoniacally attacking people and "You shouldn't make everybody free like that, you know."

And these people will step on ashtrays, upset chairs, come late, get up in the middle of a group session and open and close windows, open and close doors, and then we discover, of course, that *they don't want to have beingness granted to them.* But particularly, they are worried about the group session going on with this individual granting all that beingness to all these people and improving all these people, and if all these people improved, why, goodness knows what would happen—something horrible would happen, competition would get too high or something of the sort, or something dreadful would occur. That's the computation that it's running on when bad auditing commands are used, and don't ever think otherwise. No, don't say, Well, he just doesn't know. Every one of those homo sapiens, individualized the way he is to an Only-One computation, has some facet of *his* beingness which is refusing to *grant* beingness. Every man alive has it to some degree, otherwise he'd never have a game or a contact. There's always "the other side". He isn't going to grant any beingness to the Princeton football team—that sort of thing. And when you exaggerate this consistently and continually you'll get somebody who doesn't want to have any beingness granted to anybody anywhere, and so before he does some group auditing he won't bother to read over the way you do it. And if he does he'll do something else. And he won't study up on his subject, he won't look over his people, and he won't audit in such a way as to make them improve or win, and you will find, by the way, that his group session will not be well attended. A group auditor's group session cannot be anything but well attended. They will be continually well attended, and they will increase in their attendance, to the degree that the individual is willing to grant beingness to people, in other words, do a good job.

That's the long and short of it, and that's a very uncompromising statement, and one could say that there are a lot of things which mitigate this statement, but I'll argue you out of them. The truth of the matter is that it comes down just to the granting of beingness. He will or he won't.

Now, can that be remedied with him? Yes, when he has a little more freedom. Just a standard auditing session as given in the Group Auditor's Handbook will bring him up to a point where he will grant more beingness to people. It will do this.

You could run this as a straight process, as a group session—just "grant some beingness to the front walls", "some beingness to the back walls". You could do this if you wanted to. But again this is putting too much significance into the process.

The reason anyone is not granting beingness is that he himself is enchained and enslaved and he feels himself attacked to some degree by the environment, and you've got to get him up to the point where he has a little more operating margin in his own survival, and if he has a little survival margin he's willing to let somebody else survive. He begins to treat survival as a commodity. There are only five quarts of it in the world, and he's darned if anybody's going to get any part of those five quarts, because he *knows* he needs it all himself. Right on this point you can tell immediately a good auditor and a bad one. So there is a case computation at the bottom of group auditing ability.

An individual who is afraid of effort is an accurate measure of this. People recognize instinctively, that a fear of effort, an unwillingness to put out effort, goes right along with "bad off", "won't grant beingness", "got to slow other people down too". So, do we have a group auditor who sits back and puts his feet on the desk and audits a group? Oh no, we don't. The group won't get better, won't recover, won't do anything. Why? They'll sit there and run the commands because they've heard that Scientology is a good thing, but they will say, This guy doesn't care. He isn't interested.

There is no necromancy involved here. We don't have a beam of energy coming out from the group auditor settling like a little star over the head of every person. That is not the case in point. But there's another case in point:

There's the simple matter of *duplication of the communication.* Why do people recognize this rather instinctively, that a person doesn't care, if he hasn't energy or effort. Well, here's this individual. He seems to have some vitality. The communication line has as its Source Point VITALITY. And whatever there is at Effect point at the beginning, it will at least wind up at the end with vitality. If you've ever talked to somebody for a while in a rather bored tone of voice, you found *them* after a while getting bored. This is just "Q and A" (Q and A: From "Question and Answer". This term originally referred to the fact that *the answer to the question is the question.* Q and A has been used as the term for "changing when the preclear changes". It here refers to the preclear duplicating the beingness of the auditor). Have you ever listened to somebody who was very electrifying—a William

Jennings Bryan sort of a speaker—pound and howl and so forth—and when you look at an audience that's been talked to this way—they're aroused, they definitely are aroused. The man didn't say anything logical at all at any time during the whole time he was talking, and yet just simply the fact that they are duplicating a speaker who seems to have some vitality comes on through to the audience and seems to give *them* some vitality. But does it give them some vitality —no, they are simply duplicating it.

Now a group auditor could sit down, and talk to the group. As a matter of fact (this is a very dangerous thing to tell a group auditor) this actually brings about a little bit better duplication, because the group is sitting down. But if he is sitting down, think of how much now his voice has to do. He can't depend on anything else to do anything for him. *Everything* he does must be contained in his voice. Everything he THINKS must be contained in his voice. Oh, you say, this then requires an actor. Yep. If you're not willing to *be* various things, and if you can't be various things at will, you actually haven't even got any business *auditing*. Why? Because in that case you're trying to *keep* things from being. And the first person you're trying to keep from being is you. And if you're trying to keep *you* from being, to any marked degree, you will, on a duplication basis, restimulate this fact on the other end of the line. You'll keep others from being. So a group auditor *could* sit down. I don't mean he should or must.

As a matter of fact the best results I have ever gotten in group auditing sessions was actually walking up and down in front of a group and picking them out every now and then singly—"Did you get that all right?" etc. And the group tone just starts going *up,* and then the fact that they are doing drills which are just dynamite of course in themselves will just practically lift them right straight out of their heads. In one of the last broad group auditing sessions I did I came away from the mike and I was simply talking to the crowd and I was really trying to do something for their cases and so forth, and I was quite interested because it was getting on down toward the end of the series of group sessions. And I got the report afterwards: that there were more people exteriorized during that particular session than in any other single session I had given. Well, here I was feeling more alive, interested, urgent about what was going on, and that in itself was communicating, and it was communicating very strongly.

A group auditor who has no wish to have anything happen, however, will be disappointed if he sits there and reads the commands in a flat dull dead voice out of the Group Auditor's Handbook, to a crowd of people. He will still get some results. This has been tested out. We took the worst group auditor you ever saw or ever heard of and gave him some commands that were not too well written and we sent him out to audit. His style was, "Well, I've got some commands here now . . . I've got some commands . . . let's see now . . . uh . . . let's see . . . hum . . . uh . . . look at the front of the room . . . it says here . . . lookattherightwall . . ." And this guy still got some *results*!

So what we're doing with just the processes themselves is fabulous.

Something important to know about group auditing is this: If you're afraid of a crowd, you won't want to grant beingness to them, because that's *why* you're afraid of them. You're sure that they're about to interrupt you. You're sure that they're about to jump over the seats and attack you. If you're in that frame of mind toward a group, you will not be heard clearly through the group, you'll have a tendency to change techniques, and your attention hunger will probably cause you to drop ashtrays, lose your place, and other wild things.

Now let's look at this thing called "stage fright", and how a person could resolve it. One way he could resolve it is simply by some kind of creative processing. Just do mockups on being scared to death—body reacting, jumping, and so forth—but that's a very crude way to handle stage fright.

The *best* way to cure stage fright is to walk up on a stage before a vast number of people and do your best, and after you've done that a few times you recognize that this is an As-is-ness, this condition, and generally everything connected with it, the strain and so forth, will blow. You just recognize clearly that you're under strain when you talk to this audience. You're just under strain and so what. "So I'm under strain when I talk to the audience"—and you won't be. All it is is fear of what you will do, that you might do something unpredicted, or something strange might occur, and after you've done this a few times you discover that no strange things occur, that you get away with it every time. You survive, and you become quite accomplished.

There's something else that you could do to improve your capabilities as a group auditor. And that is beingnesses. If you could just practice beingness. You could be actors and be therapists and be swamis and be this kind of thing and be that kind of thing, and just work on it on kind of a gradient scale until you got the idea you could be anything. You could have this run on you, you see, in processing, and this would handle stage fright too, because a person with stage fright is being somebody who has stage fright. That's all there is to it. The answer to the problem is the exact problem.

The whole subject of Group Auditing, then, involves itself today not so much with a knowledge of technique, but involves itself with a stage presence on the part of the group auditor and his command over the group itself. If he's willing for the group to make gains, they'll make gains. If he's interested in giving them wins, they'll have wins. If he's interested in having a group, he'll have one. It's a very odd thing, but the best auditors have no difficulty in collecting groups.

Now, you can't have a feeling of embarrassment toward your fellow man actually and be able to walk up to him on the street and tell him anything or get him to do anything. As long as you have an embarrassment toward people you'll have difficulty collecting a group or running a group or anything of this sort. Well, what is this quantity called embarrassment? It's a matter of exhibition.

Here we have *appearance* and *disappearance* as a dichotomy. And a group auditor is somebody who has to be *willing to appear,* and if one has been compulsively made to appear many, many times against his will—one of his mother's favorite phrases might have been, "Look at you. Here you are dirty from head to foot and I just cleaned you up. Look at you! You're appearing, you little swine!"—some gentle upbringing of this character will tend to promote embarrassment. But you shouldn't go looking, for the answer to embarrassment, into deep-seated significances. The embarrassment is that the fellow is there, kind of apologizing for his presence, and trying to disappear, at the same time. That's the As-is-ness of embarrassment. And that's *just* an As-is-ness. We don't care where it came from. He's apologizing. So one of the first things you could do is simply not apologize for your presence. You might expect people to apologize for theirs but don't you apologize for yours. You're here, and their hard luck they're there too or their good luck that they're there.

But if a fellow's in really good shape, why this is the sort of an atmosphere that goes around a group session—this atmosphere says: "I'm here and you're right there and I'm real glad to see ya and you're sitting there and that's awful unlucky for you if you're sick because you're going to get well anyway and you could come in and sit down and not run any of the commands at all and you'd still improve, naturally. That's a matter of course. And I'm sorry you've got some things to be ashamed of, but you know, I haven't got a single one"—that sort of an atmosphere. A fairly calm atmosphere rather than an excited, ecstatic atmosphere. But even an excited, ecstatic atmosphere or a swami atmosphere or an Amie Semple McPherson atmosphere is better than somebody standing there and saying, "You know I'm sorry I'm up here visible."

So the best way to get into the groove of group auditing is to get your case in good shape just exactly as you *would* get your case into good shape, just with standard processing—nothing peculiar, nothing slanted, nothing odd or unusual run on it, just get in good shape. You're a little freer, and as you become freer then you are more competent to let yourself appear.

And the other thing that goes right along with that and is not at all dependent on you getting your case in good shape, is the fact that you just go on making public appearances and group auditing people with this postulate: Everybody's glad to see me, they're very happy to hear me talk, and I'm here and I know at the same time I'm scared to death and that's the As-is-ness of it, so what, but I'm putting on a good show anyhow —and the next thing you know, why, all of that is gone, all that feeling of strain and tension is gone, and you'll go on and give the group a session.

But you give sessions to people to make them better, not to be somebody standing on a stage running off a set of words. You have reason, purpose and meaning in what you are doing and consider it a personal affront if somebody in this group did not immediately get totally improved after a couple of hours' processing. That's a personal affront, and you treat it as such when they tell you about it. "You mean you've come to one of my sessions and not gotten big gains? Humph!" and, "Well, I'll let you come to another session but don't pull this again."

CHAPTER TWENTY-FIVE

SCIENTOLOGY AND LIVING

The application of Scientology to one's everyday life is a vast subject, and the best method of doing this is simply using the A-R-C triangle, with its consequent Chart of Human Evaluation, in everyday living. This takes into account most of the manifestations one sees and which one can evaluate quickly.

This, of course, includes the Communication Formula, and an understanding of that Communication Formula would be an understanding of Cause, Distance, Effect, and the fact that people who are at the Cause point or Source point are very often very reluctant to be Cause, and people who are at the Effect point are very often very reluctant to be an Effect, in both cases of anything.

So they will do various things in communication, such as to move out onto the *distance between* Cause point and Effect point, and so become a message. People get stuck very easily with this. You can carry all the wisdom you want, anywhere, to anybody, without yourself *being a message*. Have the message in your hand, put the message on the line, but don't yourself *be* the message. People as they go between these two points get closer and closer to arrival, and there is the fellow who doesn't dare arrive—*he doesn't dare get to that Effect point*—and there's the fellow who doesn't dare leave, or go any further from that Cause point, and he'll get further and further then from *being* Cause and he will be more and more an

Effect. And you could get these two points pulled together more and more tightly until, although they were not quite the same point, nevertheless you get this series of manifestations.

An understanding of the Communication Formula is very useful in every day life, very useful in understanding life. You'll see somebody who—everything he's the cause of he becomes the effect of. This goes back a long way down the track. "The Second Law of Magic", it could have been said to be, which is: *Don't be the effect of your own cause.* Well, of course it's impossible not to be the effect of your own cause, so that in itself is a booby trap. A fellow's a fool if he thinks he can cause something without becoming one way or the other the effect of it. He can cause anything he pleases as long as he is willing to be the effect of what he causes. You are a static, you are a personality, you don't have mass, meaning or mobility as yourself (you're using a body rather than being a body) and you naturally are capable of causing almost anything—but supposing you were standing there protecting a body, being a body, hiding in a body, and you *cause* something which you wouldn't like to have happen to the body. Supposing you pick up a book and throw it at somebody and give them a big bruise in the face or something of the sort—you don't like the effect, so you begin to resist being an effect, and you resist being an effect more and more and more. Actually you're making one body resist being an effect, and after a while, because of the make-up of this universe, where eventually (*Anything you resist you get, Anything you resist you become*—the favorite motto of this universe), you become it. In the absence of processing and understanding—let's modify that to that degree —if you understand this and if there is processing, that ceases to occur. But here we have people becoming very, very unwilling to be the cause of anything. You'll find they won't give anyone orders because they themselves do not want to be the effect of receiving orders. They'll do all sorts of very remarkable things to avoid upsetting people in their vicinity. Why? Because they're afraid themselves of being upset. They've learned by experience the overt act-motivator sequence (*Overt act-motivator sequence*: the sequence wherein someone who has committed a harmful or contra-survival act has to claim the existence of "motivators", which are then likely to be used to justify committing further overt acts). If you want to know why people get nervous, it's just because when they make the faintest overt act, they get this tremendously exaggerated package of facsimiles saying, No, no, no, no. "Oh, no, you'd better not talk to those people hard like that or it'll really cave in on you." Well, that is fairly normal in a society. It's one thing to be polite because you can be polite, and it's quite another thing to let yourself be walked all over, and it's still quite another thing to be reactively in apathy.

There is another manifestation which is even more curious, which you will see once in a while, and that is: anything that happens in the vicinity at all, the person *knows he is the cause of it*. Now it starts with anything that happened to him he knew he basically caused it, which of course happens to be a salient truth. It is true that anything that happened to him he was basically the cause of, but that's *way up scale* on the chart, and now he just feels this reactively—that he has become an effect, therefore he caused it. Just automatically. You've got Cause and Effect here so close together that they short circuit. If there is an effect, he caused it, and that spreads out to the broad environment, until you will find an insane person, worrying like mad—for having caused all of World War II. He must have done something, because there was World War II. It must have been him. He's playing the Only One very hard at this point. Even children will react on this one occasionally. On the death of an ally (*Ally*: a person who sympathized with or appeared to aid the survival of an individual when he was ill, injured or unconscious and whom the individual now reactively regards as necessary to his continued existence and well being) we see a child walking around worrying, and wondering what on earth he did that killed his grandmother or his sister or whoever. He *must* have done something. He was the *effect* of it, wasn't he? He must have done something.

And we get that as the entering wedge into superstition. "Let's see, I'm a victim, therefore I must be guilty of something"—and they dream up something on the order of "original sin". It's all bad, therefore you must be the effect of it, and that becomes "repent, repent". Well, actually, an individual only needs to accept the responsibility for his own acts, this will take care of things very nicely, and if he recognizes clearly the effects which he does cause, and if he's perfectly willing to cause effects which he dares be the effect of himself, he can walk through this bramble and brush with great ease even as a body. There is a mode of conduct which is available.

Well, I want to call your attention to the Chart of Human Evaluation, which was organized very early in 1951, which has various columns, and which gives behavior characteristics. It is plotted out mathematically on the basis of ARC. When you raise the affinity of a person you will raise his reality and raise his communication. When you raise his communication you will raise his affinity and raise his reality. When you raise his reality of something you will raise his affinity and raise his communication. That is a very good chart to use in order to predict people. It is particularly important for an auditor to use this chart, but it is a chart that can be used in everyday living.

An auditor at one time had studied this chart as just theory on a course. He found it quite interesting And having studied all this why, it never occurred to him that it was true or real or anything like that. He was perfectly in agreement with it as a mathematical study.

Then one day the thought struck him, that this might be applicable to life at large. What if this chart were *true*! Of course, people really wouldn't act like that. But he went into a bank and looked around, just watching people go by in the bank lobby, and watching the people behind the desks, and he talked to a couple of people and so on, and he started placing them on the Tone Scale. Well, he did this all one morning, and he came back to class pretty horrified. This Chart was absolutely accurate! It applied to every one of those people out there right across the columns. But what horrified him wasn't the Chart but the fact that people consistently obeyed these levels *all* the time, *didn't* know they were doing it or what they were doing and had no slightest inkling of what was going on. One fellow was "1.5-ing" (*1.5*: numerical equivalent on the Chart of Human Evaluation for the person who is in *Overt Hostility*. Anger is his standard state. He is capable of taking destructive action and is characteristically *trying to stop things*). He was acting exactly as a 1.5 should act, reacting across the boards. This auditor went so far, toward the end of morning, as to ask the fellow who was 1.5-ing just casually how his arthritis was, and the fellow said, "Oh! It's terrible!" Arthritis *would* be a way of stopping something, wouldn't it? An auditor spots these things just in everyday fashion as casually as he'd pick up a blotter.

But this auditor had all of a sudden walked into *a completely predictable world!* That is good, but you want to beware of this trap: Let's just avoid "the reason why". The reason why they're doing what they are doing is ARC, and the reasons they *give* are the reasons which justify them against the social pattern in which they live. That is the totality of "the reason why." For instance, the cop acts the way he acts because he is a cop. The bank president has to act the way he acts because he is a bank president. His first excuse is his beingness or position and his next few excuses down the line might have been causative things in his life—it's true that a person put in a position that requires for instance, a 2.0 (antagonism) is likely to at least *dramatize* being a 2.0 right across the Chart, but this is the curious thing: that he doesn't have to believe it, too. You see, he could be a 2.0 straight across the Tone Scale but he doesn't have to believe it. It's only when he becomes all this seriously that he gets onto this scale. Remember that it's ARC, then, not reasons why. If you fall into reasons why, you can just figure-figure with the rest of them forever.

Just look at this ratio: how much space does the person have on that Communication Formula? How much space has he got? What's his general affinity toward life at large? What's his reality? What is he basically in agreement with? And we look at that, and actually we see these three corners of the triangle forming a plane, and as his space gets greater he goes right on up the scale and right on out the top of the scale, and as his space gets less, why the Source

Point and Receipt Point of the Communication Formula come almost together, but it's like walking half way to Chicago. Every time you walked half way to Chicago you of course never got to Chicago. The Source Point and Receipt Point do not ever coincide. They will and can coincide perfectly at the top of the scale, at which moment you've achieved a condition which might be rather poetically stated as a brotherhood with the entire universe, but that's a *total* affinity, and it is not an enforced or impelled affinity. Affinity which is compelled and enforced does not persist, it simply goes down scale. A free affinity for all of life is quite a different thing.

Now every once in a while an individual may start worrying about his sympathy for life. He realizes that he has some inkling of what ants think about and do. And he knows that a cactus has a certain emotion about it too, and he's likely to start worrying about this and try to pull back. He's afraid he will become these things fixedly, if he goes into sympathy with them all.

But his passport to freedom is his sympathy for all life and its forms. Not compulsive, just his free sympathy. If he were being forced to feel sympathetic towards young boys, we would be certain he would eventually, if he were a thetan, become a young boy.

We recognize in this chart that we have a successful method of prediction, and in ARC in general we have a good scale of prediction, and an individual cognizant of these things can predict the activity of those about him.

In view of the fact that these three items, A, R and C, combined together, are symptomatic of understanding, the degree of understanding which a person has of existence is the degree that he has distance possible in his Communication Formula, therefore we find understanding of existence increasing and increasing and increasing as he goes upscale and decreasing, decreasing, decreasing as he goes downscale. Of course we could add every factor of Scientology into this, but let's add beingness into this, and we find out that an individual is at first, on middle scale, completely free to be anything, and then as he goes downscale, he's more and more compulsively being made to be something and he finds himself *something,* and this makes him unhappy because he feels that it is not by his own choice. We actually know by As-is-ness and the necessity of altering As-is-ness that he had to appoint an other-determinism to keep something, and this makes him unhappy because he feels that it is not by his own choice. We actually know by As-is-ness and the necessity of altering As-is-ness that he had to appoint another determinism to keep something to go on persisting, and he's more and more avoiding motionlessness, because motionlessness is dangerous to him. Therefore a consistent, continual beingness as something is something he begins to fear, and when an individual is to a point where he has the horrible feeling that if he stood still for a long time in one place, he'd sort of grow roots, or he'd do something peculiar like this, something bad would happen to him. Or if pain turns on because he has to stand still for a while, you would have a condition there where you have compulsive beingness jibing with this one, which is the same thing—fear of motionlessness—and that fear of motionlessness is making him more and more motionlessness. The more frantically this individual goes into motion, the more he becomes a symbol. And, of course, the more he becomes a symbol, the more mass he accumulates, and the more meaning he accumulates.

And when you get him down around about .5 (apathy) on that tone scale his "reasons why"—would be utterly nonsequitur, but boy would they be *significant!* Mass, meaning and mobility, then, fits in there. Beingness fits in there. To understand life and human beings at large one should recognize this—that every human being there is, is *a thetan being a human being.*

An individual would never have become selectively and enforcibly a human being if he had no overt acts against human bodies. He has enormous numbers of overt acts against human bodies—and as a result he is very, very pressed on the subject of protecting bodies. He mustn't let a body be an effect of anything. He now must protect the body from such things as himself. As he goes down tone scale, whereas he may worship some powerful spirit that throws lightening bolts at him, as far as individual thetans are concerned, to let anyone be three feet back of his head or something like that, is intolerable to him and means that a body is likely to be attacked. You see? "Thetans attack bodies." He knows. They're bad. On the subject of exteriorization this person will pull a trick like this: "Be three feet back of your head." "*Are* you three feet back of your head?" "Well, you're *sure* you are, now?" etcetera. And he'll say right at that moment: "Well, put your attention on your nose. Make your nose move down a little bit" . . . and the person is sitting there saying "Whaaat?" A sudden change of pace. And it'll just land the preclear in that particular moment in time. We get that kind of a manifestation.

Then there is the subject of something-or-nothingness. A thetan is perfectly at liberty to have all the somethingnesses he wants to and any of the nothingnesses he wants to. He can communicate with somethingnesses with great ease. A thetan is something which is above something-and-nothing. A thetan isn't just nothing, you see. He is something which can *monitor* somethingnesses and nothingnesses. Well, if this is the case then we find that people would be doing one of two things when they get extremely down scale. They would either be trying to concentrate on all somethings, or they would start concentrating on all nothings. As a matter of fact as they go down scale they do this alternately. They fall out of all something, something, something, and they go into a strata where it *must be nothing,* nothing, nothing, must be something, something, something, and then MUST be nothing, and then MUST be something, and going on down through these strata you'll find human beings around who are utterly compelled to make nothing out of bodies, to make nothing out of cars, manuscripts, any remark which you make, any action. They've got to make nothing out of it. It would just kill them if they couldn't ridicule it. Ridicule is the very lightest method of slapping you to pieces. You'll come up with a favorite joke of yours and it's always been funny to other people around, and all of a sudden this person takes it apart with a snide remark. And you have just won the track meet and boy you're sure happy. You've got a ribbon about a yard long and you're proud of it, and everything's fine. This person says to you, "Do you know your shoes are muddy, and you have some dirt on your face, too." NOTHING. Make nothing there if we possibly can. Well, this is the biggest allowable nothing they can make, and they're being prevented from making nothing of things. They don't know any mechanisms to use to unmock things. Really it's by effort—energy. They've got to make nothing out of things with energy. The harder they try that the further down they go. Now, when they've got to make *something,* because they have to have something, they'll get into the same kind of situation. A thetan who is in very good shape could mock up a solid steel pyramid, and if he was in *wonderful* shape, you could probably see it too. But downscale, he just compulsively has to mock up something, then all of his automaticity is gone into making something, and he's objecting to it. He's objecting to every part of it as he goes down. To understand people, then, we would have to understand what kind of cycle this person is on. Is he on a somethingness cycle or a nothingness cycle? Neither one is any worse than the other, but the truth of the matter is that sane people—and we categorize that just overtly as above 2.0 on the tone scale—sane people make somethings and nothings at will. They don't have to. They do it to get some action, life, and so forth. And they can change their minds. They're not compulsively making somethings and compulsively making nothings, continually. Their conduct has a little randomity and difference to it.

There is not really such a condition as "insanity". There really is no such condition as neurosis. These are simply two arbitrary words that were thrown into the society and they were never defined, and the society so variously understands them, that kids just as sane as anybody stand there calling each other crazy. It's just a slang. There is an *emotion,* however, called the "Glee of Insanity" ("*Glee of Insanity*": Also called the "glee of irresponsibility". Manifestation which takes the form of an actual wave emanation resulting basically from an individual dramatizing the condition of "Must Reach—Can't Reach, Must Withdraw—Can't Withdraw"), which is an intolerable thing for a person.

We could say a person in such a state in relationship to energy that he could not take care of himself, couldn't feed himself properly or take care of his body, we could call *that* person insane. But again this is just an arbitrary thing. It really has no definition in this society.

But to understand and predict people at large it is only necessary for you to know whether they make something or nothing out of things, and then remember if you please that their conduct is consistent. They might have a lot of reasons why. They might be doing something unpredictable. But they have a motive which underlies their conduct just to this degree: *something,* or *nothing*. They are doing one or the other.

Now there are two other categories of human beings, and one is the category up scale where things can be bad, good at will. The categories from Know to Sex on the upper scale can be good, but when they're low on the scale, everything from Know to Sex—and low scale this is all Mystery—is BAD. And when you get someone where everything on the Know to Mystery Scale is bad, you have a case which is very inverted. It's well below 2. It's all bad. That's why "we've got to make nothing." This is your 1.5. He is actually operating there one hundred percent. He can only operate on emergencies. "We are about to have this tremendous disaster and therefore we are going to have to have this emergency legislation," and therefore, "We can make this huge army," so as to make nothing.

They have lost the concept of doing something because it's fun, and there's your last keynote. Individuals who can do things, no matter whether good, bad or indifferent or outrageous, simply because they're fun. An individual who can freely and with a clear heart do things because they're fun is a very sane person. He's in good shape.

You can notice the amount of laughter which a

person laughs. Laughter has a number of harmonics down the line, but we're not talking about the harmonics. This is rather upper scale laughter. He doesn't laugh because he's embarrassed. He laughs because he thinks something is funny, and if a person laughs fairly often and is very easy in that laughter you've got a sane man. Down scale they laugh less and less and less, or laugh more embarrassedly, or compulsively or obsessively, more and more and more, as we get way down to the bottom, and the person there just doesn't laugh. He doesn't live, either. He just lies there —mass, meaning and no mobility. He's not even a symbol any more.

There in essence if you care to study it, is the Chart of Human Evaluation, and if you care to apply this information to life as a whole, you'll find out that you can know human beings.

But remember you shouldn't expect them to know you. If their distance in that communication formula is very close together, they won't understand you, but that doesn't prevent you from understanding them.

GLOSSARY

ACCEPTANCE LEVEL: The degree of a person's actual willingness to accept people or things, monitored and determined by his consideration of the state or condition that those people or things must be in for him to be able to do so.

ANATEN: An abbreviation of "analytical attenuation", meaning a diminution or weakening of the analytical awareness of an individual for a brief or extensive period of time. If sufficiently great, it can result in unconsciousness. It stems from the restimulation of an engram, which contains pain and unconsciousness.

A-R-C, PRINCIPLE OF: The "A-R-C triangle" is Affinity, Reality and Communication. The basic principle here is that as one raises or lowers any of the three corners of this triangle, the others are raised or lowered, and that the key entrance point to these is Communication. Understanding is composed of A-R-C.

AUDITING: The application of Scientology processes and procedures to someone by a trained auditor. The exact definition of auditing is: The action of asking a preclear a question (which he can understand and answer), getting an answer to that question and acknowledging him for that answer.

AUDITOR: Trained Scientologist. Means "one who listens" and is a person who applies Scientology auditing technology to individuals for their betterment.

THE AUDITOR'S HANDBOOK: This was the manual current at the time of the Phoenix Lectures which contained the Axioms and the Route One and Route Two processes of Intensive Procedure. It forms the basis of and is wholly included in *The Creation of Human Ability* by L. Ron Hubbard, with a great deal of additional material. *The Creation of Human Ability* is a major text and is available from all Hubbard Scientology Organization bookstores. See book list and organization address list in back of this book.

BANK: A colloquial name for the Reactive Mind.

BETWEEN-LIVES AREA: The experiences of a thetan during the period of time between the loss of a body and assumption of another. Given in *A History of Man* by L. Ron Hubbard (see book list).

"BLACK V": A heavily occluded case characterized by mental pictures consisting of masses of blackness. This is a "Step V" in early procedures much as Standard Operating Procedure 8.

CHART OF ATTITUDES: A chart on which in 1951 L. Ron Hubbard plotted with the numerical values of the Emotional Tone Scale the gradient of attitudes that fall between the highest and lowest states of consideration about life. Example: top—CAUSE: bottom—FULL EFFECT.

CIRCUIT: A part of an individual's bank that behaves as though it were someone or something separate from him and either dictates or takes over his actions. Circuits are the result of engramic commands.

COMMUNICATION FORMULA: Communication is the interchange of ideas or objects between two people or terminals. The Formula of Communication and its precise definition is: Cause, Distance, Effect with Intention and Attention and a duplication at Effect of what emanates from Cause. (The ability to communicate is the key to success in life; therefore, this definition should be studied thoroughly and understood. Read Dianetics 55! by *L. Ron Hubbard* for a full practical treatise of communication. See Scientology Book List following.)

COMM LAG, AND "COMM LAG IS FLAT": Comm Lag is Communication Lag: The time it takes for a preclear to give an answer to the exact auditing question or to carry out the exact auditing command. "Flat Comm Lag" is the point at which the auditing question or command is no longer producing change of communication lag.

CYCLE OF ACTION: The creation, growth, conservation, decay and death or destruction of energy and matter in a space. Cycles of Action produce *time.*

DIANETICS: Means through thought, or mind. Dianetics is Man's most advanced school of the mind, and is that branch of Scientology which treats of mental anatomy.

DIANETIC RELEASE: One who in Dianetic auditing has attained good case gains and stability, and can enjoy life. Such a person is "keyed-out" or in other words released from the stimulus-response mechanisms of the reactive mind.

DRAMATIZATION: Thinking or acting in a manner that is dictated by masses or significances contained in the Reactive Mind. When dramatizing, the individual is like an actor playing his dictated part and going through a whole series of irrational actions.

DYNAMIC: The urge, thrust and purpose of life—*SURVIVE!*—in its eight manifestations.

THE FIRST DYNAMIC is the urge toward survival of self.

THE SECOND DYNAMIC is the urge toward survival through sex, or children. This dynamic actually has two divisions. Second Dynamic (a) is the sexual act itself and Second Dynamic (b) is the family unit, including the rearing of children.

THE THIRD DYNAMIC is the urge toward survival through a group of individuals or as a group. Any group or part of an entire class could be considered to be a part of the Third Dynamic. The school, the club, the team, the town, the nation are examples of groups.

THE FOURTH DYNAMIC is the urge toward survival through all mankind as all mankind.

THE FIFTH DYNAMIC is the urge toward survival through life forms such as animals, birds, insects, fish and vegetation, and is the urge to survive as these.

THE SIXTH DYNAMIC is the urge toward survival as the physical universe and has as its components Matter, Energy, Space and Time, from which we derive the word MEST.

THE SEVENTH DYNAMIC is the urge toward survival through spirits or as a spirit. Anything spiritual, with or without identity, would come under the Seventh Dynamic. A sub-heading of this Dynamic is ideas and concepts such as beauty, and the desire to survive through these.

THE EIGHTH DYNAMIC is the urge toward survival through a Supreme Being, or more exactly, Infinity. This is called the Eighth Dynamic because the symbol of Infinity stood upright makes the numeral "8".

8D: Standard Operating Procedure 8D (1954). Primarily for heavy cases, the goal of this procedure was "to bring the preclear to tolerate any viewpoint". See *The Creation of Human Ability* by L. Ron Hubbard.

EMOTIONAL TONE SCALE: See TONE SCALE.

ENGRAM: A mental image picture of an experience containing pain, unconsciousness, and a real or fancied threat to survival; it is a recording in the reactive mind of something which actually happened to an individual in the past and which contained pain and unconsciousness, both of which are recorded in the mental image picture called an engram.

ENGRAM BANK: A colloquial name for the reactive mind. That portion of a person's mind which works on a stimulus-response basis.

EXTERIORIZATION: The state of the thetan being outside his body. When this is done, the person achieves a certainty that he is himself and not his body.

FACSIMILE: A mental image picture.

FACSIMILE BANK: Mental image pictures; the contents of reactive mind; colloquially, "bank".

FEAR MERCHANTS: The aberrative personality. This was an early description of what is known as a Suppressive Person, or the Anti-Social Personality.

FILE CLERK: Dianetic auditor's slang for the mechanism of the mind which acts as a data monitor. Auditors could get instant or "flash" answers direct from the "file clerk" to aid in contacting incidents.

G.E. (GENETIC ENTITY): A composite of all the cellular experience recorded along the genetic line of the organism to the present body. It has the manifestation of a single identity. It is not the theta being or "I".

"GLEE OF INSANITY": Also called the "glee of irresponsibility". Manifestation which takes the form of an actual wave emanation resulting basically from an individual dramatizing the condition of "Must Reach — Can't Reach, Must Withdraw — Can't Withdraw".

GRAND TOUR: The process R1-9 in The Creation of Human Ability by L. Ron Hubbard.

GROUP AUDITOR'S HANDBOOK: This was a 1954 compilation of group auditing sessions resulting from the Advanced Clinical Courses of that year.

INTENSIVE PROCEDURE: The Standard Operating Procedure, 1954, given in THE CREATION OF HUMAN ABILITY by L. Ron Hubbard.

KEY IN (verb): An earlier moment of upset or painful experience is activated, restimulated, by the similarity of a later situation, action or environment to the earlier one.

KEY-OUT: Release or separation from one's reactive mind or some portion of it.

KNOW-TO-MYSTERY SCALE: The scale of Affinity from KNOWINGNESS down through LOOKINGNESS, EMOTINGNESS, EFFORTINGNESS, THINKINGNESS, SYMBOLIZINGNESS, EATINGNESS, SEXINGNESS, and so through to not-Knowingness—MYSTERY. The KNOW-TO-SEX SCALE was the earlier version of this scale.

LOCK, SECONDARY, ENGRAM: A *lock* is a mental image picture of a non-painful but disturbing experience the person has experienced and which depends for its force on an earlier secondary and engram which the experience has restimulated. A *secondary* is a mental image picture containing mis-emotion—encysted grief, anger, apathy, etc., and a real or imagined loss. These contain no physical pain—they are moments of shock and stress depending for their force on earlier engrams which have been restimulated by the circumstances of the secondary. An *engram* is a mental image picture of an experience containing pain, unconsciousness, and a real or fancied threat to survival.

MEST UNIVERSE: The physical universe, from the initial letters of matter, energy, space, time.

MOCK-UP: A mental model, construction or picture created by a thetan. A mock-up is distinct from a facsimile in that it is created volitionally, does not necessarily copy any previous experience, and is under the control of the thetan.

"1.5": Numerical equivalent on the CHART OF HUMAN EVALUATION for the person who is in *Overt Hostility*. Anger is his standard state. He is capable of taking destructive action and is characteristically *trying to stop things*.

OVERT ACT: A harmful or contra-survival action against one or more dynamics.

OVERT ACT-MOTIVATOR SEQUENCE: Overt-motivator sequence: The sequence wherein someone who has committed an overt has to claim the existence of "motivators". The motivators are then likely to be used to justify committing further overt acts.

PRECLEAR: A person who through Scientology processing is finding out more about himself and life.

PROCEDURE 30: The special auditing procedure of which Opening Procedure by Duplication (R2-17 *Creation of Human Ability* is the first step.

PROCESS: A set of questions asked by an auditor to help a person find out things about himself or life. More fully, a process is a patterned action, done by the auditor and preclear under the auditor's direction, which is invariable and unchanging, composed of certain steps or actions calculated to release or free a thetan. There are many processes and these are aligned with the levels taught to students and with grades as applied to preclears, all of which lead the student or the preclear gradiently to higher understanding and awareness. Any single process is run only so long as it produces change and no longer.

PROCESSING: That action or actions of an auditor, governed by the technical disciplines and codes of Scientology, of administering a process to a preclear in order to release or free him.

"PROCESS IS FLAT": A process is continued as long as it produces change and no longer, at which time the process is "flat".

Q AND A: From "Question and Answer". This term originally referred to the fact that *the answer to the question is the question.* Q and A has been used as the term for "changing when the preclear changes", and refers in Chapter Twenty-four on page 291, to the preclear duplicating the beingness of the auditor.

REACTIVE MIND: That portion of a person's mind which works on a stimulus-response basis, is not under his volitional control and exerts force and the power of command over his awareness, purposes, thoughts, body and actions.

REPEATER TECHNIQUE: This refers to the Dianetic technique using repetition by the preclear of a word or phrase in order to produce movement on the time track into an engram containing that word or phrase.

RIDGES: Solid accumulations of old, inactive mental energy suspended in space and time.

R2-40: Route Two, Process Number 40, Conceive A Static. See THE CREATION OF HUMAN ABILITY by L. Ron Hubbard.

SOMATICS: Perceptions, stemming from the Reactive Bank, of past physical pain or discomfort, restimulated in present time.

SONIC: The ability to recall a sound so that one can hear it again as he originally heard it—in full tone and volume.

SOP: Standard Operating Procedure.

STRAIGHT WIRE: Direct memory processes, or a class of processes found in both Dianetic and Scientology auditing procedures.

THETA CLEAR: An individual who, as a being, is certain of his identity apart from that of the body, and who habitually operates the body from outside, or *exteriorized.*

THETAN: From Theta, the Static. Word taken from Greek letter θ, *theta,* traditional symbol for thought or spirit. The thetan is the individual himself—not body, mind or anything else; that which is aware of being aware; the identity that IS the individual.

TONE SCALE: A scale measuring and relating the various factors of behavior, emotion and thought to levels on the scale. (The book, Science of Survival, by L. Ron Hubbard contains a full description of the tone scale and its applications in life.)

VALENCE: The assumption by an individual of a beingness other than his own.

VISIO: The ability to see in facsimile form something one has seen earlier so that one sees it again in the same color, dimension scale, brightness and detail as it was originally viewed.

For more books contact

PUBLICATIONS DEPARTMENT

Church of Scientology of California
The American Saint Hill
Organization
2723 West Temple Street
Los Angeles, California 90026

Or Your Local Church of Scientology

Church of Scientology
20005 W. 9th St.
Los Angeles, California 90006

Founding Church of Scientology
1812 19th St. N.W.
Washington, D.C. 20009

Church of Scientology
49 West 32nd St. New York
New York, 10001

Church of Scientology
414 Mason St., Room 400
San Francisco, California 94102

Celebrity Centre
1809 W. 8th St.
Los Angeles, California, 90057

Church of Scientology
19452 Livernois
Detroit, Michigan

Church of Scientology of St. Louis
4221 Lindell Blvd.,
St. Louis, Missouri

Church of Scientology
3007 Nicollet Ave.,
Minneapolis, Minnesota 55408

Church of Scientology
985 S.W. First St.
Miami, Florida

Church of Scientology
5000 Burnet Road
Austin, Texas

Church of Scientology
910 Elliott Ave. W.
Seattle, Washington 98119

Church of Scientology
143 Nenue St.
Honolulu, Hawaii 96821

Church of Scientology
308 E. Charlston Blvd.
Las Vegas, Nevada 89105

Church of Scientology of Boston
714 Beacon St.
Boston, Mass. 02215

Church of Scientology of San Diego
7440 Girand
La Jolla, California 92037

Church of Scientology of Buffalo
960 Kenmore Ave.
Buffalo, New York 14216

IN CANADA

Church of Scientology
116 Ave Road
Toronto 5, Ontario, Canada

IN EUROPE

Hubbard College of Scientology
Saint Hill Manor, East Grinstead,
Sussex, England

Church of Scientology of Brighton
15 Preston Street
Brighton, Sussex, England

Church of Scientology
68 Tottenham Court Rd.
London, W.1. England

H.A.P.I. Scotland
13 Queen Street
Edinburgh 2, Scotland

Church of Scientology of Denmark
Hovedvagtsgade 6, 1103
Copenhagen K, Denmark

Church of Scientology of
Copenhagen
Henningsens Alle 68, 2900
Hellerup, Copenhagen, Denmark

Scientology Eskilstuna
Eskilsgatan 1, 633 56
Eskilstuna, Sweden

Scientology Orebro
Oskarsvagen 2, 702 14
Orebro, Sweden

Scientology Stockholm
Arvodesvagen 5, 12646 Hagersten
Stockholm, Sweden

Scientology Goteborg
Ostra Hamnegatan 4, 41109
Goteborg, Sweden

Hubbard Scientology Organization
58 rue de Londres, 75 Paris 8
France

NEW ZEALAND

Church of Scientology
16–18 View Road
Auckland 3, New Zealand

AUSTRALIA

Church of the New Faith
28 Restormae Ave.
Fularton, Adelaide 5000
South Australia

Church of the New Faith
137 Cleaver St.
West Perth, Australia

Church of the New Faith
69 Old South Head Road,
Bondi Junction, Sydney
N.S.W. 2022,
Australia

SOUTH WALES

Hubbard Scientology Organization
20 Henrietta St., Swansea
Glamorgan, Wales, Great Britain

SOUTH AFRICA

Church of Scientology in S.A.
(Pty.) Ltd.
99 Polly St., Johannesburg
South Africa

Church of Scientology in S.A.
(Pty.) Ltd.
Old Netherlands Bldg.,
335 Smith St.
Durban, South Africa

Church of Scientology in S.A.
(Pty.) Ltd.
19 Parliament St., Port Elizabeth
South Africa

Church of Scientology in S.A.
(Pty.) Ltd.
224 Central House
Cnr. Central & Pretorius Streets
Pretoria, South Africa

Church of Scientology in S.A.
(Pty.) Ltd.
2 Darter's Road, Cape Town
South Africa

RHODESIA

Church of Scientology
23 Bindown Court
Borrow St., Bulawayo
Rhodesia

The Advanced Organization
916 South Westlake
Los Angeles, California 90006